The Abolitionists

THE ABOLITIONISTS

THE FAMILY AND MARRIAGE UNDER ATTACK

Ronald Fletcher

ROUTLEDGE
London and New York

First published in 1988 by
Routledge
a division of Routledge, Chapman and Hall
11 New Fetter Lane, London EC4P 4EE

Published in the USA by
Routledge
in association with Routledge, Chapman and Hall, Inc.
29 West 35th Street, New York, NY 10001

Set in 10/11½ point Times & Optima
by Witwell Ltd, Southport
and printed in Great Britain
by Billings Ltd, Worcester

Library of Congress Cataloging in Publication Data

Fletcher, Ronald.
    The abolitionists: the family and marriage under attack / Ronald
Fletcher.
        p.   cm.
    Bibliography: p.
    Includes index.
        1. Family.   2. Marriage.   3. Marxist criticism.   4. Feminist
criticism.   I. Title.
    HQ518.F56   1988   88-2953
    306.8'5——dc 19   CIP

British Library Cataloguing in Publication Data

Fletcher, Ronald
    The abolitionists: the family and
    marriage under attack.
    1.   Families – Sociological perspectives
    I.   Title
    306.8 ' 5

ISBN 0-415-00855-7
ISBN 0-415-00875-1   PB

The ancient trinity of father, mother, and child has survived more vicissitudes than any other human relationship. It is the bedrock underlying all other family structures. Although more elaborate family patterns can be broken from within or may even collapse of their own weight, the rock remains. In the Götterdämmerung which over-wise science and over-foolish statesmanship are preparing for us, the last man will spend his last hours searching for his wife and child.

Ralph Linton, 'The Natural History of the Family', in *The Family: Its Function and Destiny*, ed. Ruth Nanda Anshen, 1949

v

Contents

Contents

Preface

May I ask the reader to consider this book in close conjunction with *The Shaking of the Foundations: Family and Society*? The two were written together, and are, therefore, in the fullest sense, companion books.

R.F.

Acknowledgments

Grateful acknowledgments are due to authors and publishers for the use of quotations as follows:

In Chapter 1: Edmund Leach, G. M. Carstairs and the BBC (from *The Listener*); Peter Laslett and Methuen (from *World We Have Lost*); Ronald Blythe and Allen Lane (from *Akenfield*).

In Chapter 2: R. D. Laing, A. Esterson, Tavistock Publications and Penguin Books (from *Sanity, Madness and the Family, The Leaves of Spring*); R. D. Laing, David Cooper and Tavistock Publications (from *Reason and Violence*); David Cooper and Allen Lane (from *The Death of the Family*).

In Chapter 3: Robin Blackburn and Penguin Books (from *Student Power*); Juliet Mitchell and Penguin Books (from *Woman's Estate*); Frederick Engels and (a) Allen & Unwin (from *The Condition of the Working Class in England in 1844*), (b) Charles H. Kerr & Co (from *The Origin of the Family*); Karl Marx and (a) William Glaisher Ltd (from *Capital*), (b) Lawrence & Wishart Ltd (from *Economic and Philosophic Manuscripts of 1844*, and *Karl Marx: Selected Works* – a reminiscence of William Liebknecht).

In Chapter 4: Betty Friedan and (a) Penguin Books (from *The Feminine Mystique*), (b) Abacus, Sphere Books Ltd (from *The Second Stage*); Kate Millett and Abacus, Sphere Books Ltd (from *Sexual Politics*); Germaine Greer and (a) Grafton Books, The Collins Publishing Group (from *The Female Eunuch), (b) Pan Books (from Sex and Destiny, The Politics of Human Fertility*); Debbie Taylor, Angela Davis and Methuen (from *Women: A World Report*); Catherine Itzin and Virago Ltd (from *Splitting Up*); Elaine Morgan and Souvenir Press (from *The Descent of Woman*).

In Chapter 5: Gerald Leslie and Oxford University Press (from *The Family in Social Context*); M. E. Spiro and Harvard University Press (from *Children of the Kibbutz*).

Introduction

New and radical criticisms: a strange reversal

This book has one simple aim: to take issue with those criticisms of the past twenty years which have advocated (or, in some cases, have *seemed* to advocate) the abolition of the family and marriage, and to demonstrate that – radical as they are – they are also radically mistaken. This, however, to be fully understood, must be seen within a certain context.

Without any doubt whatever, the Divorce Reform Act of 1969 marked a juncture of the greatest significance in the changing and developing nature of the family and marriage in Britain. Passed only after the most searching deliberation, coming into effect in 1971, it had been formulated within the long-continuing controversies springing from the concerns felt about the condition of the family during the two decades following the Second World War, and the many criticisms which had then been raised about it. Taking shape within this many-dimensioned controversy, it embodied many of its considerations and judgments. Some of its provisions (for example: that of making 'the irretrievable breakdown of marriage' the one basic ground for divorce, and considering the earlier grounds of the 'matrimonial offence' as elements to be referred to as giving proof of this, and that of deliberately allowing attempted reconciliation within the law, to prevent the law from standing in the way of reconciliation, and in the hope of eliminating the 'adversarial' nature of divorce proceedings) made very considerable changes. Even more controversial, perhaps, were the provisions for divorce after specified periods of separation (two years with the agreement of both parties, five years without such agreement) – which seemed tantamount to allowing divorce by consent, with the danger, perhaps, of penalising

1

an innocent party. All these were not only changes in the grounds for terminating marriage, they seemed also to alter the very nature of the institution of marriage itself – in quite fundamental ways – and this may well have been more profoundly true than was then realised, despite the prolonged and painstaking discussion. The issues at stake in the Bill were certainly very widely debated both inside and outside Parliament – in the press, in conferences of churches, among panels of 'experts', and even in 'trials' on television. No Private Members Bill (Mr Leo Abse was its dedicated protagonist) ever enjoyed more detailed scrutiny. As a piece of legislation, it was well considered in direct relation to a careful appreciation and judgment of social facts, seeking to bring the law into closer touch with the actualities of social life and conditions. Its aim, too, was undoubtedly that of *serving* and *supporting* the family in society. It was, said the Law Commission:

> ... to buttress rather than undermine the stability of marriage, and, when regrettably a marriage has broken down, to enable the empty legal shell to be destroyed with the maximum fairness and the minimum bitterness, distress, and humiliation.

Nothing could have been more clear. Yet all that followed (like the outcome of so many statutory provisions) was such as to make one wonder how successful legislation can ever be in achieving certain desired qualitative ends by trying to change social facts within a given context of collective conditions. If sociology finds itself having to emphasise the collective conditions of a society in seeking an accurate appraisal of the nature of the specific social facts within it, it finds itself having to emphasise equally the unforeseen consequences of deliberate social action, and this reform, like others, bore out the necessity and wisdom of this caution. It was clearly expected, too (nobody was naively unaware of this), that when the Act came into effect, it would at once be followed by a large increase in the incidence of divorce – simply because it would immediately make possible a long-awaited legal recognition of an earlier *de facto* situation. But no one could see beyond that, and know what could follow this initial response. Given the radical nature of the changes and the expected immediate outcome, some earlier feelings of disquiet and apprehension about the possibly disintegrating nature, growing instability, and deteriorating qualities of the family continued. Among some, the old uneasinesses remained, and the facts and trends which followed – which have continued until the later 1980s – have been thought, by them, to have fully justified all such anxieties. Here, however, it is not to our purpose to examine the *facts* and enquire into the *explanations* of this situation.* It is on one other notable and accompanying aspect of it that I want to concentrate.

Playing about, and within, these long-gathered storm-clouds of controversy – rather like conspicuously licking and flashing tongues of lightning – were certain new elements of criticism, new sources and positions of critical appraisal, which were different from those which had been common earlier. These, now, were decidedly *radical* in nature, attacking the family rather than lamenting its possible demise. The voices of those who advanced them, too, were loud and exhibitionist in their manner of presentation and display – striding demonstratively to the centre of the stage, and, with their assertiveness, bringing a new tone and character to the discussion. Each was distinguishable from the other, each posed a distinctive and well-defined point of view, and yet, taken together, they brought to bear on the whole assessment of the place of the family and marriage in society a new focus and direction of criticism, resting their arguments on new grounds, adopting a new stance. Some were interpretations of supposedly old ideological positions (e.g. Marxism); some pressed to new extremes already well established social movements (e.g. Feminism); but all – both separately and combined – sought and gained very striking prominence, exerted considerable influence on public attitudes, and, in particular, shared one conspicuous feature: *a complete 'about-turn' of argument* when contrasted with the judgments which had dominated the thinking of the 1950s and early 1960s. *Then* (not more than ten years previously) *all* the prevailing criticisms had seemed to bewail the *decline* of the family. It was the weakness, the deterioration, the rapid decay of the family which was held to be the source of all our personal and social ills. Society rested on the basic domestic group of the family. This was the primary group which maintained the community's values, within which values were first and most deeply experienced and individual character was formed. The family was the very foundation of society, and since the family was now in dangerous disarray, so was the entire moral order of society. It is not too much to say that such views commanded a very widespread consensus of judgment, and to make this clear it is worthwhile to recall some of them.

Sometimes stemming from the generalisations of sociologists and philosophers (among whom, again, there seemed to be substantial

*For this, see *The Shaking of the Foundations: Family and Society* Routledge, 1988.

agreement),[1] sometimes from the moralistic pronouncements of representatives of the several churches, sometimes from social workers, journalists, judges, such criticisms had grown, cumulatively, into a loud and almost continuous chorus of denunciation. Articles in the press, talks on the radio, mushroomed into what amounted to an almost frenzied condemnation of the parents and young people of post-war Britain: accusing them of a downward slide of moral deterioration since the end of the war. 'Englishmen,' Mrs Knowles had once written,

... are always despondent about their own times, and it would be easy to quote contemporaries in every period so that their testimony would show that we had gone downhill ever since the time of the Norman conquest.

In this one respect (if in no other) British society had certainly not changed! Evidence abounded to prove Mrs Knowles right. According to these very vocal critics, we were still going to the dogs – and fast! Here, a few examples will show their character. Some, as might have been expected, came from prominent clergymen.

Dr Leslie Weatherhead delivered his considered judgment that we were a nation 'in dire moral peril' owing to the spread of 'sexual depravity' – a danger to modern youth which was, he said, 'a greater danger than nuclear war'.* The kind of evidence he gave was the testimony of an un-named headmistress of a large un-named girls' school in London who, by un-named methods, had discovered that not one girl in her sixth form was a virgin, and the fact that – after the notorious court-case over its publication – *Lady Chatterley's Lover* had sold 'over a million copies'. This, he said, did not rest on a suddenly developed taste for 'the alleged literary ability of D. H. Lawrence'. In 1956, a Reverend Crawford Walter told delegates at a Methodist Conference in Leeds that:

... in the last half-century we have seen *a moral landslide....* Moral positions which our fathers thought were indisputable and impregnable have been swept away.... The slogan of popular opinion has become: it doesn't matter what you do so long as you can get away with it.

In a later New Year Message (which he, too, associated with the *Lady Chatterley* case) a Reverend Edward Rogers spoke of 'the

---

*Is this not an astonishing judgment to come from a Christian clergyman?

seedy, dingy moral apathy of our time', describing the moral climate of Britain as 'poisonous'.

A definite direction in this denunciation of the British public had become clear. The main targets for attack were increasingly the *family* and the *Welfare State*. All the ills from which our 'sick' modern society was suffering (crime, delinquency, the disreputable behaviour of some teenagers) were laid at the door of 'the growing instability of marriage', the 'decline of the family', the 'continual increase of divorce'... and this 'deterioration' of family life was held to be closely connected with the easy-going irresponsibility, the moral laxity, engendered by the Welfare State. We had 'gone too far, too fast'. It was time that we looked back to the moral stability and integrity of the past, before people 'had things too easy'; when the family and society at large possessed a dignity, and nobility which it had now lost.

Towards the end of the war and shortly after it, the Reverend E. C. Urwin had declared that 'the stability of the family is in real peril'; that 'the moral failure of the home' was responsible for some of our worst social problems. A few years later, Dr David Mace maintained that marriage counselling had become necessary because, among other reasons, '*the decay of the close-knit family associations of the past* had made people unwilling to make confidants of parents or relatives' (my italics). In 1957, at a national conference on social work, Professor Richard Ellis raised the question '*whether the Welfare State was in any way responsible for a weakening of parental responsibility*'. The writer of a front-page article in the *Times Educational Supplement*, too, commenting with approval on Sir John Wolfenden's contribution to the same conference, said:

> Many parents are now happy to let the state and the schools do things for their children that they would not have dreamt of allowing before the war. There have always been slack parents, but many people feel that *the Welfare State merely gives equality of opportunity for parents to be irresponsible. They fear that we shall soon begin to wonder what parents are for*...as a benevolent state *has taken more and more of their functions* (my italics).

In 1960, a secondary modern school headmaster (writing on basic training in modern schools) commented on the new material prosperity enjoyed by the British people. There was, he said:

> ... a complete and all-out worship of money and what it can

buy, and the saddest effect of this is *in the time taken from the home and its life* in pursuing this aim. *Many parents are now too engrossed to live with or for their children*, and the individual child is becoming more and more isolated, often even from his brothers and sisters as well as his parents ... [When the consequent lack of values in children leads to trouble] ... *it is often repaid by blows from the parent who has been too indifferent or too busy to help or advise* (my italics).

These opinions were so widespread, so taken for granted, that even a film reviewer could preface his remarks with the unquestioned assumption that the 'problems of teenagers' were the result of *'the breakdown of family life as we used to know it'*, and an influential editorial could say:

If adolescents are half as criminal and as vicious as the publicity given to them suggests, the root cause, *as is generally agreed*, must lie *in the breakdown of family life and social standards generally* (my italics).

In decrying this 'decline' of the family, some critics also clearly questioned, and seemed to regret, the improved status of wives and mothers. One letter in the 'Dr Weatherhead correspondence' said:

The decline in moral standards during the past fifty years has been coincident with *the gradual emancipation of our women*. Is it not time we asked ourselves *how far it is consequent upon it?* (my italics)

Such criticisms were advanced in the most influential quarters by the most prominent people. The then Archbishop of York, Dr Coggan, said in an address to a National Union of Teachers' Conference:

It is part of the sickness of modern society that *many parents have abdicated from their responsibilities in the upbringing of children*, and, consequently, the school teacher today finds himself necessarily concerned *with the total health and character-formation of the child in his care* (my italics).

No less a person than Lord Shawcross, in a speech to the Royal Society of St George in London, asked whether *the Welfare State was making the British people too soft*. We must see, he said, that the changes taking place 'did not destroy *the great permanencies, hitherto deeply ingrained through all the generations of our people*,' and, he concluded, '... *it is the parents who frighten me most*' (my italics).

6

Brought together and summarised, these charges seem – do they not? – the most astonishing indictment of a whole generation. According to them, the men and women who had married and become parents during and after the war were in a state of moral decay, lacking firm convictions on the basis of which they could bring up their children, having lost 'those permanencies which had been ingrained in all earlier generations'; so absorbed in their own selfish pursuit of wealth as to ignore and ill-treat their children, 'having taken advantage of their new equality of opportunity to become irresponsible'. The emancipation of women, in particular, had contributed to this moral deterioration. Indifferently, uncaringly, with neither affection nor concern, mothers, as well as fathers, handed their children over to the care of expert but now over-burdened school teachers. A black generation indeed!

We will not stop, in this place, to consider the truth or falsity of these accusations (whether, for example, even if this appraisal of the moral standards of society as a whole was reliable, it could correctly be laid at the door of the family) or look into the reliability or otherwise of the grounds on which they rested.[2] Our purpose, here, is only to note very clearly the one important and unquestionable point: that the prevailing view up to the early 1960s was that the family in Britain was in a condition of decline, decay, and deterioration, and it was because of this that the future and quality of our entire society was in danger. The family was 'on its way out' – and the whole of society was suffering from its eclipse.

How strange then, that, in the later 1960s – no more than a few years later – the position outlined by a newly emerging and strengthening set of criticisms was *exactly the reverse*! Now, the strength of the family (previously found so wanting) was seen as the source of all our ills. Far from seeing it in a condition of decline, the new criticism deplored its tenacity; its obduracy, durability, and deep-rooted resilience in resisting those social changes believed necessary for human improvement. The family was now an obstacle to social change; the most conservative group of all. A few years earlier society had been imperilled by the failure of the family; now, it was the most powerful barrier to society's further progress: the one group standing intractably in the way of revolution and reform; the last intransigent bulwark of an inhuman industrial capitalism; the chief instrument of that pernicious process of personality-conditioning which enslaved individuals to the requirements of the social system, so ensuring its perpetuation. Individual persons – with all their manifold dimensions and potentialities for free fulfilment – were destroyed by an intrusive character-formation which instilled, within the intense private world of the home, the worst 'bourgeois' values. So deeply entrenched a social group was the family, so firmly established a social institution was marriage, that both had to be actively attacked, disrupted, broken out of their age-old moulds, destroyed, replaced by some alternative, by some much more open kind of relationships, if the desired objectives of a humane revolution – the liberalising of individual persons (particularly women), the raising to equality and dignity of subjected social classes, for example – were to be attained.

I do not know whether this complete reversal of judgment, of critical appraisal, seems odd to you? It certainly seems odd to me – so much so that it is this that I want to emphasise and take as the starting-point of this enquiry.

How could the family in Britain possibly have been supposed to have changed so radically in so short a time? How – so quickly – could it have been transformed from a decadent weakling, threatening the stability of the entire social order, to that well nigh indestructible tower of strength which was chiefly responsible for preserving society's existing nature? How could critics of such eminence, so conspicuous in the forefront of their several areas of thought and activity, come to such widely divergent conclusions about it? What sort of explanation could the views of these critics be? What degree of seriousness and reliability, what weight, what validity could be attached to such positions – which could blame on the one hand the fatal weakness, and on the other the indomitable strength, of the family, for society's disorders? Might it be, perhaps, that the weakness, the vacillations, lay not so much in the family as in the pontifications of the critics themselves? Might it perhaps be that the family itself was standing with comparative firmness and constancy – as a much-assailed and much-battered but nonetheless enduring rock within the seas of social change – and that it was the critics themselves who, borne on the shifting tides of fashion and controversy, driven by their own moral and ideological persuasions, were dashing themselves into an ever-changing foam of consternation about it?

One thing is certain. The newly emerging criticisms were very different from – indeed diametrically opposed to – those of the past, and deserve the fullest and most careful consideration for a number of reasons. First, no detailed examination of all of them, taken together and seen in relation to each other – fully scrutinising their claims, the evidence on which these rest, the validity or otherwise of their sequences of argument – has yet been conducted. Second, the most strident criticisms in the entire field of discussion – lending themselves more readily than others to sensationalist coverage by the media – came to dominate it throughout the 1970s and 1980s, and are dominant still. Third, and because of this, the most superficial attitudes to marriage and the family (attitudes I shall later call 'half-baked') have spread from them throughout society, infiltrating every level, quarter, and corner of the community – like ripples spreading outwards from the central splashes of publicity. And fourth, so much in the public eye have they been, that – for better, for worse – their pronouncements have been taken (though no doubt differently by differently interested groups) to be authoritatively representative of their several movements, and truly drawn from the sources in which they claim to be rooted. Thus, what some 'neo-Marxists' have said on the supposed basis of 'Marxism' has been thought to be authoritatively true of what Marx and Engels themselves actually said, and what they desired. Similarly, the most extreme assertions of some influential women writers (Germaine Greer, Kate Millett, for example) have been thought to be – whether approved of or not – representative views of the 'New Feminism' or the 'Women's Liberation Movement'. It is high time, therefore, that a searching enquiry into all their claims was carried out, and this is what this book attempts.

Some of these positions were voiced and outlined during the second half of the 1960s (Edmund Leach's Reith Lectures were delivered in 1967; Laing, Cooper and Esterton stated their position in a number of books from about 1965 onwards; the 'New Feminism' began with Betty Friedan's first book, *The Feminine Mystique*, first published in Britain by Penguin Books in 1965), but all were gathering power at the same time as the deliberations preceding the 1969 Act were taking place, and have remained very influential from that time to this – in the case of some, of course, like the New Feminism, changing with varying emphases as new contributions have been made. *Five* such positions can be clearly distinguished, and we can examine each one fully in turn.

'The source of all our discontents': Edmund Leach

One of the most prominent and condemnatory criticisms of the family in society could well be called Edmund Leach's 'Reith Sentence'. Delivered in the third of his Reith Lectures in 1967,[1] it was, in fact, the last sentence of a short passage. The passage itself was this:

The family looks inward upon itself; there is an intensification of emotional stress between husband and wife, and parents and children. The strain is greater than most of us can bear. *Far from being the basis of the good society, the family, with its narrow privacy and tawdry secrets, is the source of all our discontents* (my italics).

This final sentence had the middle-men of communications throughout the country agog. It was immediately caught up and endlessly repeated in weekly colour supplements, radio discussions, television programmes, and the repetition went on *ad nauseam* for many years. Towards the end of 1972, to give just one example, no less a person than Dr Carstairs, the psychologist, was saying in a radio talk published in *The Listener:*[2]

...the authority of the family has been seriously challenged – and not only by teenagers. It was Edmund Leach, in his 1967 Reith Lectures, who described the family 'with its narrow privacy and tawdry secrets' as 'the source of all our discontents.'

The 'Reith Sentence' went on! For many years, Edmund Leach loomed large like some great oracle whose one pronouncement was pregnant with insight for the diagnosis of the sickness of our society. But one simple question was never asked. Dr Leach was a social scientist. What evidence, then, did he provide as the ground for his statement? What evidence was it which persuaded those who heard him of its importance? The astonishing answer is: none! – none whatever! Comb the Reith Lecture, and you will find no evidence at all.

The truth is that the lecture ('Ourselves and Others') was not specifically about the nature of the family at all – but about the nature of violence in our society and particularly about the supposed rebelliousness and disorderliness of the young (the teenagers) and the perceptions of them and attitudes towards them of older people. Leach's discussion of the family arose simply because it was so often the breakdown of the family which was blamed for the violent behaviour of the young, and, in scathingly rebutting this claim, he spoke not in the vein normally expected of scholarship but provocatively, in the most loosely provocative way, and this it was, it seemed, which had the appeal of the 'sensational', and consequently appealed to editors, journalists, and television and radio producers whose very nature is to be always on the alert for a telling phrase and a sensational story. It is important, then, since the selective quotation became, and has remained, so influential, to see what exactly Leach *did* say about the family, because some of the points he made were quite different from the positions he was commonly supposed to hold.

In the first place, it is interesting to see that he entirely rejected the view that any misbehaviour of the young could be explained by the *breakdown* of the family. On the contrary, Leach was quite sure that the family had been *strengthened* by social changes and reforms, not at all disrupted, and that family life and 'family cohesiveness' were, in fact, very securely established – indeed, from his point of view, too much so! These were his own words:

> Some people will tell you that youthful disorder is just a symptom of the breakdown of family life. I can see no justification for this view. Nearly all the large-scale social changes which have been taking place over the past century have been of a kind that should have brought the children closer to their parents rather than the other way about. The shortening of hours of work, improvements in housing standards, paid holidays, the prohibition of child labour, the extension of formal day school education, the disappearance

of domestic servants, should all, on the face of it, have helped to intensify family cohesiveness.

This, plainly, is very much in agreement with the kind of account we ourselves put forward earlier, in defending the modern family against the critics of the 1950s.* But, Leach argued:

> ... in practice it seems to work out the other way: the adults are now inclined to treat the teenagers as alienated ruffians – and not wholly without cause. Teenage gang warfare and the wrecking of public amenities is a reality. What has gone wrong?

Might it not be, he suggested, that the family had become too well established as a privatised group in society, was now too cohesive, and that it was the very closeness and intensity of family life itself, together with a change in the nature of family values, which were responsible for implanting the seeds of social disorder – instilling, for example, attitudes of envy between social classes.

It is in the bosom of the family that we are first carefully taught to recognise and react to signals which indicate class difference, so any attack on social class will be felt as an attack on family values. Also, many of the more futile and unpleasant forms of youthful protest – vandalism in churches and public parks, for example – are intentional acts of sacrilege designed to shock the respectable family man. 'Oh dear, what are we coming to? Why can't parents instil a sense of public decency into their children?' And the criticism is fair comment, for family values have become increasingly focused on private status rather than public good.

Perhaps, he argued, it was *the family itself that needed to be changed*, and it was here that he launched into his criticism of the family which developed, in fact, into an outright attack upon it. This attack had several elements, and, for accuracy's sake, it will be best to state and assess each one separately.

First, Leach was at pains to make it clear that the present form of the family in Britain was not (throughout the world) the universal and necessary basis of human society. Let us look at his own words, since these justify the criticism that he was loosely provocative. He wrote:

*See: *The Family and Marriage in Britain.*

Psychologists, doctors, schoolmasters and clergy-men put over so much soppy propaganda about the virtue of a united family life that most of you probably have the idea that 'the family', in our English sense, is a universal institution, the very foundation of organised society. This isn't so. Human beings, at one time or another, have managed to invent all sorts of different styles of domestic living and we shall have to invent still more in the future.

This, of course, deserves no comment. Enough has been written about the universality of the family in society, and also about the variety of its forms, to see how superficial Leach's comment is, and, of course, no one has ever claimed that the modern British family is the only viable form of the family in existence, or put out any 'soppy propaganda' to this effect. The idea, too, that human beings can 'invent' (or have 'invented') forms of the family is a very dubious one when stated in this unqualified way, and even the form of the family in Britain today is by no means simply one form – easily invented – among countless others, but a form which has been persistently worked for, over several generations and in the teeth of much resistance (much political, religious, and legal opposition) in order to improve the status and relationships of husband, wife and children in the direction of greater equality, mutuality of consideration, freedom and fulfilment – and all within the context of pressing collective conditions. It has been one essential part of the task of making a new and more just society out of the many-sided turmoil accompanying and then developing out of industrialisation.

On this point, it is worthwhile to note that – going beyond Leach himself – an altogether too loose, casual and superficial an appreciation of what more than a century of reform has won for us is abroad – and among some anthropologists who, immersed in supposedly altogether factual comparative studies, have ceased to pay any attention to (i.e. are uninformed in) moral philosophy, and who no longer even consider its relevance to the study of social facts. In a conference on 'The Family and its Future' in 1970,[3] for example, Robin Fox spoke of the modern 'nuclear family' in this way:

So much is written about the breakdown of the family, about family failures and conflicts, neuroses and the like, that is inspired by a kind of mystical functionalism which sees the nuclear family as a God-given system that would work if only things didn't happen to spoil it. On the contrary, what is remarkable about so fragile an institution is that it works at

13

all. The failures are probably simply those families which refuse to ignore the natural conflicts inherent in the situation, while the successes are the families with the greatest capacity for collective self-delusion.

The failures are the clear-sighted and realistic members of society. The successful are those wedded to delusions. And no thought whatever is given, in such statements, to the *moral* improvements in human relationships which the new form of the family embodies, or to the question as to how far other known forms of the family, in other societies, provide as satisfactory a basis for the same qualities of human relationships. Later, we shall come back to the importance of this point.

To come back to Leach, however, it is quite clear that having pointed to the social changes which had shaped the form of the modern British family – which had established its strength and cohesiveness – he by no means approved of it. All the improvements – the increased economic opportunities and better standards of material life and comfort; the opportunities for greater geographical and occupational mobility which gave families a new material and social independence; the increased autonomy of the family and its lack of dependence on wider kinship relationships; the more intense and demanding relationships between wife and husband which had resulted from this family autonomy and the equal status they enjoyed – were all things resulting in a state of affairs and a condition of the family which he deprecated. This is how he put his position:

> Up until the First World War a major part of the working population, both in the towns and in the countryside, was residentially immobile. The variety of possible occupations open to working-class people was small, and although there was a steady drift from the villages to the towns, most people had nothing much to gain by moving around from one town to another ... In the old days, bonds of neighbours, kinship and occupation tended to coincide; most people spent their whole lives close to the place where they were born, so they were always surrounded by kinsfolk. Moreover, the girl whom a man married was often a near neighbour, and the two families were quite likely to be related already even before the marriage ... but the general pattern is fast disappearing.
>
> The effect of this change is as much psychological as social. In the past, kinsfolk and neighbours gave the individual continuous moral support throughout his life. Today the

domestic household is isolated. The family looks inward upon itself; there is an intensification of emotional stress between husband and wife, and parents and children. The strain is greater than most of us can bear. Far from being the basis of the good society, the family, with its narrow privacy and tawdry secrets, is the source of all our discontents....

This was the particular context of Leach's 'Reith Sentence', but in his statement the grounds for two immediate criticisms stand out very clearly. First, like all the 'right wing' criticisms of the past (with which I cannot believe he would like to be associated) – though now in a different way – this clearly blames the family for far too much. And secondly, it commits the 'Earlier Community Fallacy'.

'The narrow privacy ... the tawdry secrets ... the source of all our discontents ...' One has only to stop for a brief moment to see how selective and over-weighted this denunciation is. Is the privacy of the family *narrow* privacy compared with the close involvement in relationships of power and the manipulations of influence in other groups? Are 'tawdry secrets' confined to the family in our society? Are there no tawdry secrets, let us say, in the administration of education (at all levels) – among Vice-Chancellors and small inner cliques of professors; between ministers of education, administrative officers, governors of schools, head-teachers and staffs – in the manipulation of affairs in trade unions – in industrial legislation and the attempts to circumvent it – in the handling of power in political parties – in the affairs of government itself? The point is obviously an absurd over-simplification. The entire institutional fabric of our society is rife with roguery. Corruption is writ large. The newspapers of every day are filled with evidence of it, and we all know this very well. Yet the family is selected for this curiously central weight of blame. For some of us, at least, exactly the reverse could be argued: that the family is the one area of peacefulness, humanity, sanity within which – confidently as whole persons – we can share our lives with others; in which privacy is a relaxed and enriching thing; within which secrecy is minimal; in which we do genuinely enjoy community in all things – the place and context of a deeply explored experience on which we can rely, in a society where wider activities and involvements are sickeningly fevered, manipulated, and false, and where – increasingly it seems – we can rely on nothing. This, too, is far from being a purely personal observation, and one of the strange things is that Dr Leach seemed completely to ignore all the evidence – both that of common experience and that of scholarly research – which proved, on the contrary, that *privacy* in the family and the supportive context of family affection, was exactly what most people *valued* and *wanted*. Thinking of 'common experience', during the period of growing redundancy and unemployment, press, radio and television interviews have been full of examples in which men who were experiencing the devastating effects of long-drawn-out unemployment (e.g. in the north-east) laid special emphasis upon the strength and loyalty they had found in their families. It was almost as though the worth and character of family affection and loyalty was something they had come to realise more deeply than ever in their adversity. Despite completely altered and worsened social conditions, despite so radical a change in status as to shake their personal confidence down to the roots, they found complete firmness and support in the collective and shared responses of their wives and children. The same closeness of the family bond was also clearly in evidence among miners during the prolonged and pointless strike of recent years. In a world of social deterioration, the private world of the family had held firm. But family privacy was clearly something that Dr Leach disliked and frowned upon. It is, he claimed, something that separates men from each other, creating unnecessary grounds of alienation and conflict. Our present society, he said:

> ... is emotionally very uncomfortable. The parents and
> children huddled together in their loneliness take too much
> out of each other. The parents fight; the children rebel ...
> Privacy is the source of fear and violence.

He believed that people should live, and children should grow up, in wider domestic groups, in more closely knit communities, and, like all writers advancing this point of view, he mentioned the Israeli 'kibbutzim' and the Chinese 'communes'. This whole question of the erosion of community-experience, and of the degrees (and kinds) of social isolation experienced by families in our society, is, of course, an important matter, and one to which we must return, but, for the moment, let us notice the evidence of reputable research (going beyond common experience) which seems positively to disprove what Leach was claiming. And this can be introduced by asking a simple question. If privacy in the home and the family is so appalling an experience, so 'emotionally uncomfortable', with stresses and strains 'greater than most of us can bear', how does it come about that the majority of people actively want and choose it? Many pieces of research – some available when Leach was writing, some published since that time – are quite decided in their answer to this.

The well known findings of Geoffrey Gorer – first published in 1955 and confirmed and extended in 1970* – showed how much home life and family life were wanted, and how, indeed, it was the new closeness and companionability of marriage which had its strongest appeal among young people. In the early 1970s, these findings were entirely borne out in the surveys conducted by Mark Abrams for the Social Science Research Council. Investigating social indicators of greater or lesser degrees of satisfaction associated with certain patterns of expenditure (of consumers' outlay), he identified eleven chief *domains*. It is enough here to note that the three most important domains were unquestionably Marriage, Family Life, and Health (in that order). These were closely followed by Standard of Living, and House. In short, marriage, home and family life were far and away the chief realms of satisfaction, and the rate of satisfaction found in their own marriage (among respondents) was 'easily the highest rating accorded to any of the domains of life dealt with in the interview'. The same findings emerged from studies which were not initially directed at the family at all. Whilst studying newly affluent industrial workers, for example, to discover whether or not their attitudes were moving towards those of the middle classes, Lockwood, Goldthorpe and their colleagues discovered that the chief orientation of their motives was towards their home and their family life. Their work itself and their attendance at their work-place were ceasing to be something in and for themselves and were becoming increasingly instrumental: their objective being the provision and enjoyment of a better home and a richer family experience. 'Higher standards of domestic living' were the most widespread kind of aspiration. Men showed a marked consideration for their wives and a desire to spend time with them (not to allow work or other activities to keep them too long from home). Family life was looked to as the 'major source of expressive and affective satisfaction'. Their 'over-riding commitment' was to their families. It was, quite specifically, 'a commitment to the interest of one primary group – the conjugal family – which was of an overriding kind', and, strangely enough, it was, in fact, the very quality of the *privacy* of the family which these authors found it necessary to emphasise. The new closeness of family relationships brought about an increased enjoyment of family life and an increasing attachment to it. In consequence of the conjugal family assuming a more 'companionate' or partnership-like form,

---

Exploring English Character, Cresset Press, 1955; '*Sex and Marriage in England Today*', Nelson, 1970.

relations between husband and wife and between parents and children would seem likely to become closer and more inherently rewarding. The *'privatised* world' of the family – its area of private experience and shared activities – was, quite plainly, what these workers wanted and most enjoyed. The same findings were reported from straightforward building surveys. One of the most important features of the homes people were seeking was the degree of *privacy* it provided. Families actively wanted their own home in their own garden in a quiet environment with a certain degree of 'elbow-room' between themselves and their neighbours. In 1968, for example, a survey was carried out by National Opinion Polls for the National Housebuilders' Registration Council. One of the questions on which they wanted information was: whether critics were right in saying that people had to live in 'little boxes' because there was no other choice. The report said that 'privacy', in fact, played a big part in the survey's findings, and concluded: 'Home-buyers *want* privacy and most of them want to live in "little boxes" to get it.' Their investigations showed:

> ... that 88% of people prefer a larger garden of 60ft by 30ft to a smaller garden of 30ft by 20ft with a communal landscaped garden shared with neighbours.
>
> 85% were willing to take a smaller house if it gave privacy.
>
> 31% would prefer a smaller semi-detached house to a bigger terraced or town house, and 54% would accept a smaller house if it gave even more privacy by being detached
> ...

– and the conclusion was quite definite:

> The charge that they buy 'boxes, little boxes' only because they are offered no choice is not supported by the evidence. The preference for privacy and the detached and semi-detached was marked.

For most people, then, privacy in their families was far from being the suffocating, undesirable experience Leach himself imagined it to be.

A final point deserves brief mention here – though we shall come back to it when considering the claims of the Women's Liberation Movement. It is this: a simple but surely telling point. Why – if the monogamous, conjugal family group as we have come ιo know it in Britain is so impoverished and unbearable a form of the family compared with the very variable traditional family-types which exist in other societies, and with which anthropologists are familiar – do subjected peoples, and particularly subjected women, opt for it when their traditional constraints are removed? Might it not be because this is by no means merely a matter of 'cultural relativity', but because the present-day process of 'modernisation' throughout the world is substantially one of 'Westernisation'? Because the same elements of social change are becoming increasingly operative the world over, the same ethical principles are increasingly seen to be applicable, and the form of the family in Britain is coming to be seen (correctly?) in terms of reason, morality, and directed social action in the making of a more humane society – protecting in the best way possible the rights of men, women, and children alike? It is a question I shall raise again.

Meanwhile, in the same way, Leach also seemed to ignore available evidence in committing the 'Earlier Community Fallacy'.

All the evidence of the historical researches of the post-war years had been such as to deny and disprove it. Indeed, if there has been any consensus of opinion in recent social history it is surely to be found on this one question, and this, too, we shall elaborate later. The picture Leach drew was of earlier communities as being much smaller, self-contained, immobile, simple, and long-abiding. People were born in them, grew up in them, married in them, lived the whole of their lives in them, and died in them. The bonds of work, kinship, and neighbourhood tended to be fused, thus giving 'the individual continuous moral support throughout his life'. Now that this close support was gone, families and individuals were more free, alone, isolated – and more prone to emotional stress. Here, I will only mention the evidence provided by Peter Laslett (in *World We Have Lost*, published in 1965)[4] and some observations drawn from Ronald Blythe's *Akenfield* to show how false and decidedly one-sided a picture this is,[5] and later we shall be able to note wider and more detailed evidence of the same kind.

Peter Laslett – giving detailed facts for a number of village communities in the *seventeenth* century – showed that the number of families having resident in-laws was very small indeed. In one (Clayworth) there were only 7 out of 98, and – late in the century – 3 out of 91. In another (Chilvers Coton) 13 out of 176 households contained in-laws – which is $7\frac{1}{2}$ per cent. The *highest* proportion he found was in Cogenhoe in which 6 out of 33 families contained in-laws. Also, these in-laws were not, by any means, all *parents* of the husband or wife of the family, and the number of children living in their old home after their marriage was smaller than that of parents living in the homes of their married children. Compared with this, what is the position today? In Woodford Green, in 1957, 23 per cent (nearly a quarter) of people of pensionable age shared their houses with the family of their son or daughter; and in Bethnal Green, in 1954, 21 per cent did so. The truth, therefore, is the reverse of the common assumption, and one obvious reason for this, said Laslett:

> ... is the lengthening of life. In Stuart England very few people lived with their in-laws, because they less often had in-laws to live with. A couple seldom had their parents living with them because their parents survived less frequently to an age where this might become necessary.

The larger proportion of the population in earlier rural communities consisted of children.

> We must imagine our ancestors ... in the perpetual presence of their young offspring. A good 70 per cent of all households contained children – this figure is remarkably constant from place to place and date to date – and there were between two and a half and three children to every household with them ... In the pre-industrial world there were children everywhere; playing in the village street and fields when they were very small, hanging round the farmyards and getting in the way, until they had grown enough to be given child-size jobs to do; thronging churches; for ever clinging to the skirts of women in the house and werever they went and above all crowding round the cottage fires.

It is an error, Laslett insisted, that the family group in pre-industrial communities in Britain was large.

> It is erroneously believed that it was large because it contained whole groups of kinsfolk living together. The impression seems to be that sons and daughters stayed with their parents after marriage and had their children there: therefore the family group must often have been multi-generational ... It is assumed that when a woman's husband died she returned to her original family group and was supported by it. A widowed mother might live with her married daughter, or a family would support various in-laws. It is also said that there would also be joint families of another type, because two married couples would often find

it more convenient to share one household, just as perhaps they shared one plot of land. In any case, and this seems to be the most deep-seated and important generalization of all, in the familial, patriarchal world the family was the source of welfare. Sickness, unemployment, bereavement were all the responsibility of the family, and so to a large extent was education. To fulfil all these functions the family in the old world would have had to be large. Something like this seems to be the general impression of family life among our ancestors.

But, he continued, the records demonstrate that their families were not large. The general rule governing the size and constitution of the family was this:

... no two married couples or more went to make up a family group; whether parents and children, brothers and sisters, employers and servants or married couples associated only for convenience. When a son got married he left the family of his parents and started a family of his own. If he was not in a position to do this, then he could not get married, nor could his sister unless the man who was to take her for his bride was also in a position to start a new family.

Laslett also presented a large array of facts which made any idea of a 'rich community life' seem very far from the truth. The simpler communities of the past clearly had another side. With regard to the extent of poverty in earlier rural communities in Britain, he wrote:

... it is probably safer to assume that at all times before the beginnings of industrialization a good half of all those living were judged by their contemporaries to be poor, and their standards must have been extremely harsh, even in comparison with those laid down by Victorian poor law authorities.

And – again reversing and contradicting many commonly held assumptions about the health of rural community-life in the past:

It seems true to say that a baby born into the Gorbals of Glasgow in 1879 probably had a better chance of surviving to its first birthday than a baby born into the entirely rural, open-field village of Clayworth in the fairly prosperous county of Nottinghamshire in 1679.

The notion of the rich, morally supported community life of the past is therefore in large part a *myth*, as is the similarly romanticised idea of what has come to be called (falsely extrapolating from the concepts of the early anthropologists) *'the extended family'*. All this, however, rested on the historical evidence of village records of the pre-industrial past, but in some parts of the country which 'missed' industrialisation (or at least the worst features of it) this same actuality came very close to our own door-step in time, and Ronald Blythe's *Akenfield* substantiates this same picture of the life of earlier rural communities – this time drawing its information from living memory. His composite portrait of the village was made up of the life-stories and experiences of the individual members of the village themselves – as given to him in their own words. The continuity of families, of crafts, even of physical characteristics of both families and the practice of crafts, were shown to be rich strands in the traditional pattern of life, but the overwhelming conclusion that emerged (from old and young people alike) was that the life of the old rural community was hard, impoverished, cruel in its work and work relationships, a struggle at the level of long-endured desperation in the sustaining of homes and families, one of burdensomeness in caring for the aged, and one of tragically limited horizons – of the sheer non-existence of education, and of no possible vistas of variety or opportunity. The village had a grasp upon individuals which none could escape. Here are just a few examples.

Fred Mitchell, an old horseman of 85, had a completely disabling accident when about 47 years old – dragged away by horses which 'jagged me all to pieces.' He had no compensation, and 'had a rough old time from then on.'

> I had a struggle to bring the family up. You had to nearly perish to bring a family up then. It was too much. There wasn't a penny for nothing. They have money now, don't they? We didn't have money. I never had no good times. Nothing began to happen until my boys were all grown up and I was getting old. But there, I wasn't the only one! The farmers were sharp with us. If you couldn't do a job you were reminded that plenty more could. So you had to be careful. I had to accept everything my governor said to me. I learnt never to answer a word. I dursn't say nothing. Today you can be a man with men, but not then. That is how it was. It will never be like that again. I lived when other men could do what they liked with me. We feared so much. We

even feared the weather! Today a farmer must pay for the week, whatever the weather. But we were always being sent home. We dreaded the rain; it washed our few shillings away.

'There is,' he said, concluding his long story, 'some comfort in the world now ... I'm pleased to think that I've lived to see such nice times.' And there was Jubal Merton – remembering the nature of hunger:

I can remember being really hungry – there are not many people who can truthfully say that now, are there? We never saw sugar at all. We used to have golden syrup in our tea and if we couldn't get that we had black treacle. We had cakes without sugar – and our bread! My grandmother still baked it, as she had always done, but now, when you cut off the top crust you could put your hand in the hole which was left ... I can remember when I was about twelve that we boys were so hungry that we used to get together, crouch down in the corn and bark. It distracted people but once we started we couldn't stop. Barking like dogs – imagine!

He, too, spoke of the fact that people never left the village, and, within it, had to suffer the power of their masters. 'The farmer had got the upper hand and wherever he could he made his worker a slave ... Have no doubt about it. No man dare open his mouth, or out he went!' An old, retired farm-worker of 80 – Samuel Guising – echoed the same resignation to submission: 'Our lives were all obedience.'

The economic and material conditions of families, the prevailing ignorance of the labouring poor, and the quality of the care given to children and the aged in this first quarter of our own century were well described by Marjorie Jope (79), a retired district nurse.

There was a great difference inside the cottages in those days. One had to explain every single thing. The most simple instructions had to be said twice over. Living conditions were very, very poor ... when the school doctor came round, I had to assist him examine the children. I knew them all so well they could have been my own children. I knew their homes and in most cases I had delivered them. There were so many dirty children in those days, dirty hair, dirty feet, impetigo. It was thought a disgrace to have a dirty head, but lots did. There's nothing like that now. Children have never been as beautiful as they are now ...

The old people were not taken care of. This is another thing which people like to think now, that grandfathers and grandmothers had an honoured place in the cottage. In fact, when they got old they were just neglected, pushed away into corners. I even found them in cupboards! Even in fairly clean and respectable houses you often found an old man or woman shoved out of sight in a dark niche. People were most suspicious at first when I called.

There was no such thing as a welcome, you had to make your own way. They didn't want anybody outside to know their business. I had to ask questions, especially about TB. They hated that. I had to collect long lists of facts about them and they were so unwilling that it often took me days. I had to feel my way, exchanging trust for trust. They had their secrets, like all families, but I had to know some of them! There were families in Akenfield who never told anyone anything. It was - their entire life, you know - all bolted up behind the back door. Not many people were taken away to the infirmaries. They were born at home and they died at home.

Hardly a picture of a closely-knit community - of a larger and more relaxed set of community relations, of a family unit morally supported by occupation, neighbourhood, and kindred. On the contrary it was a picture of families locked within narrow destinies by poverty, limitation, ignorance, and economic tyranny alike. And 'tawdry secrets', it seems, were not lacking there. The wide network of kinship relationships was as much a source of long-harboured resentments, conflicts and troubles as of mutual support and concern. A visiting nurse, then, was clearly a confidante for social and psychological disturbances.

Five years after I arrived in Akenfield it got so that I could walk in nearly every house. Sometimes they all looked so strong and well that I wondered why I had been sent for, then the worry would come spilling out. It was usually about the relations. Practically every family was related. It is the same with myself, except I don't know my own cousins. So many village marriages used to be cousin marriages. It is different now because the young men drive about all over the place and find girls. Nobody moved a yard in the old days.

It is interesting to notice, too, that there seemed to be a greater lack of sensitivity even towards adoption and 'foster-families'.

There were quite a lot of 'home' children in the village in those days – more than twenty, perhaps. They came from Dr. Barnardo's and from the Church of England Children's Home. They were all boys – nobody wanted girls.... A lot of the Barnardo boys were sent to Australia when they were fourteen and new ones came in their places. Their foster-parents didn't seem to turn a hair when the replacement happened; it always amazed me.

These examples are enough. Whatever the evidence considered – from the remote past to the recent past alike – the picture of family life that results is the same. The rural communities of the past, their families set in the networks of close kinship relationships, by no means enjoyed conditions of social life from which the modern family has fallen, but, on the contrary, conditions of harshness and limitation from which the modern family has been liberated – from a past which it has escaped – to enjoy a life, for all its members, of richer opportunities and fulfilment.

These arguments could be pursued at much greater length, and we shall return to other aspects of them later, when considering the positions of other critics. Here, however, we need only note that Dr Leach's attack upon the family rested upon no satisfactory grounds at all. It was not a factually founded criticism, but a casual and unsupported statement carrying no weight other than that of being the personal opinion of a well-known anthropologist. Strictly speaking, its wide influence was an aberration of selective quotation, mass-communications, and gullibility: nowadays a curious and dangerously increasing source of 'authority'.

Before leaving Leach, however, let us note that one or two of his points – once they have been freed from the context of his particular perspective and interpretation – can be accepted. It is true that many families in modern society have come to suffer various degrees of 'social isolation', and it is just because of the 'potential instability' brought about by the improvements in the family that such unchosen isolation can be such a source of difficulties. But this is a matter of the changed collective conditions of our whole society, not at all a matter for which the family itself is responsible, or a situation within which the family can be said to have worsened in the supposed tyranny of its 'inwardness' and 'intensity'. In many ways, as we have seen and as the evidence proves, the modern family offers far greater degrees of freedom and fulfilment to its members, far greater opportunities for wider personal and social life, than was ever possible in the earlier and much smaller communities of tightly related neighbours and near-kin. It is true, too, that, with this in mind, we do face an important task of community-making, but this should be a making of communities which preserve the qualities and liberties of the kind of family unit we have now achieved, and one appropriate to the changed collective conditions of our own society now – not in any sense a going back to 'earlier communities' or 'extended families' which were largely mythical, and which, in any event, we would find intolerable – indeed immoral – now.

The family as destroyer:
Laing, Cooper and Esterson

A second source of criticisms of the family which became extremely influential during the late 1960s and throughout the 1970s, and which seemed to reinforce Leach's view of the destructiveness of the intense privacy of the family – though resting on a theoretical position going far beyond his – was the work of R. D. Laing, D. G. Cooper, A. Esterson. The books resulting from their studies were very variable, but it is valid to regard them as a 'school' of thought on the modern family because all three authors, besides focusing on the same area of research, shared certain basic elements in their positions – and it is with these that we have to be concerned. But theirs was a much more detailed body of work than the 'Reith Sentence' of Leach, and care has to be taken over it, especially because these authors have protested from time to time that their position has been misrepresented and misunderstood. Here, I want to take issue with the misrepresentation itself – the widespread assumption that they have demonstrated the destructive evils of the family as a group in society, and have advocated and justified its 'abolition' – and also, going beyond this, to attack those actual elements of their own teaching which have given rise to this misinterpretation.

The general impression given by these authors was unquestionably that they were 'anti-family', and we will look at some of their statements later. The fashionable 'anti-marriage' and 'anti-family' cult which spread through all the media of mass-communications during the 1970s – in films, weekly colour supplements, and the like – owed much (whether justifiably or not) to them. The picture of the modern family they conveyed was of a tight, inward-looking, possessive group which – just because of its intense privacy, within which tyrannical forces were at work – was essentially *destructive of the individual*. The family was depicted as that powerful agency of society which forced the nature of the child into prescribed patterns of attitude and behaviour, and, in doing so, was chiefly responsible for conflict, disorder and misery in individual personalities – for mental disturbance and 'abnormality', for psychotic illness. In modern society, the family was the *destroyer*! – of individual freedom and individual personality alike. The assumption which seemed to follow was that the family itself had to be destroyed – to be replaced by some more humane alternative. 'The Death of the Family', to use David Cooper's much-repeated title, is what a community sensitive to the freedom and fulfilment of individual 'selves' required.

I want to argue, first of all, that this interpretation is unfounded; that these authors – despite the extremes of Cooper in particular – did not teach this at all, at least in the precise form of this statement, and then to go beyond this and argue that such an interpretation is understandable, even so, because of basic faults in the underlying ideas themselves, and because of an underlying ideological stance. Before doing this, however, let it be clear that this is by no means a matter of purely unsympathetic and antagonistic criticism, and that – whether or not we agree with all elements of it – the contribution of these authors has much of a positive kind to be said in its favour.

First, though it concentrated entirely on abnormalities of personality and family functioning (something to be questioned later) it had the great virtue of being a fresh, open, forthright questioning of the very categories of 'sanity' and 'mental illness', and this had many worthwhile aspects. It raised forcefully the whole question as to how far certain mental illnesses could be said to be clinical facts quite independent of social judgments, and, in so doing, exposed the enormous range of disagreement over the supposed 'symptoms' of mental illnesses – of 'schizophrenia', for example. Indeed, the fundamental question directing their own researches was: 'are the experience and behaviour that psychiatrists take as symptoms and signs of schizophrenia more socially intelligible than has come to be supposed?' And to answer this, they found it necessary to investigate the experience and behaviour of their patients *within the living contexts of their families*, looking at: '(i) each person in the family, (ii) the relations between persons in the family, and (iii) the family itself as a system.' Their interest, they said, was:

> ... in persons always in relation either with us, or with each other, and always in the light of their group context, which

in this work is primarily the family, but may include also the extra-familial personal networks of family members if these have a specific bearing on the issues we are trying to illumine. In other words, we are interested in what might be called the family *nexus*, that multiplicity of persons drawn from the kinship group, and from others who, though not linked by kinship ties, are regarded as members of the family. The relationships of persons in a nexus are characterized by enduring and intensive face-to-face reciprocal influence on each other's experience and behaviour.

We are studying the persons who comprise this nexus, their relationships, and the nexus itself, in so far as it may have structures, processes, and effects as a system, not necessarily intended by its members, not necessarily predictable from a knowledge of its members studied out of context.[1]

One fundamental significance of the Laing, Cooper, Esterson school, therefore, was that they had validly seen the importance of the sociological perspective for the understanding of individuals and their problems. They employed it effectively in their research, and tried to build it into new procedures for the diagnosis and treatment of mental conditions. They had clearly and fully seen what sociological theorists had meant when insisting that, at least at the level of human experience and behaviour, the processes of association were psychologically creative, and that many aspects of individual behaviour and dimensions of the individual personality could not be understood excepting within this context. They were extraordinarily close to Cooley's and Mead's analysis of the growth of the 'self' in 'society', and the emphasis placed on the importance of *social facts* and *collective conditions* (by Emile Durkheim, for example) for the understanding of the experience and problems of individuals. These authors, in short, were very decidedly *not* 'anti-psychiatry'. On the contrary, Laing's emphasis was only that the *existing* conceptions, methods, and clinical practices of psychiatry – which failed to see the 'patient' as a person within a social context – were insufficient. In both diagnosis and treatment, it was necessary that psychiatry should move out of the clinic, so that it could see and consider the individual person not as a 'patient' stripped of all social context in surgery or hospital, but as someone whose pattern of attitude and responses had taken shape – and continued to operate – within the complex relationships of a family, and this within its wider social situation. The diagnosis of a 'patient' turned out to be the diagnosis of a social situation. To be 'called in' to deal with the mental crisis of a 'patient' was to be 'called in' to a 'social crisis' (whatever its dimensions might prove to be). And unless the actual social context was observed and examined, no one in the situation, including the psychiatrist, could know clearly what that situation was. Laing's emphasis, in short, was that a sociological model of diagnosis and treatment must replace (or at least add its perspective and dimensions to) a medical model. It was an attempt at a telling reformulation of psychiatry informed by the significance of the new perspective of sociology, and this possessed the exciting possibilities not only of deeper and more correct diagnosis, but also of more effective treatment. The significance they attached to this new associational emphasis was very considerable.

We believe that the shift of point of view that these descriptions both embody and demand has a historical significance no less radical than the shift from a demonological to a clinical viewpoint three hundred years ago (my italics).

This was a large and important claim, and one which still deserves much more thought and elaboration.

It is worth mention, too, that all these detailed matters of theory, diagnosis and treatment with reference to individuals within their specific family situations were also seen within the wider perspective which sociological theorists (from Comte, Marx, Mill to Weber and Durkheim) had continually emphasised when characterising the critical transformation through which they believed that scientific and industrial society was – and is – passing. On this, too, Laing was very plain.

We are living in an age in which the ground is shifting and the foundations are shaking. I cannot answer for other times and places. Perhaps it has always been so. We know it is true today.

Modern industrial society – in its largeness of scale, its rapidity of change, its complexities, its compulsive preoccupation with the external matters of technology, organisation, control – was such, he said, that men and women had come to be 'starving' for the richness of the inner world, for some return to it, for some renewed experience of it. In their lack of contact with it, their being forced into a distance from it, lay the reason for their impoverishment. It was very much like Jung's emphasis in *Modern Man in Search of a Soul*, and, like others, Laing emphasised the notion of 'alienation', the fact of

30

modern man's enforced 'estrangement from his own being'. There is, he wrote:

... a prophecy in Amos that there will be a time when there will be a famine in the land, 'not a famine for bread, nor a thirst for water, but of *hearing* the words of the Lord.' That time has now come to pass. It is the present age.

The Laing, Cooper, Esterson 'school' was, then, wide in its humanitarian concern; couched not only in medical and psychiatric terms or even in the terms of various psycho-analytic schools (Freud, Jung, etc.), but also in terms of wider social and philosophical theories, and referring to wider sources in literature, mythology and religion; important in its appreciation and use of the sociological perspective; and of considerable contemporary significance in creating a new socially orientated psychiatry. But all this suggests that its influence should have been to emphasise the significance of the family – not the reverse; and this, indeed, is exactly what I want to argue. If this is so, however, how was the strong anti-family image of their work brought about? There are two or three clear reasons.

Focus on pathology

The most obvious reason why Laing's picture was always one of the destructiveness of the family was because he and his colleagues concentrated entirely on those families they studied which had produced schizophrenics. In following the persuasion that the 'schizophrenic' condition of the patient was in some way or other the outcome of family patterns, the concept of the 'schizophrenogenic mother' was introduced, and then, more fully, the concept of the 'schizophrenogenic family'. In *The Divided Self*, Laing wrote:

... one might do better to think of schizophrenogenic families, rather than too exclusively of schizophrenogenic mothers. At least, doing so might encourage more reports of the dynamics of the family constellation as a whole, instead of studies of mothers, or fathers, or siblings, without sufficient reference to the whole family dynamics.

And it was a detailed study of eleven such families which formed the report of Laing and Esterson – *Sanity, Madness and the Family* – in 1964. Now these families were very specially selected: they were the families of women between the ages of 15 and 40 who satisfied certain other conditions which the authors wished to investigate. They said quite plainly that they were testing no hypothesis – but only illustrating by eleven examples the ways in which the schizophrenic experience and behaviour of the patients could be seen to make social sense when seen in the context of their families. They did not test their findings in any way, they simply said that these were selected illustrations of what they had found always to be the case in over two hundred studies. And they went on to say that – if they were wrong – this could be quite readily shown by studying a few other families: 'and revealing that schizophrenics really are talking a lot of nonsense after all'.

The fact remains, however, that *all* the families studied by Laing and Esterson were 'schizophrenogenic' families, and – following upon their own conviction – such families were bound to have been such as to produce 'abnormalities' of experience and behaviour. They were – by both definition and selection – instances of psychopathology and social pathology. They focused entirely on the pathological; on the social and psychological patterns disruptive of 'normality'. Laing and Cooper both went out of their way to point out that 1 per cent of the population were likely to be diagnosed as 'schizophrenic' – meaning, presumably, that this was a large number. It may be a large number, but it was an extremely small proportion. It meant that 99 per cent would *not* be diagnosed as 'schizophrenics', and therefore – again by their own definition – the overwhelmingly large majority of families in society were *not* 'schizophrenogenic'. It is perfectly plain, then, that to characterise '*the* family in society', or *all* families in society according to the very small proportion of 'abnormal' ones was just a stark error. There were no grounds for it at all.

It may still be said, however, that there is no clear line of demarcation between the 'normal' and the 'pathological'; that the patterns of relationships in 'normal' families may not be markedly different from those in 'pathological' families; and, indeed, that the study of pathological cases may actually throw much light on the 'normal' functioning of families. Exactly so! And this is exactly why a comparative study with 'normal' families is necessary.

Let us notice one or two points before leaving this, however. It may well be that the study of 'abnormal' families would throw light on 'normal' family functioning – and some sociologists (Comte, Durkheim) have long argued that our understanding of the nature and functioning of social institutions can be much deepened and enriched by studying cases when they break down, or go wrong – but it is worth noting that *if* it proved to be the case that family processes were alike in both 'normal' and 'schizophrenogenic' families – then the Laing, Cooper, Esterson theory concerning the family aetiology of schizophrenia would be disproved.

That aside, however, it remains the case that no such comparative studies with 'normal' families were undertaken. In *The Politics of the Family*,[2] Laing saw and said clearly that this should be done. Indeed he said that it *had* been done – but no evidence was given of it. In discussing *The Study of Family and Social Contexts*, he pointed to the necessity of 'sampling' behaviour in a multiplicity of social contexts, and said:

> The emphasis has not so much been on developing a typology of family structures as on de-mystifying what we have always found to be highly mystified situations. We have compared such situations with what goes on in 'normal' families.

But one has to ask: *where* – in the published work of these three authors – are these studies of 'normal' families to be found? So far, I, at any rate, have not been able to find them. Later in the same book, too, Laing pointed to the difficulty of studying *any* family (in that one is looking at one momentary period in what is a long history of generational relationships), but especially of studying the *normal* family. 'The more smoothly they function,' he wrote, 'the more difficult they are to study.'

The truth of the matter is that the work of these authors dwelt *entirely* on the very small proportion of families within which individuals had come to be diagnosed as 'schizophrenics'. There was no comparative study at all of the overwhelming majority of families from which came the 99 per cent of the population who were 'normal'. Is it not perfectly plain, then, that to characterise the vast majority by the qualities of the small minority is an absurdity? To speak in general terms of *the family in society* as being *destructive of individual selves* on these grounds alone is quite unwarranted. And therefore such a *misrepresentation* arising from the claims of these authors is completely without foundation. And it must be said that – *on this point alone* – this *was* a misrepresentation. Neither Laing nor Esterson (we shall come to Cooper later) advocated the abolition of the family in society on the basis of their study of pathological families and individuals. At this point, however, two other factors complicate the issue.

First, this relatively limited statement based on an over-emphasis

33

upon 'pathological' families was given a much wider range of application by the ideological position which these authors had adopted – an ideological position very far removed from the claims of either psychiatry or science. And secondly, though all rooted in this same ideology, the authors varied a good deal among themselves and a distinction has to be drawn between them. The fact is that David Cooper was much more extreme in his pronouncements than Laing and Esterson, and it was his very deliberate emphasis upon *The Death of the Family* which seems to have had the widest publicity and influence. All three authors, however, were at fault.

Ideology

The shared ideology which widely publicised their picture of the family as a *destructive agency* in society was compounded chiefly of the existentialism of Jean Paul Sartre and the revolutionary notions of Marx, but many others were drawn in (from the Bible, Hegel, Ibsen, Jung) if their imagery – like that of Amos mentioned earlier – could help to touch in a supportive dimension or two. A very mixed compound it was! Laing, Cooper and Esterson were not simply putting forward a body of work resulting from their examination of the families of mentally ill people. They were engaged in an ideological attack upon society, and their own brand of 'science' was deliberately rooted in this ideology. It was this ideology which both confused and extended their notions of 'sanity' and 'madness', and gave rise to their general view of the role of the family in society. This had several important dimensions, and we will look at each in turn.

NOT 'BOURGEOIS SCIENCE' – BUT PRAXIS AND DIALECTICAL KNOWLEDGE

First of all, this ideology rejected what most of us accept as science. The entire enterprise of science – of establishing a set of concepts and methods appropriate to the exploration of a distinctive subject-matter and for the testing of hypotheses about it – was brushed aside as '*bourgeois* science'. Understanding the world in terms of tested hypotheses – establishing 'objective knowledge' – was not enough. The only genuine knowledge about men in society was dialectical knowledge: the intelligibility of the actions of men (their praxis – what they do) in continually changing the world in the conflictful

process of their historical-social relationships. This kind of orientation to 'knowledge' had both its large-scale and its more limited
application in the work of Laing, Cooper and Esterson, and had, too,
its confusions and misconceptions of the nature of science.

First: consider the large-scale conceptions of 'praxis' adopted by
Laing and Cooper in their exposition of a decade of Sartre's writing
(in their book *Reason and Violence*).[3]

> Praxis, in effect, is the passage *from* the objective through
> interiorization *to* the objective. The project, as subjective
> depassment of objectivity towards objectivity, is stretched
> between the objective conditions of the environment and the
> objective structures of the field of possibilities. It represents in
> itself the moving unity of subjectivity and objectivity, these
> cardinal moments of activity. The subjective appears as a
> necessary moment of the objective process, the objective as a
> necessary moment of subjectivity.

The implications of this for a 'knowledge' of 'praxis' in the history
of society was stated as follows:

> History always has to be rewritten, that is, detotalized and
> retotalized ... Here the individual is the only possible
> methodological point of departure. Through his praxis, the
> dialectic is not the outcome of history, it is the original
> movement of its totalization by him on the basis of its
> totalization of him ...
> Now, if history is totalization, and if individual praxes are
> the unique basis of totalizing temporalization, it is necessary
> to ask how a multiplicity of individuals produce a praxis of a
> kind through a multiplicity of totalizations. One wishes for an
> Ariadne's thread to conduct one from individual praxes to the
> diverse forms of human collectives. We shall try to trace the
> dialectical intelligibility of these transformations, whereby
> praxis become praxis-process. The individual agent enters into
> very different collectivities. We shall have to follow the
> vicissitudes and transformations of praxis from series to
> groups to series: we shall study groups of groups: class and
> the being of class. While we may take examples from the
> working class or the bourgeoisie, it is not the primary
> intention of this study to define these, or any, particular
> classes, but rather to work out the way a class is constituted,
> its totalization and detotalization, and, all the time, its

35

dialectical intelligibility, involving links of interiority and exteriority, its internal structures, relations with other classes, etc....

And here is a further example of how – with regard to alienation and struggle in history – social classes were regarded as 'crystallised praxes'.

The alienation of one's praxis through alteration and objectification being-other-for-other and being-outside-in-the-Thing, is nevertheless one's truth and reality. This being-outside (*être dehors*) constitutes itself, or is constituted, as practico-inert matter. Human praxis, in so far as it is subject to matter, can fall into social impotence, into inertia. As Marx has shown, capitalism is an antisocial force: it massifies and serializes men...

... class encumbrances can be seen variously as the passive synthesis of materiality, the crystallized praxes of preceding generations, the general conditions of social activity, the most immediate and brutal aspects of our objective reality, its predetermination in general...

Now I do not know what you make of writing like this, but it is only necessary here to see that it decidedly is *not* science, neither does it lead to anything approaching the exactitude of the methods of science. There is no testing of hypotheses here, no establishing of testable knowledge. Dialectical knowledge is a matter of one 'praxis' – in its detotalising and retotalising social activity – 'depassing' and superseding another. Not understanding and explanation – but success in the wielding of power is supreme.

All this, however, was at the large-scale level of the general ideological position of these authors, and it is only fair to say that at the much more limited level of their specific research, the concepts they borrowed from this larger rubric were far more clearly employed. Their approach to the study of families made use of these few concepts: they studied (a) what families were *doing* (their 'praxis'), (b) *what was going on* – the interconnection of events of which the members of the families might not have been aware (the 'process'), and (c) as investigators involved in the dialectic of knowledge, they sought the *intelligibility* of the experience and behaviour of individuals in terms of this 'praxis' and 'process'. This was clear enough, and the analysis they accomplished of particular families was rewarding. On this limited level, then, no great exception to their usage is necessary. I will not stop to ask why all these words from a cloudy epistemology are necessary – for, after all, what this limited scheme of analysis amounts to is simply the interpretation of action and interaction within a situation. The Sartrean fog hardly seems necessary for that. It is more relevant to our concern with the study of families, however, to move quickly to other points.

It is important to see, next, that – even at this limited level of specific researches – this ideology precluded science, and carried confusion with it. When Laing was meeting the criticism of not having scientifically tested the propositions he and Esterson were making (in *Sanity, Madness and the Family*), he explicitly renounced all effort towards science. This was his statement.

> Such criticism would be justified if we had set out to test the hypothesis that the family is a pathogenic variable in the genesis of schizophrenia. But we did not set out to do this, and we have not claimed to have done so. We set out to illustrate by eleven examples that, if we look at some experience and behaviour without reference to family interactions, they may appear comparatively socially senseless, but that if we look at the same experience and behaviour in their original family context they are liable to make more sense.

And this is what Esterson said when, at the end of a book (*The Leaves of Spring*)[4] on the study of *one* family, he tried – honestly – to meet the demand that he should be scientific. Why, he asked, should he have chosen this particular family (the 'Danzigs') as his 'paradigm'? His answer was:

> Simply because I was moved to do so. The dialectic is a movement in the observer and the system observed, and is fully realized when so experienced. And the scientist who allows himself to be moved, and later discovers the why and wherefore, is acting correctly dialectically. . . .
> Dialectical knowledge is knowledge of the dialectic, and as such it is reflective knowledge in, through, and for social and historical action. A dialectical paradigm is validated if it helps others to reason and act dialectically. Subsequent students will judge.

All one can say is that this is not science, and nothing approaching scientific testability was offered here. There were other quite fundamental confusions over the use of the term 'dialectic' that went unnoticed (for example the equating of 'dialectical science' with 'the human sciences' as distinct from 'natural science', and then opposing 'dialectical science' to 'positivism') and this is something widely shared among all those who adopt a left-wing 'radical activist' point of view – all those who want to make changing the world, rather than the understanding of it, the bedrock of their theory of knowledge – but the exposition of these would take us too far from the study of the family. There was – and is – however, sheer error at the heart of it.

All this, indeed, may well seem a great distance from assessing the place of the family in society, but it is not so, and the direct relevance of this ideological position insisted upon by Laing, Cooper and Esterson to their statements about the family can now be made very clear.

FUSING IDEOLOGY WITH PATHOLOGY

The fact is that these authors – having reconsidered the definitions of 'sanity' and 'madness' within the wider context of society; having argued that they must be understood within the context of the family; and having shown the destructive power of the family in relation to 'schizophrenics' in particular – then fused this position with their larger ideological position that the modern family was the constraining 'socialising' agency of 'bourgeois capitalism'. With this fusion (which is no fusion really), the family in society (i.e. the nuclear family as an institution appropriate to capitalistic society) was held, in general, to be destructive of the individual 'self', imposing this necessitous 'alienation' upon him, grinding him into the shape required by the exploitative machine. Let us now look at some of the actual statements which were made.

Laing himself wrote this:

It is not enough to destroy one's own and other people's experience. One must overlay this devastation by a false consciousness inured, as Marcuse puts it, to its own falsity.

Exploitation must not be seen as such. It must be seen as benevolence ... we have to interiorize our violence upon ourselves and our children and to employ the rhetoric of morality to describe this process.

In order to rationalize our industrial-military complex, we have to destroy our capacity both to see clearly any more what is in front of, and to imagine what is beyond, our noses. Long before a thermonuclear war can come about, we have had to lay waste our own sanity. We begin with the children. It is imperative to catch them in time. Without the most thorough and rapid brain-washing their dirty minds would see through our dirty tricks. Children are not yet fools, but we shall turn them into imbeciles like ourselves, with high I.Q.s if possible.

From the moment of birth, when the stoneage baby confronts the twentieth-century mother, the baby is subjected to these forces of violence, called love, as its mother and father have been, and their parents and their parents before them. These forces are mainly concerned with destroying most of its potentialities. This enterprise is on the whole successful. By the time the new human being is fifteen or so, we are left with a being like ourselves. A half-crazed creature, more or less adjusted to a mad world. This is normality in our present age.

Love within the family was definitely conceived by Laing as a 'moralistically justified' violence perpetrated on the child in the service of exploitation. This was what Laing actually said. The family, and the parental love within it, destroyed the child: making him into a 'half-crazed' creature. And let us note here that a switch had now occurred. Laing was not now talking of 'mental abnormality' or 'insanity' as the condition of a small minority. The 'normal' was now the 'half-crazed' condition! And Laing, consistently and deliberately, made much of this. Insanity, psychosis, schizophrenia, were now regarded as ways in which people managed to live in this half-crazed normality. He wrote:

... it seems to us that *without exception* the experience and behaviour that gets labelled schizophrenic is a *special strategy that a person invents in order to live in an unliveable situation.*

These are Laing's own italics. Later, he went so far as to say that when future men look back on our 'age of darkness':

... They will see that what we call 'schizophrenia' was one of the forms in which, often through quite ordinary people, the light began to break through the cracks in our all-too-closed minds.

The situation was completely reversed. The 'normal and sane' were mad, and 'madness' was a glimpse – through the exploitative glass-and-concrete leviathan of society – of man's true estate. The absurdity of this entire analysis may be seen in the fact that if this was so – then Laing and his colleagues ought to have been seeking to increase the number of schizophrenogenic families in society, and increasing the number of schizophrenics – as bearers of the true vision, rather than seeking to cure them.

But a further fault must be mentioned here: Laing had too facile a manner of moving from near-clinical symptoms (such as the particular disorders of a schizophrenic patient) to the global efforts of men to understand and grapple with the enigma of nature and the complex judgments to be taken in meeting human destiny. There may be analogies to be drawn between psychotic symptoms and the doctrines, rituals, and symbolic significances of religion and philosophical systems, but to treat them as being homologous (as being qualitatively the same thing) is a grave mistake.

It is time now, however, to demonstrate these same faults in the work of David Cooper, because it was his more extreme statements which had, perhaps, the greater degree of publicity.

The extreme position of David Cooper

It is hard to believe that anyone could have taken *The Death of the Family*[5] seriously, but that it was so can best be seen (though its being very widely reviewed will be well remembered) by looking at the publisher's 'blurb' on the book's jacket. Usually, an author has some hand in the preparation of such blurb, but this, surely, reads as though the publisher actually believed it.

The family is the model for the greater part of our social organization, so much so that we often speak in familial terms of our country, or even of a group of countries. The modern family, often called the nuclear family, is structured in such a way as to produce the most intolerable stresses on its members. Hints of how this is so have appeared in earlier work by both David Cooper and by R. D. Laing, but here the problem is examined in detail. This formidable and vividly-expressed book is not only concerned with the destructive nature of the bourgeois nuclear family in itself, but also with those situations which reproduce the nuclear

40

family pattern: offices, factories, schools, churches, industrial corporations and so on.

The Death of the Family seeks to make people look at the situation in which they live, to make them understand the nature of their mutual gangsterism and the way in which the family compels us to form particular unfree roles. For in this understanding is also to be found the road to new forms of communal existence freed of the deadly restraints of familial fear....

This is not a quiescent or comfortable book. Passionately and finely written, it amounts to a manifesto for revolutionary social change in First World countries over the next two decades. The 'new men' of which revolutionaries so often speak cannot easily spring from families where the conditioning, even when it is very subtle, is towards the bourgeoisification of its members. The vanguard of revolution will itself take things only part of the way. For revolution to succeed, new and open structures must be created, specifically to replace the existing family....

This 'blurb' is an excellent example of what I mean when saying that it is the extreme statements of figures like Edmund Leach and David Cooper which seem to suit the fashionable conceptualisation of the middle-men of communications. And so – the most question-able assertions come to be given the hallmark of accepted authority. In this case, for example, the blurb clearly accepted without criticism the proposition that the 'nuclear family' was 'structured in such a way as to produce the most intolerable stresses on its members'. It echoed the 'destructive nature' of the 'bourgeois' nuclear family. It accepted the idea that 'mutual gangsterism' existed among members of the modern family, and that they were conditioned into 'bourgeoisification'. It seemed to accept, too, the desirability of a successful 'revolution' and some sort of 'replacement' of the existing family. In short, the blurb was as bad as the book itself – and no other book on the family can ever have been as bad and unbalanced as this one.

It contained, first of all, sociological absurdities. The form of the family was said to be that basic form running through the entirety of the social structure for the explicit purpose of domination. The power of the family, Cooper wrote:

resides in its social mediating function. It reinforces the effective power of the ruling class in any exploitative society by providing a highly controllable paradigmatic form for every social institution. So we find the family form replicated through the social structures of the factory, the union branch, the school (primary and secondary), the university, the business corporation, the church, political parties and governmental apparatus, the armed forces, general and mental hospitals, and so on. There are always good or bad, loved or hated 'mothers' and 'fathers', older and younger 'brothers' and 'sisters', defunct or secretly controlling 'grandparents'. Each of us, in terms of Freud's discovery, transfers bits of our original family experience in the 'family of origin' on to each other in our 'family of procreation' (our 'own' wife and children) and on to each other in whatever situation we work.

Again, he said, 'The family is endlessly replicated in its anti-instinctuality throughout all the institutions of this society.' The superficiality of such a view simply does not deserve serious comment.

Second, there was a complete confusion over perfectly clear sociological terms. 'Marriage', for example, was given this definition:

Now, as regards talking about the topography of love – that is to say where love is at, if anywhere, today – I shall take, as a paradigmatic case, the word 'marriage'.

Beyond the obvious legal and social-contractual senses of the word, marriage can mean any sort of more or less lasting, socially objectified conjunction between personal entities. If we recognize that each of us is filled with a world of others who are not quite them and at the same time not quite us, we can envisage the possibility of some marital arrangement within one person. If we go back in the tradition of phenomenological investigation of human experience we recall the definition of intentionality running through the work of Husserl and Sartre in particular. Any primary datum of experience arising as a thinking, feeling, striving movement is of something, towards some object that both constitutes and is constituted by the initial movement in consciousness as a unitary and self-uniting entity in the world.

And this is the kind of discussion that stemmed from it:

One has to see through one's parents' marriage and one's own state of, in some sense, being married to their marriage and one's own marriage to each of one's parents in turn.

Also one's marriage to each of one's siblings and to each of
the 'other significant persons' (and to their marriage to
oneself, since marriage can be entirely non-reciprocal – one
can feel married to oneself). Then, before one arrives at any
marital relationship with other people in the world outside
one's family one has to go through a whole lot of divorce
proceedings with each of these people to a more or less
partial or total degree. One may have to get finally divorced
from one's relationship with one of one's parents or divorced
from one's infatuation with their marriage and so on, *seriatim*
through the sibling ranks and the ranks of 'significant others'.

The book also contains psychological absurdities, but, rather than
give examples of this, it is enough to give one example of sociological
and psychological nonsense combined. This was Cooper's brief
exposition of 'evacuation greed'.

The next sort of greed we must look at is *evacuation greed.*
This refers to the need excessively to shit or fart on other
people, to piss on them from a great height, spitting in
someone's face in excess of the provocation of the other. It
reaches psychotic limits, to use the term in its conventional
sense, with bombs and guns, as at the My Lai massacre in
Vietnam, which was a clear display of evacuation greed.
Whether someone is going to be greedy enough to drop the
H-bomb, or unleash chemical warfare, is another matter.

It was within this kind of analysis that Cooper most certainly did
advocate the death of the family as one indispensable element in 'the
revolution'. His position was very similar to that of Laing,
mentioned earlier, and it is important to see that this *is*, indeed, what
they did actually say.

The family over the last two centuries has mediated an
invasiveness into the lives of individuals that is essential to
the continued operating of imperializing capitalism ... The
time to write our last Will and Testament is now, and only
one clause is essential and urgent. Nothing is to be left to the
Family.

Nothing could be more definite than that! And the essential
destructiveness of the family (as Cooper saw it) could be shown in
many other quotations.

The Bourgeois nuclear family unit (to use something like the language of its agents – academic sociologists and political scientists) has become the ultimately perfected form of non-meeting ... This is all about communication and the failure of communication that characterizes the family system ... Bringing up a child is like bringing down a person ... The main task to be accomplished if we are to liberate ourselves from the family in both the external sense (the family 'out there') and the internal sense (the family in our heads) is to see through it ... All one has to do then, having seen through the family, is to see through oneself into a nothingness that returns one to oneself in so far as this nothingness is the particular nothingness of one's being....

It seems, without much stretching of the point, that the death of the family is indistinguishable from death itself: the journey back to the 'oceanic feeling' whence we came. The heads of revolutionary ostriches may well be buried not so much in the sand of 'continuous revolution' as in the warm beatings of the womb in which they were once untroubled. And there is certainly no doubt that Cooper, like Laing, regarded 'insanity' as a vision which penetrated through the shrouding and obscuring details of 'normality'.

Madness is a tentative vision of a new and truer world to be achieved through de-structuring – a de-structuring that must become final – of the old, conditioned world.

Only one conclusion can be drawn from a full analysis of the Laing, Cooper, Esterson 'school': that is – that it offered no valid criticism of the family in society at all, and certainly provided no case whatever for the abolition of the family.

It was faulty on many counts. Its research focus was entirely on a small minority of pathological families, which is the reason for the unbalanced emphasis on the destructiveness of the family which it gave. No study of 'normal' families was offered at all,[6] and there was never any consideration whatever of the possibility that the family might fulfil positive and worthwhile functions for individual and society alike: that it might be a context for other-regarding (not tyrannical) love and affection; for co-operative activities of a constructive and enjoyable kind both within and beyond the home; for the experience of loyalties and desirable qualities of character, support and mutual aid; for a beneficial growth of the individual personality. Perhaps a context defined by prescribed limits is a necessary foundation for secure growth as well as something which, abused by aberrations of possessiveness and power, can become a place of imprisoned torments, but such possibilities were not even entertained. The pathological and destructive emphasis was raised to the level of a general creed by its confused and unwarranted linking with an ideology for which no substantiating grounds were ever given: an ideology which was such as to vitiate all claims of testable science and lead to extremes such as David Cooper's – which were simply lamentable.

Though based on a larger theoretical apparatus than the broadcast comments of Leach, the views of Laing, Cooper and Esterson can therefore be placed in the same category. They constituted no seriously based criticism of the modern family at all.

In their case, too, it is interesting to point to some strange inconsistencies.

Personal testimony

It is not curious that this outright attack on the family as 'destroyer', on familial love as the masquerading face of exploitative violence, should be belied by personal testimony?

Laing dedicated *The Divided Self*: 'To my Mother and Father'. Why? Because they destroyed him? Because – their love veiling their violence – they moulded him for a lifelong submission to capitalist society? He dedicated *The Politics of Experience*: 'For my Children'. Why? Why for his *own* biological children more than for the children of others? Was it because of his guilt in having them? Because of having to socialise them into the mould of capitalism by his own violence masquerading as love? The case of David Cooper was even more strange. Having completed his total denunciation of the family; having – with nothing to salvage whatever – appealed for, and advocated its death; he, too, wrote a dedication on the very last page.

During the end of the writing of this book against the family, I went through a profound spiritual and bodily crisis that amounted to the death and rebirth experiences of renewal that I speak of in these pages. The people who sat with me and tended to me with immense kindliness and concern during the worst of this crisis were my brother Peter and sister-in-law Carol and their small daughters. Just as a true family should.

'... just as a true family should'. A true family? – what could he possibly have meant by that? These, surely, are inconsistencies quite inexplicable in terms of all that had been said before.

But Laing himself, during the 1970s, seemed to be contracting out of some of his earlier positions. In newspaper interviews he 'publicly dissociated' himself from what he called many misconceptions. He disclaimed the title of 'anti-psychiatrist' (and this, as we have seen, *was* a misrepresentation of his position). But he also disclaimed the linking of his left-wing ideological commitment with his attack on the family, which, he said, stemmed from a talk on the Dialectics of Liberation which was delivered in 1967 and published without his permission. His reported words were:

> It suited people to be able to pin me out there in that ideological position just as it suited them to use me in the attack on families. I'm not against families. I have a very nice one here. And although I have tried to show how families go wrong, I think they are one of the best relics of a crumbling system we have to hang on to.

But this will not do. The quotations I have used here are drawn from his book jointly written with David Cooper (*Reason and Violence*), and, in particular, his book *The Politics of Experience*, which – he said in his acknowledgements – was written over a period of three years, and, published first in 1967, was reprinted at least four times between then and the time of his 'retraction'. This, in short, was the considered and committed position he had long held. The opinion people had formed of his position was fully justified in terms of what he himself had written.

He also came to claim (in the same interview) that he had never meant to imply that madness was superior to 'normality'; that:

> ... madness is superior to true sanity. I'm sorry if I put that idea into people. I would never recommend madness, although I do think that some people can come through a regression and a new birth into a good place.

The upshot seems to be that Laing now quite specifically claims that the family, far from being the destructive agency of capitalist society, is 'the best relic of a crumbling system we have to hang on to'. He is *not*, therefore, a destructive critic of the family in society after all. The Laing, Cooper, Esterson 'school', long thought to have advocated and justified the abolition of the modern nuclear family, can be seen, when all is taken into account, to have done nothing of the kind. What they have proved, on the contrary, is the enormous strength and power of the family – for good, or for ill – and their own particular contribution has been to show what deeply rooted agonies and tragedies can be caused when the family goes wrong.

The abolition of the family:
Marxism and the New Left

A third call for the abolition of marriage and the family which was trumpeted loudly at the very end of the 1960s (1969) and during the early 1970s was that supposedly based on 'Marxism' and came from various exponents of the 'New Left' who, quite literally, were, at the time, involved in the rash of campus-campaigns and campus-revolutions in the universities. They were opposed to the universities. They were opposed to 'sociology' within the universities. Sociology, too, was a subservient hand-maiden of capitalist society, helping in 'the practice of organizing capitalism'. 'All boycotts of courses to help us in this are welcome' – was their italicised cry. And . . . could anything else be expected? – they were opposed to marriage and the family. Just as Laing, Cooper and Esterson had rested their case on a 'dialectical' ideology rooted in Marx and Sartre, so these exponents of the New Left – stating their own brand of 'Marxism' – called upon the position of Laing, Cooper and Esterson to reinforce their own view. The family, they claimed, was the entrenched agency of exploitative capitalism, destroying the individual 'self' by the imposition of its bourgeois demands, moulding individuals in the service of the system. It is enough to look briefly at just two examples of this because it is much more to the point to explode the myth of Marxism itself – or at least (on this one particular subject) to see what Marx and Engels themselves actually did say.

Robin Blackburn

In his essay 'A Brief Guide to Bourgeois Ideology',[1] Robin

Blackburn devoted a section to 'The Family and Domestic Mystification', not failing to attack, within it, 'bourgeois sociologists' (by which, presumably, he meant *all* sociologists who were not Marxists)* for discovering: 'within the tiny compass of the family the realm of self-realization for the citizen of the modern capitalist democracy'. It was almost an echo of the Leach criticism that the family was held up and defended as a little private world existing in social isolation and therefore with a limiting and destructive intensity. Now though some sociologists (then only a few) had pointed to the substantial improvements in the nature of the family over a century or so of reforms, and had indicated the important functions which it had now come to fulfil in close interdependence with the wider fabric of social institutions, *no* sociologist had (or has) *ever* regarded the family as an encapsuled unit within which self-realisation could take place in isolation from wider activities and responsibilities in society. Blackburn argued, however, that it had not occurred to bourgeois sociologists:

> ... to assess the functioning of the family as the key primary institution of our society. It is, for example, a fact that the family is the main arena of deliberate physical violence as even a cursory look at the statistics on cruelty to children or on murder show. It is also the case that one family in five has some history of 'schizophrenia' that comes to the attention of the medical authorities.

And then – following the fashion of self-selective reinforcement of the time – he selected a quotation from *Sanity, Madness and the Family* by Laing and Esterson.

> The needs of the Good Folk to define themselves as sane lead them to project their anxiety, disturbance and conflict into a sub-community which is furtively but progressively labelled as mad and then confirmed as such by all the agents (often well intentioned, 'sincere' people) of an alienated society – police, judges, welfare officers, social workers, psychiatrists, and so on, until they become 'chronic institutionalized mental patients'. In this curious dialectic between 'sanc' society and 'crazy' individual the mediation is usually provided by the family. In the family the whole bog of social

---

*It deserves mention that *all* sociologists in the nineteenth century were bourgeois sociologists – including Marx himself.

mystification, re-ification, alienation, bad faith is filtered ... Those who receive less of this precious mess are placed in a situation in which they must rebel and assert the fact of their difference. When they do this they invite the fatal label. A young man has only to look a little cross with his manipulative incestuously demanding mother to end up on a detention order as 'dangerous to others'...

The family was the agency for 'the whole bog of social mystification'; a 'precious mess'. It spoke significantly of the standards of argument, of intellectual judgment, that satisfied Blackburn that he could accept this kind of writing – and with approval. He condemned even the 'well-adjusted, happy family' because it:

... creates, by exclusion, those who might yearn for its cosy consolations – the illegitimate child or the unwanted grand-parent. Finally the social regulation of sexuality which the family provides is exposed by the proliferation of 'Playboy Culture', which seeks to rob sex of its erotic character.

The 'Playboy Culture' reference was to a point made by Cooper, and – again indicating the standards of argument he found satisfactory – he also accepted Cooper's general estimation of the family completely.

As Cooper indicates, the family transmits alienations which originate in the whole structure of capitalist society and one cannot separate its micro-dynamics from this function.

The family was the bulwark of capitalist society, of bourgeois values; the *conservative* institution, the agency of *conservation*, par excellence; the obstinate, resistant block to revolutionary advancement.

Juliet Mitchell

Another example of the use of 'Marxism' to launch an attack on the family (this time blended with the popular arguments of the Women's Liberation Movement) was that of Juliet Mitchell in her book *Woman's Estate* (1971).[2] She echoed exactly Blackburn's conception of the essentially conservative nature of the family.

The family ... embodies the most conservative concepts available: it rigidifies the past ideals and presents them as the

50

present pleasures. By its very nature, it is there to prevent the future. No wonder revolutionaries come up with the vulgar desperation: abolish the family – it does seem *the* block to advance, *the* means of preserving a backwardness that even capitalism makes feel redundant, though, of course, it is essential to it.

Though not as extreme as some, Juliet Mitchell, too, saw the contradictions of capitalist society reflected in the contradictions of the family and its relationships, and (again) called in Laing, Cooper and Esterson to illustrate the destructive pathological outcome of these conflicts in the lives and personalities of individuals. There was, she maintained (arguing her case on a very simple notion of the distinction in Marx's analysis of society between the 'economic base' and the 'ideological super-structure'), a contradiction between the ideology of the family (valuing privacy, unity and individualism) and its basic social nature – which was determined by the necessary economic involvement of its individual members in the productive forces of society. So, she wrote:

... the ideological concept of the family embodies a paradox which reflects the contradiction between it and the dominant, capitalist method of organizing production ... this method of organizing involves social production (a mass or 'team' of workers), and the family provides the relief from the confiscation of this social production by apparently offering individual private property. Now the same contradiction is today contained within the family itself.... What (under feudalism) had hitherto been a *united* unit became, because of changing social conditions, a *divided* one. The peasant family works together for itself – it *is* one. The family and production are homogeneous. But the members of a working-class family work separately, for different bosses in different places and, though the family interest unites them, the separation of their place and conditions of their work fragments, perforce, their unity. Part of the function of the ideology of the family under capitalism is to preserve this unity in the face of its essential break-up. However, in doing this, it ties itself in knots....
The woman's task is to hold on to the unity of the family while its separate atoms explode in different directions.... it seems possible that within this dual contradiction lies the

eventual dissolution of the 'family', a future already visible within the conditions of capitalism.

There was no lack of clarity about this diagnosis. The family, striving for its continued unity, was confronted with its 'essential break-up', its 'eventual dissolution'. Changed collective conditions would defeat the conservative ideology.

In these sorts of ways, the 'Marxists' among the new critics either told of the doom (the coming dissolution) of the family, or advocated its abolition*. They did not say what would, or should, replace it, for this, of course, is never the concern of those who believe in 'continuous revolution'. New social forms can be left to arise within the context of new economic conditions. They do not say what Marxist theory has to say about what social forms will replace the present ones when revolutionary change takes place, for Marxist theory (according to them) is too wise to predict, to conjecture, to indulge in 'Utopianism', to try to foresee what these might be. Marxist theory is not, Blackburn tells us, *just* some rival school of social science (rival, one supposes, to the 'bourgeois' schools of social science): '*It is the theory of the practice which is changing the world*' – a definition so vacuous as to take you, as we have seen, in whatever direction you wish to go within the continually calculated expediencies of the struggle for power.

So much for the kinds of criticism then being offered by representatives on the New Left. Rather than spend more time on them, however, it is much more worthwhile to go to the two great originators in whose work they claim that their own theories are rooted; to question the fundamental assumption on which their own positions rest. It has, in fact, come to be so widespread an assumption as never, now, even to be questioned, that the teaching of Marx and Engels was that marriage and the family were institutions which had been necessarily bound up (in all historical societies) with modes of production, property relations, and social classes; that this was so within the conditions of industrial capitalism, and that they would disappear and be abolished with the destruction of capitalism and the abolition of private property. The question I want to ask is – quite simply – *is this so*? And the answer – equally simple – is a decided *no*! When the writings of the two men are scrupulously examined, it is plain that this interpretation of them is decidedly *not* true! I hope

---

*This will be qualified, as far as Juliet Mitchell is concerned, a little later.

(though this is very optimistic) that we might be able to both kill and bury an unwarranted myth here.

Marx and Engels

What the term 'Marxism' actually means nowadays, of course, is a question open to interminable – and almost always pointless and mystifying – conjecture. Like 'Christianity', it can be discussed, interpreted, assessed, in very many ways and at many different levels. Indeed (like Christianity), as an entire system, an entire position, it does not exist. I shall therefore leave Lenin, Stalin, Mao Tse-tung . . . and Marcuse, Gramsci, Althusser, and other contemporary 'Neo-Marxists' . . . severely alone. They can all be shown to be philosophically threadbare – of the nature of ideological programmes for political action and the pursuit of political power rather than systems of ideas containing scientific theories admitting of *test*. But, whilst setting such large-scale considerations aside, it is nonetheless possible, in the thick of this always continuing revolutionary 'mystique' (i.e. – as with Sartre – fog!) to do at least two things: first – *to see what Marx and Engels themselves said* (a necessary beginning, one would think?), and second – *to assess the truth and worthwhileness of some of the specific things they said* – quite apart from attempting to prove or disprove the sufficiency of any over-all 'system' they might be supposed to have established. This, we can manage to do here. Our first question, then, is simply this: what did Marx and Engels actually say about marriage and the family in society?

The statement which has most given rise to the common assumption that their 'teaching' is opposed to the continuity of marriage and the family is their joint statement in the *Manifesto of the Communist Party*, published early in 1848. Attacking the 'selfish misconception' that led the 'bourgeoisie': 'to transform into eternal laws of nature and of reason, the social forms springing from the present mode of production and form of property . . .', they went on to counter and criticise the supposed 'bourgeois' support for one of these social forms – 'the family'. This is their statement in full.

Abolition of the family! Even the most radical flare up at this infamous proposal of the Communists.

On what foundation is the present family, the bourgeois family, based? On capital, on private gain. In its completely

53

developed form this family exists only among the bourgeoisie. But this state of things finds its complement in the practical absence of the family among the proletarians, and in public prostitution.

The Bourgeois family will vanish as a matter of course when its complement vanishes, and both will vanish with the vanishing of capital.

Do you charge us with wanting to stop the exploitation of children by their parents? To this crime we plead guilty.

But, you will say, we destroy the most hallowed of relations, when we replace home education by social.

And your education! Is not that also social, and determined by the social conditions under which you educate, by the intervention direct or indirect, of society, by means of schools, etc? The Communists have not invented the intervention of society in education; they do but seek to alter the character of that intervention, and to rescue education from the influence of the ruling class.

The bourgeois claptrap about the family and education, about the hallowed correlation of parent and child, becomes all the more disgusting, the more, by the action of modern industry, all family ties among the proletarians are torn asunder, and their children transformed into simple article of commerce and instruments of labour.

But you Communists would introduce community of women, screams the whole bourgeoisie in chorus.

The bourgeois sees in his wife a mere instrument of production. He hears that the instruments of production are to be exploited in common, and, naturally, can come to no other conclusions than that the lot of being common to all will likewise fall to the women.

He has not even a suspicion that *the real point aimed at is to do away with the status of women as mere instruments of production.*

For the rest, nothing is more ridiculous than the virtuous indignation of our bourgeois at the community of women which, they pretend, is to be openly and officially established by the Communists. The Communists have no need to introduce community of women; it has existed almost from time immemorial.

Our bourgeois, not content with having the wives and daughters of their proletarians at their disposal, not to speak

54

of common prostitutes, take the greatest pleasure in seducing each other's wives.

Bourgeois marriage is in reality a system of wives in common and thus, at the most, what the Communists might possibly be reproached with is that they desire to introduce, in substitution for a hypocritically concealed, an openly legalised community of women. For the rest, it is self-evident, that the abolition of the present system of production must bring with it the abolition of the community of women springing from that system, i.e., of prostitution both public and private (my italics).

Now on the face of it, this does seem a radical attack on the family, and an outright manifesto for its abolition, but a careful reading of it, especially bearing in mind the context of the social conditions they were attacking, makes it clear that this is not so. If the statement is read with care several points are completely clear.

First: Marx and Engels were attacking the 'bourgeois' family: the nature of marriage and the conception and practice of family life among the property-owning and manufacturing 'ruling' classes. It was this social form of the family that they wished to see abolished.

Second: they were especially attacking the subordinate status of women in this type of family: the fact that within the family, a woman was herself an item of property, and that (a corollary of this) beyond the family women were also a species of property – prostitutes – whose availability for sexual gratification could be bought. The entire family system was one which entailed the use of women as objects of property: whether as sexual objects or as domestic utensils and (as and when respectable ostentation demanded it) ornaments of status-display.

Third: they were also attacking this type of family *and* the supposed family among the labouring classes in the spirit of mockery. They attacked the 'bourgeois' family itself for its sheer hypocrisy: pointing to the sexual licence carried on by the property-owning and manufacturing employers – both in the sexual exploitations of the girls and women economically dependent on them in the factories, and in the wider resort (the very extensive resort) to prostitution – despite the church-mouthed protestations of the holiness and respectability of marital and family relationships. And they made a mockery of the very idea of the family among the proletarians, because (they claimed) *this simply did not exist*. The exploitation of men, women and children alike in the early development of 'the industrial (and agrarian) revolution' was so unbelievably harsh and far-reaching that to speak of a 'family unit' among the labourers was nothing short of a bad joke. This is what Marx and Engels meant when they railed against 'the bourgeois claptrap about the family and education'. And when they said: 'Do you charge us with wanting to stop the exploitation of children by their parents? To this crime we plead guilty ...' – they were referring, obviously, to the sheer exploitation of children, in domestic industry as well as in the context of the new mines, factories, and towns, to all of which parents were driven by sheer, grinding economic necessity.

And *fourth*: the real crux of their attack was the point I italicised in the quotation: '... *the real point aimed at is to do away with the status of women as mere instruments of production.*'

Very clearly, then, this was *not* an attack upon *any* form of the family. It did not advocate the abolition of the family *as such* – in *any* form. It simply argued that there was nothing 'eternal and "natural" about the form of marriage and the family which has grown up within the context of industrial capitalism;' and, indeed, that this form was evil in the several kinds of exploitation (but especially that of women) that it embodied. It was the abolition of the bourgeois family that Marx and Engels advocated, and the abolition of those economic and social conditions which made any decent family life among the working classes utterly impossible. And it is worthwhile to note that these attacks held, and still hold, much humanity and validity quite apart from any larger ideological system of 'dialectical and historical materialism' and political revolution which Marx and Engels (combined) put forward. The truth or falsity, the ethical and political value, of particular points they made or particular stands they adopted on social issues, do not stand or fall with any over-all acceptance or rejection of their wider ideology.

This interpretation of their attack upon the family in early nineteenth-century Britain is thoroughly understandable and largely substantiated when it is seen within its historical context. Much of what they said about the bourgeois family was true; much of what they said about the absence of anything approximating to satisfactory family life among the labouring classes – in country and town alike – was true ... *at the time in which they were writing*. It is interesting to note, that none of the examples I used in *The Family and Marriage in Britain* to draw the harrowing picture of family life among labourers in the early nineteenth century – in rural areas, lace-making, blanket-weaving, cotton-spinning, nail-making homes and workshops, and in the new larger factories and mines alike – were taken from the work of Marx and Engels. They were all drawn from other observers of the time – from the reports of the various commissions, and from other social historians. But it is interesting to see that the picture all these sources provide is exactly that given by Marx and Engels, and for the very simple reason that they were witnessing the same scene and drawing many of their general facts from the same government reports. In these sections of their work, Marx and Engels were simply good social recorders, social historians, social commentators, and, in fact, Engels was the more original of the two in this respect. Engel's book *The Condition of the Working-Class in England in 1844*[3] is still one of the most graphic accounts of the economic and social conditions of that period, and, apart from many personal observations and the use of a wide range of sources – including newspaper reports and statements of clergymen, Members of Parliament, etc. – he drew especially upon official reports, such as that of the Health Commission, the 'Report concerning the sanitary condition of the working class' (in Manchester), that of the Children's Employment Commission, and many others. This book was first published in Germany in 1845, and was referred to (in its German edition) by Marx in volume 1 of *Das Kapital* (1867). In this book, too, Marx drew on the same sources depicting the conditions of the workers when he was arguing the various aspects of his theories of value – the nature of the 'working day', the expropriation of 'surplus-value', the 'law of capitalist accumulation',* etc. In the work of both writers the information on which they based their attack on 'the family' was amassed together.

It is also worthwhile to note that – in drawing upon the reports of government commissioners, factory inspectors, and the like – Marx did, in fact, have a very high estimation of their ability and integrity. In his preface to *Capital*,[4] he wrote this, for example, in upholding English records against those of continental Europe.

The social statistics of Germany and the rest of Continental Western Europe are, in comparison with those of England, wretchedly compiled. But they raise the veil just enough to let us catch a glimpse of the Medusa head behind it. We should be appalled at the state of things at home, if, as in England,

---

*The chapters in *Capital* (vol. I) on 'The Working Day' and 'Machinery and Modern Industry' are well worth reading for these historical details and will give much evidence relevant to what I called the 'Earlier Community Fallacy' – the picture given by Leach of an earlier condition in which families were morally supported in close communities. Marx and Engels are good dispellers of such a dream.

our governments and parliaments appointed periodically commissions of enquiry into economic conditions; if these commissions were armed with the same plenary powers to get at the truth; if it was possible to find for this purpose men as competent, as free from partisanship and respect of persons as are the English factory-inspectors, her medical reporters on public health, her commissioners of enquiry into the exploitation of women and children, into housing and food. Perseus wore a magic cap that the monsters he hunted down might not see him. We draw the magic cap down over eyes and ears as a make-believe that there are no monsters.

It is also worthwhile and relevant to the claims I want to make about the position of Marx and Engels to notice that both of them believed that – in England, among all capitalist countries – the transformation from industrial capitalism to a more humane society could be accomplished peacefully. The 'revolution' could be bloodless. In his preface to the English translation of *Capital* (1886), three years after Marx's death, and when the volume of unemployment seemed to be increasing year by year, Engels wrote:

Surely, at such a moment, the voice ought to be heard of a man whose whole theory is the result of a life-long study of the economic history and condition of England, and whom that study led to the conclusion that, at least in Europe, England is the only country where the inevitable social revolution might be effected entirely by peaceful and legal means. He certainly never forgot to add that he hardly expected the English ruling classes to submit, without a 'pro-slavery rebellion,' to this peaceful and legal revolution.

It is not necessary to give a large number of examples of the picture which both Engels and Marx painted of the family condition of the 'ruling' and 'exploited' classes in their own time – because their books are there to be read. But (since many people do not know these books) it is worthwhile to glance at just a few such examples, partly to show the general nature of their conclusions (to justify the interpretation I have suggested above), and partly to show the agreement of Marx and Engels with the kind of analysis which we ourselves set out and considered earlier.*

*These examples of Marx and Engels can be compared with the description given in the chapter on 'The Family and Industrialization in Britain' in *The Family and Marriage in Britain*, pp. 67–138.

From Marx, let us take just three examples: one of domestic industry, one of manufacturing industry, and one of the employment of women in the mines. The example of domestic industry is that of straw-plaiting in parts of Buckingham, Bedford, Hertfordshire and Essex in 1861 – just over a hundred years ago.

> In the place of ... lace-schools we find here the 'straw-plait schools.' The children commence their instruction in straw-plaiting generally in their 4th, often between their 3rd and 4th year. Education, of course, they get none. The children themselves call the elementary schools, 'natural schools,' to distinguish them from these blood-sucking institutions, in which they are kept at work simply to get through the task, generally 30 yards daily, prescribed by their half-starved mothers. These same mothers often make them work at home, after school is over, till 10, 11, and 12 o'clock at night. The straw cuts their mouths, with which they constantly moisten it, and their fingers. Dr. Ballard gives it as the general opinion of the whole body of medical officers in London, that 300 cubic feet is the minimum space proper for each person in a bedroom or work-room. But in the straw-plait schools space is more sparingly allotted than in the lace-schools, '12⅔, 17, 18½ and below 22 cubic feet for each person.' The smaller of these numbers, says one of the commissioners, Mr. White, represents less space than the half of what a child would occupy if packed in a box measuring 3 feet in each direction. Thus do the children enjoy life till the age of 12 or 14. The wretched half-starved parents think of nothing but getting as much as possible out of their children. The latter, as soon as they are grown up, do not care a farthing, and naturally so, for their parents, and leave them. 'It is no wonder that ignorance and vice abound in a population so brought up ... Their morality is at the lowest ebb, ... a great number of the women have illegitimate children, and that at such an immature age that even those most conversant with criminal statistics are astounded.' And the native land of these model families is the pattern Christian country for Europe ...[5]

This is the kind of thing Marx had in mind when mocking the very existence of the 'family' among people labouring in such conditions, and when denouncing the exploitation of children by their parents.

The example of manufacturing industry – with its effect upon girls, women, and family life – is that of brick and tile making.

Between May and September the work lasts from 5 in the morning till 8 in the evening, and where the drying is done in the open air, it often lasts from 4 in the morning till 9 in the evening. Work from 5 in the morning till 7 in the evening is considered 'reduced' and 'moderate'. Both boys and girls of 6 and even of 4 years of age are employed. They work for the same number of hours, often longer, than the adults. The work is hard and the summer heat increases the exhaustion. In a certain tile field at Mosley, for example, a young woman, 24 years of age, was in the habit of making 2000 tiles a day, with the assistance of 2 little girls, who carried the clay for her, and stacked the tiles. These girls carried daily 10 tons up the slippery sides of the clay pits, from a depth of 30 feet, and then for a distance of 210 feet. 'It is impossible for a child to pass through the purgatory of a tile-field without great moral degradation – the low language, which they are accustomed to hear from their tenderest years, the filthy, indecent, and shameless habits, amidst which, unknowing, and half wild, they grow up, make them in after life lawless, abandoned, dissolute ... A frightful source of demoralization is the mode of living. Each moulder, who is always a skilled labourer, and the chief of a group, supplies his 7 subordinates with board and lodging in his cottage. Whether members of his family or not, the men, boys, and girls all sleep in the cottage, which contains generally two, exceptionally 3 rooms, all on the ground floor, and badly ventilated. These people are so exhausted after the day's hard work, that neither the rules of health, of cleanliness, nor of decency are in the least observed. Many of these cottages are models of untidiness, dirt, and dust ... The greatest evil of the system that employs young girls on this sort of work, consists in this, that, as a rule, it chains them fast from childhood for the whole of their after-life to the most abandoned rabble. They become rough, foul-mouthed boys, before Nature has taught them that they are women. Clothed in a few dirty rags, the legs naked far above the knees, hair and face besmeared with dirt, they learn to treat all feelings of decency and of shame with contempt. During meal-times they lie at full length in the fields, or watch the boys bathing in a neighbouring canal. Their heavy day's work at length completed, they put on better clothes, and accompany the men to the public houses.' That excessive insobriety is prevalent from childhood upwards among the whole of this class, is only natural. 'The worst is that the brickmakers despair of themselves. You might as well, said one of the better kind to a chaplain of Southallfield, try to raise and improve the devil as a brickie, sir!'[6]

That example was selected by Marx from the report of the Children's Employment Commission (1866). And finally, it may be of interest to give one of the 'question-and-answer' sequences from the 'Report from the Select Committee on Mines', because this is revealing both of the attitudes of the members of the investigating committee and of the miners themselves. This concerned the continued employment of girls and women (chiefly the wives, daughters and widows of working miners – from the ages of 12 to 50–60) on the 'pit-banks': sorting, and drawing tubs on the canals and railway wagons.[7]

'What is the feeling among the working miners as to the employment of women?'
    'I think they generally condemn it.'
'What objection do you see to it?'
    'I think it is degrading to the sex.'
'There is a peculiarity of dress?'
    'Yes ... it is rather a man's dress, and I believe in some cases, it drowns all sense of decency.'
'Do the women smoke?'
    'Some do.'
'And I suppose it is very dirty work?'
    'Very dirty.'
'They get black and grimy?'
    'As black as those who are down the mines ... I believe that a woman having children (and there are plenty on the banks that have) cannot do her duty to her children.'
'Do you think that those widows could get employment anywhere else, which would bring them in as much wages as that (from 8s. to 10s. a week)?'
    'I cannot speak to that.'
'You would still be prepared, would you,' (flint-hearted fellow!) 'to prevent their obtaining a livelihood by these means?'

'I would.'

'What is the general feeling in the district ... as to the employment of women?'

'The feeling is that it is degrading; and we wish as miners to have more respect to the fair sex than to see them placed on the pit bank ... Some part of the work is very hard; some of these girls have raised as much as 10 tons of stuff a day.'

'Do you think that the women employed about the collieries are less moral than the women employed in the factories?'

'... the percentage of bad ones may be a little more ... than with the girls in the factories.'

'But you are not quite satisfied with the state of morality in the factories?'

'No.'

'Would you prohibit the employment of women in factories also?'

'No, I would not.'

'Why not?'

'I think it a more honourable occupation for them in the mills.'

'Still it is injurious to their morality, you think?'

'Not so much as working on the pit bank; but it is more on the social position I take it; I do not take it on its moral ground alone. The degradation, in its social bearing on the girls, is deplorable in the extreme. When these 400 or 500 girls become colliers' wives, the men suffer greatly from this degradation, and it causes them to leave their homes and drink.'

'You would be obliged to stop the employment of women in the ironworks as well, would you not, if you stopped it in the collieries?'

'I cannot speak for any other trade.'

'Can you see any difference in the circumstances of women employed in ironworks, and the circumstances of women employed above ground in collieries?'

'I have not ascertained anything as to that.'

'Can you see anything that makes a distinction between one class and the other?'

'I have not ascertained that, but I know from house to house visitation, that it is a deplorable state of things in our district ...'

'Would you interfere in every case with the employment of women where that employment was degrading?'

'It would become injurious, I think, in this way: the best feelings of Englishmen have been gained from the instruction of a mother ...'

It is surely quite plain from the miner's comments here and from Marx's evident sympathy, that the emphasis was not in the direction of *abolishing* the family, but entirely upon *the desirability of its very existence*!

Engels amassed wide evidence of exactly the same kind and there is no point in repeating this. From him, we will select only two examples: one of similar conditions among the families of agricultural areas, and one giving his general conclusions about the 'family' among the working classes in the new industrial towns. The statement he gave of families in 'agricultural districts', who must struggle along: 'with 6, 7 or 8 shillings a week, and at times have nothing ...' was as follows.

An English agricultural labourer and an English pauper, these words are synonymous. His father was a pauper and his mother's milk contained no nourishment. From his earliest childhood he had bad food, and only half enough to still his hunger, and even yet he undergoes the pangs of unsatisfied hunger almost all the time that he is not asleep. He is half clad, and has not more fire than barely suffices to cook his scanty meal. And so cold and damp are always at home with him, and leave him only in fine weather. He is married, but he knows nothing of the joys of the husband and father. His wife and children, hungry, rarely warm, often ill and helpless, always careworn and hopeless like himself, are naturally grasping, selfish, and troublesome, and so, to use his own expression, he hates the sight of them, and enters his cot only because it offers him a trifle more shelter from rain and wind than a hedge. He must support his family, though he cannot do so, whence come beggary, deceit of all sorts, ending in fully developed craftiness. If he were so inclined, he yet has not the courage which makes of the more energetic of his class wholesale poachers and smugglers. But he pilfers when occasion offers, and teaches his children to lie and steal. His abject and submissive demeanour towards his wealthy neighbours shows that they treat him roughly and with suspicion, hence he fears and hates them, but he never will injure them by force. He is depraved through and through, too far gone to possess even the strength of despair. His wretched existence is brief, rheumatism and asthma bring him to the workhouse, where he will draw his last breath without a single pleasant recollection, and will make room for another luckless wretch to live and die as he has done.[8]

It might be thought that this was a heavily biased account by a youthful and very left-wing Engels (he was 24 years old at the time). It was, however, *not* Engels at all – but a statement which he himself quoted, and which was taken, in fact, from a pamphlet *Swing Unmasked: or, the Cause of Rural Incendiarism* (1831) by E. G. Wakefield, a *Liberal* Member of Parliament. Engels's own over-all conclusion was this:

> Thus the social order makes family life almost impossible for the worker. In a comfortless, filthy house, hardly good enough for mere nightly shelter, ill-furnished, often neither rain-tight nor warm, a foul atmosphere filling rooms overcrowded with human beings, no domestic comfort is possible. The husband works the whole day through, perhaps the wife also and the elder children, all in different places; they meet night and morning only, all under perpetual temptation to drink; what family life is possible under such conditions? Yet the working-man cannot escape from the family, must live in the family, and the consequence is a perpetual succession of family troubles, domestic quarrels, most demoralising for parents and children alike. Neglect of all domestic duties, neglect of the children, especially, is only too common among the English working-people, and only too vigorously fostered by the existing institutions of society. And children growing up in this savage way, amidst these demoralising influences, are expected to turn out goody-goody and moral in the end![9]

Accounts such as this surely show all our present-day criticisms of the 'inwardness', 'intense, unbearable, privacy', and 'destructiveness' of the modern family (whether offered by Leach, David Cooper, or whoever else it might be) to be flagrantly mistaken. Would any of us exchange our own families now, no matter how problematical, for the experience and conditions of families then? The slightest histor-ical knowledge makes the whole basis of such criticism absurd. However, we must confine ourselves for the moment to our assess-ment of the position of Marx and Engels.

It is surely abundantly clear from these few examples and comments alike, that these two authors – utterly opposed to the hypocrisy of the 'bourgeois' family, and certainly seeking the abolition of this – were far from being opposed to family life for the working people. Their position was entirely one of outrage and disgust that decent family life for the labouring poor was made impossible. And – throughout – their emphasis was essentially *this*: that the social form of the family which involved the treatment of women as items of property, and the exploitation of women and children alike – both in and beyond the family, was inhuman and evil, and that it should be replaced by a more humane form in which individuals were treated as *persons* possessing equal rights and status. Let us bear in mind, too, that they believed that this could be brought about in England by peaceful and legal means, and, indeed, that, even by the end of the nineteenth century, very great improvements had been made. In his preface to the English publication of *The Conditions of the Working-Class in England in 1844* (in 1892) Engels wrote this: 'The state of things described in this book belongs today, in many respects, to the past, as far as England is concerned ...' In particular, he was impressed and heartened by the 'revival of the East End of London' which had come about with the extension and development of the trade union movement. There were no half-measures in his joy and pride in this achievement.

That immense haunt of misery is no longer the stagnant pool it was six years ago. It has shaken off its torpid despair, has returned to life, and has become the home of what is called the 'New Unionism'; that is to say, of the organisation of the great mass of 'unskilled' workers. This organisation may to a great extent adopt the form of the old Unions of 'skilled' workers, but it is essentially different in character. The old Unions preserve the traditions of the time when they were founded, and look upon the wages system as a once-for-all established, final fact, which they at best can modify in the interest of their members. The new Unions were founded at a time when the faith in the eternity of the wages system was severely shaken; their founders and promoters were Socialists either consciously or by feeling; the masses, whose adhesion gave them strength, were rough, neglected, looked down upon by the working-class aristocracy; but they had this immense advantage, that *their minds were virgin soil*, entirely free from the inherited 'respectable' bourgeois prejudices which hampered the brains of the better situated 'old' Unionists.

And thus we see now these new Unions taking the lead of the working-class movement generally, and more and more taking in tow the rich and proud 'old' Unions ...

For all the faults committed in past, present, and future, the revival of the East End of London remains one of the greatest and most fruitful facts of this 'fin de siècle', and glad and proud I am to have lived to see it.[10]

It might be said, however, that though it may be clear that Marx and Engels were attacking the bourgeois family in the *Communist Manifesto*, I have by no means proved my assertion that they were not opposed to the family in general, and that they did not wish to abolish the family as such. For this, it is necessary to look at other writings, and here the date of the *Communist Manifesto* – 1848 – is significant. This was undoubtedly an attack on the conditions of the family as they saw them between 1848 (with Engels's book on the *Condition of the Working Class*) and 1867 (with Marx's *Capital*). It is worthwhile to note, however, just before leaving this, that elsewhere in the *Manifesto* they made it plain that it was *not* the family as such to which they objected, but the way in which the new 'ethos' of the bourgeoisie reduced all human relationships – including those of the family – to the term of the market-place: to terms of property owner-ship, money, and economic transactions. The following quotation shows quite clearly their conviction that the new commercialism had debased work and family relationships which would otherwise be dignified and humane.

The bourgeoisie has stripped of its halo every occupation hitherto honoured and looked up to with reverent awe. It has converted the physician, the lawyer, the priest, the poet, the man of science, into its paid wage labourers.

The bourgeoisie has torn away from the family its sentimental veil, and has reduced the family relation to a mere money relation ...

This seems perfectly plain. But there is better evidence of the full conceptions of both Marx and Engels. My first quotation from the *Manifesto* still rather suggests that they viewed without much concern any possible 'community of women'. But Marx himself had gone out of his way to make it clear that this notion of a 'community of women', following the abolition of private property was itself a conception of *'crude* communism' which he completely rejected. In the *Economic and Philosophic Manuscripts of 1844*,[11] he wrote that the movement:

... of counterposing universal private property to private property finds expression in the bestial form of counterposing to marriage (certainly a form of exclusive private property) the community of women, in which a woman becomes a piece of communal and common property. It may be said that this idea of the community of women gives away the secret of this as yet completely crude and thoughtless communism.

And he attacked the crudity of this conception – arguing that the quality of the relationship between man and woman in a society was so central and important as to be regarded as the best possible index of the level of humane development of that society as a whole. His essential conception was that the relationship between man and woman could only be satisfactory and ethically upheld when sexual gratification as such (as of a man with an object) was replaced by a mutually needed and desired communion between two equal persons. This was his own statement.

In the approach to woman as the spoil and handmaid of communal lust is expressed the infinite degradation in which man exists for himself, for the secret of this approach has its unambiguous, decisive, plain and undisguised expression in the relation of man to woman and in the manner in which the direct and natural procreative relationship is conceived. The direct, natural, and necessary relation of person to person is the relation of man to woman. In this natural relationship of the sexes man's relation to nature is immediately his relation to man, just as his relation to man is immediately his relation to nature – his own natural function. In this relationship, therefore, is sensuously manifested, reduced to an observable fact, the extent to which the human essence has become nature to man, or to which nature has to him become the human essence of man. From this relationship one can therefore judge man's whole level of development. It follows from the character of this relationship how much man as a species being, as man, has come to be himself and to comprehend himself; the relation of man to woman is the most natural relation of human being to human being. It therefore reveals the extent to which man's natural behaviour has become human, or the extent to which the human essence in him has become a natural essence – the extent to which his human nature has come to be nature to him. In this relationship is revealed, too, the extent to which man's need has become a human need; the extent to which, therefore, the other person as a person has become for him a need – the extent to which he in his individual existence is at the same time a social being.[12]

This, plainly, was no objection to marriage as such, but only to these forms of marriage (and sexual relations related to them) based upon crude conceptions of private property and communal property alike. It was the upholding of a kind of marriage which – all considerations of property set aside – was a mutually chosen union between equal persons. And this was Marx's conception at the time the *Communist Manifesto* was written. If my interpretation is still thought too forceful, we can look at Engels's fuller statement in his book *The Origin of the Family*, published in 1884.

Both he and Marx had been impressed with Lewis H. Morgan's book on *Ancient Society*, which gave an account of the 'Lines of Human Progress from Savagery, through Barbarism, to Civilization' and which included an analysis of the parallel development of *forms* of the family. We need not look at the full argument of this book, nor the way in which Engels used it. Briefly he gave an account of 'stages' of family development – from 'group marriage' in the simplest societies ('savagery'), to the 'pairing family' in early 'barbarism' (in which one man and one woman married within a system of patriarchial authority, within which polygamy and occasional adultery remained male privileges) to 'monogamy' in 'civilization', in which one man and one woman were the 'legally united pair' but where the woman was still the husband's property, and where his sexual desires could be supplemented by adultery and prostitution. It is of interest to notice that Engels discussed the expected adultery of the recent monogamous family type as 'hetaerism' (sexual intercourse of men with unmarried women outside the monogamous family*) and quoted Morgan with approval to the effect that: 'it still follows mankind in civilization as a dark shadow on the family.'

What is of central interest to us, however, is what Engels especially had to say about the 'monogamous family', because the 'bourgeois family' was the recent form of this which he and Marx hated and despised so much. It was in this that he saw 'contradictions' appearing, and this, therefore, that he thought was doomed to disappear. Let us see, first, that though Engels saw the monogamous

*Open concubinage.

family as a correlate of the progressive economic forces (conditions of production) of 'civilization', he by no means saw it as an ethical advancement, but, on the contrary, as the first family system requiring the total subordination of women as a class. Monogamy, he wrote:

> by no means enters history as a reconciliation of man and wife and still less as the highest form of marriage. On the contrary, it enters as the subjugation of one sex by the other, as the proclamation of an antagonism between the sexes unknown in all preceding history. In an old unpublished manuscript written by Marx and myself in 1846, I find the following passage: 'The first division of labor is that of man and wife in breeding children.' And to-day I may add: The first class antagonism appearing in history coincides with the development of the antagonism of man and wife in monogamy, and the first class oppression with that of the female by the male sex. Monogamy was a great historical progress. But by the side of slavery and private property it marks at the same time that epoch which, reaching down to our days, takes with all progress also a step backwards, relatively speaking, and develops the welfare and advancement of one by the woe and submission of the other.[13]

This brought with it, he thought, the 'double standard' of sexual morality. Adultery and prostitution were thought to be expected indulgences of men, in no way diminishing their reputations, whereas the women of which they made use were ostracised and made social outcasts. It also, however, brought with it the seriousness of the wife's adultery. Engels wrote:

> ... you cannot have one side of the contradiction without the other, just as you cannot have the whole apple after eating half of it. Nevertheless this seems to have been the idea of the men, until their wives taught them a lesson. Monogamy introduces two permanent social characters that were formerly unknown: the standing lover of the wife and the cuckold. The men had gained the victory over the women, but the vanquished magnanimously provided the coronation. In addition to monogamy and hetaerism, adultery became an unavoidable social institution – denounced, severely punished, but irrepressible. The certainty of paternal parentage rested as of old on moral conviction at best, and in order to solve the

unreconciliable contradiction, the code Napoléon decreed in its article 312: 'L'enfant conçu pendant le mariage a pour père le mari'; the child conceived during marriage has for its father – the husband. This is the last result of three thousand years of monogamy.[14]

But it was the economic contradiction in the monogamous family on which Engels placed his greatest emphasis. On the one hand, women had become – as a class – the domesticated property of men. On the other hand, the new complexity of the division of labour of developing capitalism made increasing demands upon the employment of women. Women were removed from the home to the extent that they had to enter the labour market. Among the labouring classes this had been extended to the point of destroying any viable family life. Among middle-class women, the 'domestication' had been more complete, and the re-introduction to the 'public' industries was still to come. When it did come, however, this would toll the death knell of the monogamous family.

As in the factory, so women are situated in all business departments up to the medical and legal professions. The modern monogamous family is founded on the open or disguised domestic slavery of women, and modern society is a mass composed of molecules in the form of monogamous families. In the great majority of cases the man has to earn a living and to support his family, at least among the possessing classes. He thereby obtains a superior position that has no need of any legal special privilege. In the family, he is the bourgeois, the woman represents the proletariat. In the industrial world, however, the specific character of the economic oppression weighing on the proletariat appears in its sharpest outlines only after all special privileges of the capitalist class are abolished and the full legal equality of both classes is established. A democratic republic does not abolish the distinction between the two classes. On the contrary, it offers the battleground on which this distinction can be fought out. Likewise the peculiar character of man's rule over woman in the modern family, the necessity and the manner of accomplishing the real social equality of the two, will appear in broad daylight only then, when both of them will enjoy complete legal equality. It will then be seen that the emancipation of women is primarily dependent on the re-introduction of the whole female sex into the public industries. To accomplish this, the monogamous family must cease to be the industrial unit of society.

He went on:

> We are now approaching a social revolution, in which the old economic foundations of monogamy will disappear ...
> Monogamy arose through the concentration of considerable wealth in one hand ... a man's hand – and from the endeavour to bequeath this wealth to the children of this man to the exclusion of all others. This necessitated monogamy on the woman's, but not on the man's part ... Since monogamy was caused by economic conditions, will it disappear when these causes are abolished?[15]

It will be noticed that Engels did not say that the monogamous family would cease to exist but that it would cease to be the industrial unit of society, and this is an extremely important point on which much hangs. He said again, later, that the monogamous family would cease to be the economic unit of society, but – he added – the private household would be changed to a social industry. The care and education of children would come, increasingly, to be a public matter, and the family would increasingly become a unit of intimate relationships between equal persons based upon affection.

It is here that we must follow Engels's argument very closely, for, far from arguing that the family would be abolished, he argued, on the contrary, that the existing evils of the 'bourgeois' monogamous family would be removed, and that the monogamous family would thus continue in a new and improved form. In answer to his own question: 'Since monogamy was caused by economic conditions, will it disappear when these causes are abolished?' – he answered quite plainly: 'One might reply, not without reason: not only will it *not* disappear, but it will rather *be perfectly realised.*' And he then argued that it was the change towards these modern socialised conditions that made possible the fusing of 'individual sex love' with 'marriage'. Astonishingly, his position was exactly that later stated by G. M. Trevelyan! – and it is of great interest to compare the two. Engels wrote:

> Here a new element becomes active, an element which at best existed only in the germ at the time when monogamy developed: individual sexlove.
> Before the middle ages we cannot speak of individual sexlove.

He then went on to show how, in the Middle Ages, the intensity of personal sexlove was confined to the adulterous affairs of the knights – and not thought to belong to marriage, which was a practical matter of property arrangements by elders. 'From this love endeavouring to break through the bonds of marriage to the love *destined to found marriage*, there is a long distance which was never fully traversed by the knights.' Gradually, however (this was Engels's argument) the bourgeois ethics which upheld 'freedom of contract' came to affect the nature of the marriage contract itself. The 'arrangement' of marriage by elders or others itself became questioned.

> If perfect freedom of decision is demanded for all other contracts, why not for this one? Did not the two young people who were to be coupled together have the right freely to dispose of themselves, of their bodies and the organs of these? Had not sexual love become the custom through the knights and was not, in opposition to knightly adultery, the love of married couples its proper bourgeois form? And if it was the duty of married couples to love one another, was it not just as much the duty of lovers to marry each other and nobody else? Stood not the right of lovers higher than the right of parents, relatives and other customary marriage brokers and matrimonial agents? If the right of free personal investigation made its way unchecked into the church and religion, how could it bear with the insupportable claims of the older generation on the body, soul, property, happiness and misfortune of the younger generation?[16]

The idea of personal love became not only associated or fused with that of marriage, but regarded as *the only justifiable basis for it*. G. M. Trevelyan's comments on the way in which marriage had come to be reconstituted as *an institution in its own right* resting on personal affection, deserves full statement here simply to demonstrate how completely it is in agreement with what Engels had to say.

As to the medieval 'love' associated with chivalry and the distance of this from what was expected in marriage, Trevelyan wrote this:

> ... to some vaguely accustomed to think of the Middle Ages as a period of chivalry and love, with knights ever on their knees to ladies, it may come as a shock to realize that, in the knightly and gentle class, the choice of partners for marriage had normally nothing whatever to do with love; often the

bride and bridegroom were small children when they were pledged for life, and, even if adults, they were sold by their parents to the highest bidder.

The Pastons and other county families regarded the marriages of their children as counters in the game of family aggrandisement, useful to buy money and estates, or to secure the support of powerful patrons. If the victim destined for the altar resisted, rebellion was crushed – at least in the case of a female ward – with physical brutality almost incredible. Elizabeth Paston, when she hesitated to marry a battered and ugly widower of fifty, was for nearly three months on end 'beaten once in the week or twice, sometimes twice in one day, and her head broken in two or three places.' Such were the methods of her mother Agnes, a highly religious, respectable, and successful controller of the large Paston household. Many parents seem to have cared very little who married their children, provided they themselves got the money ...

These old-established medieval customs, still vigorous in the fifteenth century, may at first seem inconsistent with the tone of medieval literature ... But this poetry of love, from its most heavenly flight in Dante's chaste worship of another man's wife, to the more usual idealization of courtly adultery had seldom anything to do with marriage ...

But with later developments, this fusion of 'romantic' love with marriage actually took place.

... Could this precious concept of the medieval poets be allied, by a further revolution, to the state of marriage? Could the lovers themselves become husband and wife? Could the bond of young love be prolonged till age and death?

This change has actually taken place in England in the gradual evolution of the idea and practice of marriage ... the arranged marriage has given place to the love-match; the parents have yielded to the children the choice of their own destiny.

Engels, then, is not only in agreement with present-day 'bourgeois sociologists', he is also in agreement with one of the most popular 'bourgeois' social historians of recent times. For him, as for them, marriage – with the remedying of the worst conditions of industrial capitalism – has been reconstituted, improved as an institution in its own right, and the family has been remade as a unit of husband, wife and children whose continued relationships rest upon affection and mutually recognised personal obligations. Engels's final conclusion is worth quotation in full, because it included statements which are nowadays made by quite eminent and respectable bodies in those Church of England study groups which were set up quite recently to investigate questions of marriage and divorce.

Since sexlove is exclusive by its very nature – although this exclusiveness is at present realized for women alone – marriage founded on sexlove must be monogamous.

This advance implied, historically, a deterioration in the position of women and a greater opportunity for men to be faithless. Remove the economic considerations that now force women to submit to the customary disloyalty of men, and you will place women on an equal footing with men. All present experiences prove that this will tend much more strongly to make men truly monogamous, than to make women polyandrous.

However, those peculiarities that were stamped upon the face of monogamy by its rise through property relations, will decidedly vanish, namely the supremacy of men and the indissolubility of marriage. The supremacy of man in marriage is simply the consequence of his economic superiority and will fall with the abolition of the latter.

The indissolubility of marriage is partly the consequence of economic conditions, under which monogamy arose, partly tradition from the time where the connection between this economic situation and monogamy, not yet clearly understood, was carried to extremes by religion. To-day, it has been perforated a thousand times. If marriage founded on love is alone moral, then it follows that marriage is moral only as long as love lasts. The duration of an attack of individual sexlove varies considerably asccording to individual disposition, especially in men. A positive cessation of fondness or its replacement by a new passionate love makes a separation a blessing for both parties and for society. But humanity will be spared the useless wading through the mire of a divorce case ...

The full freedom of marriage can become general only after all minor economic considerations, that still exert such a powerful influence on the choice of a mate for life, have been removed ... Then no other motive will remain but mutual fondness.[17] *

There is absolutely no doubt, then, that Marx and Engels did *not* advocate the dissolution or abolition of marriage and the family. They advocated the *improvement* of the monogamous family. They wanted to remove its relationships from the calculating grasp of property considerations. They wanted to give women a status equal with that of men so that marriage could be a partnership between persons, entered into and sustained on the basis of love and affection. They wanted the family to cease to be an industrial, economic unit, so that – aided by public services for child care and education – it could be essentially a social communion of persons. And they wanted to see greater freedom in the law for the termination of marriage if it so happened that love within it ceased to exist.

It is perfectly clear, too, that the reforms of the past century have all been exactly in these directions. We are therefore led to the conclusion that Marx and Engels would wholeheartedly approve of the many reforms that have been achieved, and would undoubtedly uphold the nature of marriage and the family in present-day Britain as against anything that existed previously. If they had any argument at all, it would be in the direction of improving the status of women, the nature of the family, and the quality of family life, still further. We can therefore embrace them (in these respects at least!) as good bourgeois sociologists like ourselves who have arrived at the same conclusions.

It is only fair, however, to make one or two final qualifications. First, it is true that Engels refused to predict what the *future* form of the family might become. This, however, was only because he thought it impossible to foresee what new generations of men and

* We have noted – with some astonishment – Engels's agreement with G. M. Trevelyan. It may be of equal interest – and perhaps of greater astonishment! – to note his similar agreement with no less a person than Herbert Spencer. Spencer too, pointing to similar economic, social and legal changes, concluded:

> ... whereas, hitherto, the union by law was regarded as the essential part of marriage and the union by affection as non-essential; and whereas at present the union by law is thought the more important and the union by affection the less important; there will come a time when the union by affection will be held of primary moment: whence reprobation of marital relations in which the union by affection has dissolved.

women – freed from the economic and social conditions out of which earlier generations had had to fight their way – might make of their social institutions. And this we can accept. His sole insistence was that they should rest upon the choice and affection of equals. And second, though – clearly – I think that Juliet Mitchell is mistaken in her interpretation of Marx and Engels (especially with reference to the situation as it exists now), it is fair to point out that, in fact, she does not go so far as to advocate the abolition of the family so much as an attempt to provide *a variety of new forms*, and, in particular, to see the family placed within the wider context of a living and enriching community life. But we can come back to this later when considering the arguments arising from the new 'commune movement'.

To complete this argument about the position of Marx and 'Marxism' on the family, however, two final points are worth brief consideration.

Marx the man

Just as we pointed to some inconsistencies between the theories put forward by Laing, Esterson and Cooper, and the personal testimony of the dedication in their books, so there is a similar noticeable inconsistency between what 'Marxists' uphold as the theory of their leader concerning the family, and the picture they like to give of him as a person. Thus, though it has been widely assumed that Marx denounced the family and desired its abolition, when his colleagues, friends and followers have publicly commemorated his life and work, they have gone to great and genuinely felt lengths to illustrate his warm humanity by his actions and behaviour as a husband and father.

Marx had a bourgeois family of his own – and a very loyal and devoted bourgeois family it was, he himself being as devoted a member as any, just as he was a dominant male, Victorian head of the household. Abundant evidence of this is given, for example, in the reminiscences of Marx written by men like Paul Lafargue and Wilhelm Liebknecht.* Marx was affectionately nick-named 'Moor' because of his dark complexion and his black hair and beard, and

*Selections are given in *Karl Marx: Selected Works*, vol. I, published by Laurence & Wishart, pp. 81–134.

many accounts are given of the picnics and games which 'Moor', his daughters Jenny, Eleanor and Laura, his wife, Jenny von Westphalen, and Helene Dermuth, their devoted housekeeper, enjoyed on Hampstead Heath; sometimes visited by Engels and other friends. Here are just a few examples from Liebknecht.

Marx, like all persons of a strong and healthy nature, was extraordinarily fond of children. He was not merely the most tender father, who could be a child with his children for hours together – he also felt himself, as it were, magnetically drawn to strange children who came in his path, especially those who were poor and helpless. Hundreds of times, when wandering through poverty-stricken districts, he would suddenly tear himself away from us in order to stroke the hair and press a penny or halfpenny in the little hand of some child sitting in rags at a doorway ...

One had to have seen Marx with his children in order to get a full idea of the depth of feeling and childishness of this hero of science. In his minutes of leisure or on walks, he carried them about, played the maddest, merriest games with them – in brief, was a child among children. On Hampstead Heath we often played 'cavalry': I took one of the little daughters on my shoulders, Marx the other, and then we vied with one another in trotting and jumping – on occasion there was also a little fight between the mounted riders ...

... when his own children were grown up or dead, then the grandchildren took their place. Little Jenny, who in the beginning of the 'seventies married Longuet, one of the Commune refugees, brought Marx several children into the house – wild youngsters. The eldest ... was the grandfather's favourite. He could do what he liked with him and he knew it. One day, when I was on a visit to London, Johnny, whom the parents had sent over from Paris – as occurred several times every year – hit upon the brilliant idea of converting Moor into an *omnibus*, on the box of which, that is to say Marx's shoulders, he set himself, while Engels and I were appointed to be omnibus horses. And when we were properly harnessed, then there was a wild chase – I should have liked to say furious drive – in the little house garden behind Marx's cottage in Maitland Park Road ...

Marx, clearly, was no Victorian tyrant as a parent. 'Children must educate their parents,' was one of his much repeated sayings. On

Hampstead Heath, they obviously behaved as most other families have behaved, from that day to this.

One Sunday we discovered in the neighbourhood a horse-chestnut tree with ripe fruits. 'Let's see who can bring down the most,' someone cried, and with shouts of 'hurrah' we set to work. Moor was like a madman, and certainly bringing down chestnuts was not his strong point. But he was indefatigable – as we all were. The bombardment only ceased when the last chestnut had been secured amid wild cries of triumph. Marx could not use his right arm for eight days afterwards, and I was not better off.

The greatest 'treat' of all was a ride on the donkeys. What uproarious laughter and merry-making there was! And what comical scenes! How Marx amused himself – and us!

The same close bonds of family affection were experienced in relation to sickness and death. Neither Marx nor his wife Jenny ever recovered from their grief over the death of their son, Edgar. Edgar was very small, with a head too big for his body, and very affectionate and gentle. They called him 'Musch' (from 'mouche' – French for a fly – because of his smallness), but he came to be very lively, active, companionable, and had a passionate liking for singing – roaring out some comical, some revolutionary, songs in 'a terrifying voice'. He was so lively that they came to call him '*Colonel* Musch'. But when he was eight years old, he died – courageously – in Marx's arms, of 'mesenteric disease'.

Robert Payne, in his biography of Marx, tells how inconsolable the family was. In a letter to Lassalle (who had written a letter of sympathy), Marx wrote:

> Bacon says that really important men have so many contacts with nature and the world, and have so much to interest them, that they easily get over their loss. I am not one of these important men. My child's death has shattered my heart and brain, and I feel the loss as keenly as on the first day. My wife is completely broken down.

And Payne adds:

> He was to learn, as Jenny learned, that grief can endure for a lifetime. More than ten years later Jenny would write to a friend: 'The longer I live without the boy, the more I think of him, and the grief only grows greater.' She would gaze at

the children playing around here and suddenly her face would go blank as she remembered Edgar. Marx, watching her, would see the telltale signs, and he had no need to ask her what she was thinking.

The same kind of grief befell Marx during the last two or three years of his life on the death of his wife (by cancer) and of his first daughter, Jenny. The reminiscences of these events recorded by friends and members of his family (his daughter Eleanor, for example) show without any doubt the depth of affection which attended all the relationships of Marx's family. The marriage, quite apart from many periods of illness and poverty, was not without its personal difficulties and tragedies. For some time Helene Dermuth – who served the family as housekeeper throughout their various experiences, going everywhere with them – was Marx's mistress. An illegitimate son was born to her actually in Marx's home in Dean Street. This was a distasteful and tragic event in many respects, and one which Marx's wife felt deeply. Even so, it was overcome, and the close bonds among the members of the family, including Helene Dermuth, continued to the end. Indeed, in writing about Marx's well-known grave in Highgate Cemetery, Liebknecht is especially concerned to emphasise: 'Here lies Karl Marx *and his family* ... Marx's *family grave* it should more correctly be called...' And Helene Dermuth lies there too, with the several members of the family she so faithfully served.

Marx, then, was certainly not 'anti-family' in his personal life, and, as we have seen, this was no inconsistency with his own and Engels's view of the family in society in general. It was the *bourgeois family* – and all those traditional family-types in societies of the past which entailed the exploitation of women as property – to which they were opposed. My point, however, in pointing to the accounts given of Marx's family life by some of his followers is that there very often *is* an inconsistency here – when, on the one hand, Marx's view is represented and upheld as advocating the abolition of the family, whilst, on the other, his warm humanitarianism as a person is upheld by picturing him as a devoted husband and father. The truth is that neither in theory nor in personal practice was Marx opposed to marriage and the family as such.

The experience and practice of communist countries

It is worthwhile to point out as a final comment (though this has no necessary relevance to what Marx and Engels said) that no communist society in the world is opposed to marriage and the family either. In their experience of revolution, and then, more particularly, in the making of a new, stable system of institutions *after* revolution, the family always remains and is always given powerful government support. In *The Family and Marriage in Britain*, I described the situation in the Soviet Union,* and this need not be repeated. The fact is that after a brief post-revolutionary period when 'Marxism' was taken at its incorrect face value, and when public policy was such as to try to abolish the family as a 'bourgeois' institution, a reversal of policy had to be established for the simple reason that the family still remained, and it is now supported in the USSR as fully and strongly as in any other society in the world.

A more interesting case at the present time, however, is that of China. Again, in *The Family and Marriage in Britain*, I described the new Chinese Marriage Law,** but the very general view still remains that the nature of the Chinese Communes which are being established and encouraged is such as to undermine and destroy the family. All it is necessary to say about this is that the available evidence shows that it is quite untrue. It is a misconception. A reading, for example, of *China Reconstructs*, a journal published in Peking, and the many issues available from the London office of the Chinese 'Chargé d'Affaires', shows without question that the village 'Commune' is, in fact, a community of *families*. Indeed, great pride of achievement is felt in that – under the regime of the new 'collectives' – every family is now separately and satisfactorily housed, and is enabled to carry on family activities (of production, as well as leisure) of its own, in its spare time, when duties to the collective are over. Here are just a few aspects of a report on one village – 'Chiaoli Village' – and its experience of 'collectivization'.

> The expansion of collective production brought improved living for the commune members. When farming individually, the poorer peasants did not get enough to guarantee their own food grain, to say nothing of any other income. Last year the average income in the Chiaoli production team was

*pp. 48–52.
**See, also, p. 209.

close to 800 jin of food grain and 198 yuan in cash per capita. These figures do not include income from home sideline production. *Each family* raises an average of three pigs, and most also raise sheep and chickens. Two-story tiled-roof buildings of brick and wood have replaced the old thatched-roof huts, and electric lighting has replaced the dim oil lamps.

And this is the picture given of the improvement in the quality of life of individual families.

At noon, when the commune members come back for lunch and two or three hours for rest or to look after household affairs, we visited the home of Tsai Ah-shui. Hers was one of the 18 families who formed the first mutual-aid team. We found her helping her mother-in-law feed the four pigs and five sheep in the barn at the back of the house, where there was also a flock of chicks following a big hen about.

Tsai Ah-shui's husband, Teng Fu-shan, who is in charge of the team's plant protection work, had gone out visiting. Our hostess asked us to sit down and told us about herself.

Thirty-seven-year-old Tsai Ah-shui is an open and straightforward person. Like many of her generation she had a bitter childhood. When she was six years old, her father, a hired hand, could not stand the inhuman treatment he was getting from the landlord and quarrelled with him. He was beaten by the landlord's flunkey and died from the injuries. Shocked and grieved, her mother died the same year. A neighbour, also a poor family, took the orphan girl in. Tsai Ah-shui grew up in cold and hunger, going about barefoot even in winter. She married Teng Fu-shan when the village's first mutual-aid team was being formed. For her wedding she at last got on a pair of cloth shoes, but still had to borrow socks to hide her feet, swollen from years of frostbite. She also had to borrow a jacket to cover her own ragged padded one.

Now the family lives in a two-storey house they built themselves. They have no worries for food or warm clothing. Among their proud possessions is a sewing maching. 'Thirteen others of those first 18 families have bought sewing machines', she told us, and added that most of the team's 55 families have savings in the bank.*

*See pp. 208–10, and Note 2, p. 225.

There is no need to go into further detail. The straightforward truth is that in the new form of collectivisation, the family still remains as the primary domestic unit, and is *supported* by government. There is no evidence whatever in communal (or communist) theory or practice that it is threatening or seeking to abolish the family. All it is doing is to liberate women, giving them an effective equality of rights as citizens. It is the *old* type of family (the feudal family) – with its polygyny, its concubinage, its inferior status of women – that Chinese communism wishes to destroy, *not* marriage and the family as such, and it was *this* kind of family which Marx and Engels themselves attacked.

Conclusion

Our conclusion, very simple indeed, is that – whatever 'Marxism' or the various brands of 'Neo-Marxism' now say – it is a myth that Marx and Engels were opposed to the family (whether in theory or in practice) and that they either sought or advocated its abolition. Such a view is simply not true, and if 'Marxists' wish to maintain that this is a false interpretation the onus is on them to tell us where, in the work of Marx and Engels, statements to the contrary are to be found. And we have seen – again whatever present-day 'Marxist' theory might be – that communist practice bears us out in this. Communist theory and practice constitutes no attack on the family at all.

The upshot is – as we have seen, and strange though it may seem to some – that Marx and Engels would thoroughly approve of all the reforms to the nature of marriage and the family which have been accomplished in Britain by peaceful and legal means since the time of their death. They would uphold the modern British family as we are now doing, and seek only to improve it still further.

There was, then – and is – no serious criticism of the family here.

4

The family as prison: the New Feminism

Or ... to use Betty Friedan's own words: the family as *'Comfortable Concentration Camp'*. The use of this kind of language by the most moderate of the women's writers demonstrates at once that this fourth source of criticisms of marriage and the family is one characterised by the most extreme judgments and pronouncements. But also, however, it presents other large difficulties. Commonly known as *one* source of criticisms – the literature of 'The Women's Movement' or simply 'Women's Lib' – it is by now, and has become over a period of twenty years, an area of argument so extensive and complex, embracing the opinions of so many different groups, that it is well nigh impossible to cover, formulate, and judge its many positions satisfactorily. Bristling with the most aggressive as well as the most concerned and searching assertions and proposals, it contains, in fact, many strands which must be carefully distinguished if reliable judgments are to be achieved. Some of these rest on acceptable grounds, some are wild and wildly controversial, and it would require an encyclopaedic task to disentangle them and do justice to them all. Despite the problems, however, we must form some judgment of the criticisms of marriage and the family which have arisen from them – whether they are right or wrong, sound or misconceived – because the following up of their implications has wrought havoc among common attitudes, and seems set fair to wreak havoc in the law. This can only be done by assessing the different positions expressed by some of their more influential exponents, but it seems necessary to begin – even if only in outline fashion – by indicating the nature of the complexity which faces us.

An introductory outline

FEMINISM: THE 'FIRST PHASE' CONTINUED

The 'Women's Movement' – the struggle of women themselves (though with some notable men supporters) to win an effective recognition of their equal status with men as citizens of the political community – has by now had a long history: from its beginnings in the nineteenth century to the winning of 'Votes for Women' some fifty years or so ago. This was clearly a remarkable campaign, a remarkable victory, and the very fact that it took place so short a time ago – so recently within the entire span of human history – itself speaks in the most telling way of the deeply established subjection of women in all societies of the past (and which remains, of course, in many societies still). A great revolution – involving 'one half of the human race', and bound massively to affect the other half – was then begun, and now moves cumulatively, if at a varying pace, throughout the world. Its effects on the transformation of societies cannot yet be fully known or foreseen. It was, of course, a claim not only for recognised 'political citizenship', but also for everything that this entailed: the effective securing, the realisation, of 'the rights of women' in all areas of social life – for equality of consideration and treatment in education, employment, the choice and pursuit of career, earnings from employment, the ownership, management and inheritance of property, choice over the entry into and ability to terminate marriage, the division of property and income (maintenance) following desertion or divorce, etc. One centrally important strand in the Women's Movement as it developed after the Second World War – gathering force with a new and strengthened formulation during the 1960s and becoming more powerfully voted throughout the 1970s and into the 1980s – was therefore a continuing campaign for the effective achievement of the claims made in its first beginning. The early achievements became known as 'the first phase' of the Feminist Movement. Recognised and valued by women, it was thought, nonetheless, that many of its aims had not, in fact, been achieved. Its promise had not been realised. One important strand of the Women's Movement has therefore been this quite straightforward continuity of Feminism.

FEMINISM: THE SECOND PHASE

The writers who became the leading exponents of the Women's Movement during the 1960s, and then throughout the 1970s and 1980s – Betty Friedan, Germaine Greer, Kate Millett and others – all supported this continuity. But as society settled down into certain patterns after the end of the Second World War, and as certain developments became clear, they characterised their own campaign as 'the Second Phase' of Feminism: quite distinct from the first phase in calling attention to new problems, raising new issues, making new claims, and – in general, and on many quite specific matters – becoming more *radical*. 'Revolution' rather than 'Reform' was in the air, and was called for.

Betty Friedan believed that American women – perhaps too well provided for as wives and mothers (with all the gadgetry of modern technology) in the post-war focus on secure and comfortable domesticity – had become enslaved within the home under the dominating influence of 'the Feminine Mystique'. Isolated in their homes, preoccupied with the care of their husbands, babies, house, they had lost touch with their own nature as persons apart from these concerns (had lost their own identity), and become desperate in their experience of a new void they could not understand: 'the problem that had no name'. Women needed more than their life within this 'comfortable concentration camp', and had, somehow, to break out of it, asserting their right to something going far beyond it. Germaine Greer, more radically and (deliberately) with more outrageously shocking and provoking language, proclaimed women's autonomy. Each woman had her own nature apart from her relatedness to men, marriage and family, and should assert her right to a freely chosen range of sexual activity, the use of contraception and abortion, the rejection of marriage and the family – rebelling against the diminished nature and status imposed upon her as 'the Female Eunuch'. With variations of analysis and emphasis, with differing degrees of intensity, other writers followed. The Women's Movement came to have more faces than one. Even within these initial and most basic arguments themselves, however – and certainly within those of the subsequent groups which quickly established themselves, their banners waving high in the prevailing winds which blew through the halls of international conferences and over the protest-marches down the streets – many strands and concerns which were by no means identical became evident, quickly leading, indeed, to tensions, quarrels, and struggles for power within the Feminist Movement itself, and it is important to note each of these, no matter how briefly.

WOMEN'S SEXUALITY

One was simply the recognition and assertion of the existence of women's sexuality as such; the new, open admission and exploration of it; and, indeed, the publication of the new investigations into its nature. Women, it was now frankly revealed, themselves enjoyed sexual experience. Moreover – in its arousal, in the continuing dimensions of stimulation and fulfilment of it during sexual congress, and in its culminating satisfaction – this was different from that of men. The findings of the 'sexual researchers' – Kinsey, Masters and Johnson, etc. – became the new and newly available basis of knowledge. Controversies arose about clitoral orgasm, vaginal orgasm, multiple orgasm. Women (it was now held) could be active in taking the initiative in sexual experience rather than being considered only receptive and submissive in such relationships. Coupled with this was the assertion of a woman's right (if she so wished it) to seek and enjoy sexual fulfilment before marriage and to expect satisfactory sexual fulfilment within it (i.e. as a required and essential part of a satisfactory marriage). This was only one new strand of knowledge and argument in the 'second phase'. Yet even this itself was variously held and expressed: sometimes discussed in a temperate and relatively orthodox way – with reference to sensitive and mutual consideration within the marital relationship, with the improved quality of marriage in mind; sometimes asserted in an aggressive, fanatical way, in terms of what the liberated woman required or demanded of her partner or husband, and, as such, it was often flagrantly opposed to marriage and the family: not so much criticising them as violently denouncing and rejecting them.

CONTRACEPTIVE TECHNIQUES: DISCUSSED, AVAILABLE, IMPROVED

A related – but distinct – strand was the much more publicly available knowledge of contraceptive techniques: the discussion of them, the more ready availability of them, and changes and supposed improvements in them (the greater reliability of them). They were now available for use openly, at any age, both inside and outside marriage. Culminating (though this is by no means final) in 'The Pill', this gave women themselves, at last, a very considerable degree of control over their sexual and reproductive activity and the degree of liberty in their behaviour that they desired. This had, and continues to have, large and unresolved implications for changes in the orientation of responsibility and care in sexual intercourse, and the choice of pregnancy, for both men and women. The romanticised ethos of the contraceptive information given in the secretly read books of Marie Stopes (in the service of *Married Love*) was now replaced by a much more hard-headed sophistication.

ABORTION

Part and parcel of this same focus on contraception, birth control, and the extension of the sexual liberation of women – but still a matter significantly distinct from it – was the more direct and open demand for the legalisation of abortion; and this, too, immediately had its moderate and extreme exponents. Some wanted legalisation simply to eliminate the unfortunate aspects of the 'hidden abortions of the backstreets', and to recognise the need for chosen abortion in special cases (with the health of the mother and/or child in view; in cases of pregnancy by rape, etc.). Some – much more aggressively and outrightly – demanded 'abortion on demand' as the unconditional right of every woman. Women, having conceived a child (whether as a matter of course within marriage, or casually, accidentally, irresponsibly outside it) had the right to decide themselves 'what they should do with their own bodies'.

But, contraception and abortion aside, yet another demand for sexual liberty arose within this prevailing atmosphere.

HOMOSEXUALITY: MALE AND FEMALE

Quite distinct from all the considerations mentioned so far, this might well seem, at first glance, to have little to do with marriage and the family. Yet – within the same context of the new knowledge about the nature and varieties of human sexuality – it came, very decidedly, to be attached to the movement for Women's Liberation, and for some, especially, to be more or less identified with it. More narrowly, this was the claim for the recognition of 'lesbianism'; more generally, that for the recognition of 'homosexuality' (whether male or female); and this, too, was sometimes advanced in a temperate and moderate manner, sometimes fanatically – as an outright attack upon one sex by the other. In general, the demand was made and met for the legalisation of homosexual practices and relationships between 'consenting adults'. Among some women, however – a militant, derisive, and vocal minority – this was accompanied by an aggressive 'anti-man' campaign, frequently displaying a violent hatred of men. Going far beyond an insistence on the recognition of women's sexuality as such (and even of the variations of such sexuality), some lesbians (e.g. see Koedt) argued, quite literally, for 'the extinction of the male organ'. The supposed existence of the vaginal orgasm was merely a myth put abroad to serve and support the unwarranted idea that a man was required for a woman's sexual satisfaction. The rubbing of one clitoris against another proved that this (among other kinds of stimulation) was all that was necessary for satisfying orgasm. Men and the part they had hitherto played in sexual behaviour were quite unnecessary – dispensable. Women could manage quite satisfactorily alone. Not only marriage ... even heterosexuality was quite unnecessary. Reproduction, it was true (if it was desired), still needed a minimal contribution from a male, but this could be supplied quite easily in a test-tube; and, furthermore, a woman bringing about the conception of a child by this method (employing, perhaps, a sperm-bank provision from a male donor of her chosen level of intelligence) could even invent and arrange an appropriate ceremony in her home to celebrate her act of creation. Some were even ready to allow television cameras and crews into their homes to record how the deed could be done. It was only a small step from this for both women and men homosexuals to claim the right to establish their own publicly recognised long-term domestic relationships; to claim the right, in fact, to establish and enjoy families in the same way as heterosexuals – with children (if they so wished), whether, again, acquired by injection or adoption. Why should heterosexuals, or biological parents, be the only ones thought fit to bring up and care for children? This, however, could well require the provision of a new kind of 'domestic law'.

ONE-PARENT FAMILIES

Another strand of argument and practice stemmed from this – but this, too, had its several and independent roots. It was the growing assertion of the right to establish, or to continue to maintain by choice, a 'single-parent family'. The possibility of such families was, on the one hand, a straightforward corollary of the autonomy and freedom of the sexes, and was based, particularly, upon the new ability on the part of women to provide for their own livelihood and home from the earnings of their own employment and the pursuit of their own careers. Husbands – as well as wives – were, in this respect too, no longer necessary. But this was not the only ground for such families, and some cases were by no means a matter of personal choice. Many families became single-parent families because of marriage breakdown, and their number grew, obviously, with the growing incidence of divorce and separation. Usually, even for straightforward economic reasons alone, such families suffered hardships. Women or men alike left to care for their children alone, found difficulty in keeping a full-time job and undertaking satisfactorily all the many-dimensioned tasks involved in the upkeep of a home. Again, therefore, there arose a demand for new 'domestic law' and social services and provisions appropriate for the amelioration of these hardships. Quite apart from this matter of direct *need*, however (as resulting from broken families), women, it came to be argued, needed the further provision of many kinds of social support so that – on the basis of equal opportunity with men – they could effectively enjoy their right both to choose to have children, and, at the same time, to preserve their autonomy, and to choose and pursue a career for the fulfilment of their talents and abilities. Men and women alike had the right to establish one-parent families – and new social services and supports should be provided to make this possible, to make these rights effective. The recognition of these rights actually required a revolutionary re-organisation of society.

These kinds of demands – for homosexual and one-parent families – were made even more detailed by the assertion of the right of several men and women, on the basis of choice and agreement, to establish new kinds of 'collective households' and 'communes', which would make necessary even more complicated clauses in any new body of 'domestic law'.

In various ways, these newly demanded sexual freedoms, these newly recognised and asserted varieties of sexual practice and domestic relationships, led to a rejection of the normal, traditional, or 'orthodox' conception of marriage and the family (and particularly – a term I shall come to criticise later – 'the nuclear family'). Marriage was now regarded as an outmoded institution which led partners into the captivity of an intolerable and unjustifiable bondage and held them in it. It was a denial of the newly articulated 'rights'. The 'nuclear family' was the old-fashioned and equally out-moded prison itself. Newer and freer relationships were called for.

COHABITATION

Taking the place of marriage itself were new relationships of 'cohabitation'. Taking the place of the nuclear family were new household groups of 'cohabitants'. Men and women, women and women, men and men, should be able to live together without publicly recognised and registered changes of status. Still single, still free, they could live together and cease to live together as they pleased. The public ceremony – the declaration, commitment to, and recording of a marriage – was now thought unnecessary. The certificate of marriage was reduced in status to that of 'just a piece of paper'. 'What's the point of getting *married*? We can live together just as well without it. Why tie ourselves up for life? In any case, what difference does a piece of paper make?' These attitudes became, and remain, widespread. Yet strangely, and despite this casual deriding of the relationship between husband and wife, cohabiting couples still continued to make use of its language – especially when needing to make claims upon each other, or on the welfare provisions of the state, if problems arose between them. At such times, confronted with such problems, they insisted (and insist) on referring to their 'common law *wife*' or 'common law *husband*', though, in fact, no such status exists in the law. Why *wife*, or *husband*, one wonders? It is as though they demanded recourse to the law pertaining to marriage without having been prepared to recognise it or enter into it. Still, too, for some reason, they continued (and continue) to want their children to be publicly recognised as 'their own', and felt annoyed and aggrieved that they should be 'stigmatised' as being 'illegitimate' – though this, by their own deliberate choice was what they were, and what they themselves had made them. All this, again, led to the demand for a new body of 'domestic law', and recommendations were made for the drawing up of detailed 'cohabitation contracts' to regulate the claims and counter-claims members of households could make upon each other whilst still leaving personal rights and status intact. The outcome was a detailed *Cohabitation Handbook** drawn up and published on behalf of the Women's Rights Movement to guide intending cohabitants through the labyrinth of the law.

* There are now several such books, offering guidance on cohabitation, the tax law, 'social security' provisions, etc.

This already seems a forbidding array of the distinct strands which, woven together, have come to comprise 'The Women's Movement' – each of them, obviously, requiring careful consideration and judgment – but still others need mention, no matter how brief, to make it completely clear how complex the situation has become.

SUPPORTS AND DEFENCES: THE FAMILIAR SOURCES

First, as one might have supposed, all the familiar sources came to be called upon as and when they proved expedient to buttress the criticisms of marriage and the family these writers wanted to make, and to support the new claims. The ubiquitous Reith Sentence of Leach was quoted. Laing, Cooper and Esterson were uncritically drawn upon. Marxism in its various forms (sometimes the family was part of 'the economic base', sometimes it was part of the 'ideological superstructure') was used as the basic analysis of 'capitalism' and the exploitative family unit within it. Engels, too, continued to be misrepresented.

SEXUAL POLITICS

With additional grounds, too – largely supported by a detailed analysis of the work of novelists – the call was made to recognise the place of concepts of sexuality and of sexual attitudes (particularly of men towards women) in the ongoing patterns of, and struggles for, *power* in society. The most notable statement of this was that made by Kate Millett in her book *Sexual Politics*, but her language was echoed and used by many thereafter.

UNISEX

There was also (an ingredient which must not be underestimated) a connected trend towards 'Unisex', which was seized upon, cultivated, and therefore reinforced by every organ of 'fashion'. Men and women, perhaps different in some respects, were now held to be not all that different. Indeed, doubt was thrown upon the reality of any and all differences. Even those apparent differences existing in society were, in all probability, superficial social distinctions culturally induced, and not essentially different features of the basic biology and psychology of the sexes. Gender was socially created: a matter, most probably, of long-established convention and tradition, of immemorial usage. There was no real or basic reason why boys and girls should be expected to play with different toys, to want to form different groups at play, to prefer different games. Such differences were cultural myths which changes in upbringing, education and practice could stamp out. There was no reason, either, why men and women should not dress in the same kinds of clothes, have exactly the same kinds and elements of education, do the same work, achieve the same levels of skill in the same careers or in creative work in the arts, play an equal and similar part and do the same tasks in housekeeping and child-care. It was true that a child actually took shape inside a woman and issued from her, but, after the business of birth itself, everything could be done just as well by men as by women. The equality of women – for some Feminists, at least – went far beyond any question of equality of status and opportunities only, whilst continuing to recognise certain basic, important, and perhaps complimentary, differences between themselves and men. It was a more radical claim that men and women were, as a sheer matter of fact (were it not for unfortunate, long-established and distorting social infuences), in large measure the same, and so should be treated in the same way. Women needed neither protection nor privileges. Any such idea was a lingering corollary of the assumption of their inferiority. All that women wanted was autonomy and freedom; with that they could stand on their own feet.

In the wake of this emphasis came a lengthy list of demands for the changes in society which would make this possible. Those made for fundamental changes in language – in the terms to be used of the sexes in their social roles – were perhaps the most conspicuous and significant. Not 'Miss' or 'Mrs' which distinguished between the status of married and unmarried women, but (like the universal 'Mr' for men) 'Ms' should be the rule. In the procedures of committees, not 'Chair*man*' but 'Chair*person*' should be the new usage. Why, too, for example, should the woman – and not the man – be expected to change *her* surname on marriage? And why should the children of a marriage automatically adopt the surname of their father? – and not their mother? The *Cohabitation Handbook* offered detailed ways of putting such matters right. The same considerations even entered the realm of Theology. 'God', clearly, should not be thought of as 'God the *Father*'. This was not only the most elementary anthropomorphism, it was also unjustifiably slanted in its anthropomorphism – reflecting the long history of male dominance, power, and authority. The 'Divine Nature' must clearly contain all the elements of female nature too. Following upon this same line of argument, there was no reason, either, why women should not be entitled to ordination (at least within the Christian Church), and be able to serve as priests. The issue gave rise to grave and intricate ecclesiastical debates – still unresolved – in the Church of England Synod, and the matter, clearly, cannot rest there. There seems no earthly reason (or, as far as one can see, heavenly either) why 'The Vicar of Christ on Earth' should always be a man. The logic of the argument compels the question: why not a woman Pope? It might make a significant difference to the encyclicals.

These, then, were the more conspicuous strands of argument, protest, and practice which were stated and emphasised from about the mid-1960s onwards, which came into full power during the 1970s, and have remained powerful in their influence during the 1980s. In various ways and in varying degrees of intensity quite distinct, they have become welded together in public opinion as one movement: The Women's Movement or the movement for Women's Liberation. This is how these related matters are now thought of, and a common assumption seems to have become implanted – deeply and uncritically taken for granted – that the entire movement and the people, books and groups contributing to it, have rejected marriage, and advocate the abolition of the family on the basis of a number of radical criticisms which they all share. In what follows, I want to show quite simply that this is not so; that it is a misconception; and to argue, too, that very few of the criticisms of the family actually made (as distinct from attacks aggressively launched) stand up to careful scrutiny. For this, we must now turn to an appraisal of the work of each of the most influential writers – something which, I think, may contain some surprises. After this, finally, we shall be able to draw together some clear conclusions.

Betty Friedan

One notable voice heralding the second phase of Feminism had been clearly heard during the late 1940s – that of Simone de Beauvoir (in her book *The Second Sex*) – but only late in the 1960s did the new Women's Movement come to be firmly proclaimed and founded, and, by common agreement, it was the work of Betty Friedan which provided the most clearly articulated statement, and was the chief stimulation responsible for this. Juliet Mitchell called Friedan's first book (*The Feminine Mystique*, 1963) 'the single inspiration for the movement', and on the appearance of her second (*The Second Stage*, 1981)[1] she was greeted by the *Sunday Times* as 'the most influential feminist of the last 20 years'. Here, if anywhere, then – in the position set out in these two books – we could expect to find the basic criticisms of marriage and the family stemming from the Women's Liberation Movement. The surprising – indeed, the astonishing – thing: is that *it contains no criticism of marriage and the family at all!*

The Feminine Mystique became widely available in paperback form in Britain only in 1965, and 'Women's Lib' in Britain began to develop from this late in the 1960s. What did the first book say?

It stemmed from Betty Friedan's long-growing conviction that American women, in general, had become increasingly assailed by a gnawing and deepening sense of emptiness, boredom, and discontent in the experience of their lives as wives and mothers since the end of the Second World War. This was something going far beyond any ordinary work-a-day dissatisfaction. It seemed, more deeply, to lie in a growing meaninglessness of personal life, in a loss of self-identity. It began by being felt secretly, inwardly, but then with a mounting intensity of desperation which was all the worse for being not understood. Only gradually did it come to be shared as women confided in each other about it. This, however, did not imply any criticism or rejection of marriage and the family as such. It lay rather in a mistaken emphasis which had been placed upon them as a result of certain conditions prevailing in society after the war, and then deliberately fostered and furthered by various social and commercial agencies. This central mistake was the widely publicised conviction (so deeply established as to have become taken-for-granted as a fundamental truth) that the fulfilment of a woman's nature was to be found entirely in a life of domesticity: in her devotion to her husband, her children, her home. A 'feminine mystique', built up to this effect, had 'succeeded in burying millions of American women alive'. Only gradually did women come to realise that the void they themselves experienced in their confinement to their homes was not merely a personal matter – peculiar to each one of them alone – but was one shared by all the housewives and mothers throughout America. Only gradually did they become aware that it was not only something which they themselves, individually, did not understand, but that *it was not understood by anybody*. The roots and causes of it were not known. Even the consciousness of its generality had only slowly emerged. It had not even been reflected upon and articulated. It was a 'problem without a name'.

Certain conditions of life and society after the war had laid people open to this mistake; had made them vulnerable to it. The relief that the war was over, the relief of servicemen at getting safely back home, the relief of their women-folk at having them safely back home ... all this made welcome the warm focus upon family life: on the building of homes, enjoying the new-found security, settling back into work and domestic life, planning and working for the future, providing and sharing a continually improving quality of life for all the members of each home. An entire pattern of motivation and desire came to be focused upon shared and enjoyed domestic privacy. There was 'a pent-up hunger for marriage, home and children' which made men and women alike 'pushovers for the mystique'. But, given this context making for an all-too-ready response of warmth to any suggested concentration upon close familial feeling, thinking, and activities, there were also other conceptions, other social concerns, other developments of knowledge, other calculating agencies, which tended to 'cash in' on the feminine mystique and develop it in many and exaggerated ways. But let us be quite clear, first of all, what exactly this mystique was. It says, wrote Betty Friedan, that:

> the highest value and the only commitment for women is the fulfilment of their own femininity. It says that the great mistake of Western culture, through most of its history, has been the undervaluation of this femininity. It says this femininity is so mysterious and intuitive and close to the creation and origin of life that man-made science may never be able to understand it. But however special and different, it is in no way inferior to the nature of man; it may even in certain respects be superior. The mistake, says the mystique, the root of women's troubles in the past is that women envied men, women tried to be like men, instead of accepting their own nature, which can find fulfilment only in sexual passivity, male domination, and nurturing maternal love.

It actually meant, however (she complained), the same age-old image of women: 'Occupation – Housewife'! And the new conditions brought not only a retrograde moving back to this image (against which the early feminists had rebelled) but also a renewed glorification of it. The first 'passionate journey', the 'first phase', of early feminism had successfully achieved 'Votes for Women'. But there, it seemed, it had stopped. The newly publicised 'Happy Housewife

Heroine' no longer demanded equal status and opportunities in education, employment, professional careers, etc. The earlier claims were left unaccomplished and unfulfilled, and many elements had contributed to this.

The influential women's magazines had turned their backs on the 'career woman'. Their heroines now renounced their careers, having discovered after all, that what they really wanted was to be housewives. There it was that their warm fulfilment lay. And housewives were increasingly portrayed as being younger, more glamorous, more sexually attractive and sexually responsive objects to which husbands came home at night. Educationalists – in schools and colleges alike – prided themselves on providing 'relevant' courses for girls: to fit them for being successful and happy wives and mothers (and little else). Coupled with this, certain ideas were abroad – stemming chiefly from Freud and some (supposedly) 'Functionalist' anthropologists (e.g. Margaret Mead) – perpetuating the idea of woman's nature as being only capable of fulfilment in her relationship of dependence, as a partner, with man, and the idea of the domestic role of women as one which was a necessary element within the entire structure of society; one essentially integrated with 'the social system'. Education should therefore have both this nature and role of women centrally in mind, and train girls accordingly. Psychology and social anthropology alike, in short, served the feminine mystique, especially through the massively influential medium of education. But there were agencies of 'education' going beyond the educational system. Manufacturers and advertisers, too, planned their products and marketing in the light of the new image: deliberately cultivating it, enhancing its attractions, emphasising it more colourfully, making it more appealing, for two direct reasons. First, the new home itself was an enormous market for specific products: carpets and furniture, television sets and vacuum cleaners, food-mixers and dish-washers, barbecue sets and garden tools. Second, the domestic group (the advertising media now built into the living-room corner of every home) was the most easily approachable, captive, and susceptible group for inculcating a widespread demand for almost any product: motor cars, boats and trailers, caravans and swimming pools, package tours abroad, second-home holiday bungalows by the beach. The housewife was more and more flattered, more and more wooed by the advertisers, her gullibility and susceptibility deliberately cultivated and extended, as the central recipient of advertising, the centrally influential consumer. Within the home, one result of this was a particular embodiment of Parkinson's Law.

'Housewifery' with a preoccupation fully engaged on all the newly available gadgets – 'expanded to fill the time available'. With the new 'improvements' a woman's work in the house was, very truly, 'never done', leaving her 'no time for herself'. The 'motivational researchers', says Betty Friedan, were:

guilty of persuading housewives to stay at home, mesmerised in front of a television set ... drained by the sexual sell into the buying of things ...
The manipulators and their clients in American business can hardly be accused of creating the feminine mystique. But they are the most powerful of its perpetuators; it is their millions which blanket the land with persuasive images, flattering the American housewife, diverting her guilt and disguising her growing sense of emptiness ... If they are not responsible for sending women home, they are surely responsible for keeping them there.

The American housewife had become busily trapped within her 'comfortable concentration camp' – now so magnificently equipped. But another factor became important within this situation, too: the new knowledge of women's sexuality. Kinsey and others published their new findings on women's experience of 'orgasm'; some women, they claimed, being 'insatiably capable of "multiple orgasm" to the point of sheer physical exhaustion'. If American women found them-selves lacking such kinds of satisfaction in their own experience, then from teenage to middle age, they are 'doomed to spend most of their lives in sexual fantasy'. The new sexual knowledge led American women to diagnose 'the problem that has no name' as a sexual problem. That was what lay at the roots of their emptiness and discontent. And there developed among them a 'mounting sex-hunger'.

It is not an exaggeration to say that several generations of able American women have been successfully reduced to sex-creatures, sex-seekers.

Two effects, it seemed, followed from this. First, even for the women themselves, the 'promise of infinite orgiastic bliss', far from finding itself fulfilled, led to the fact that the pursuit of it became a 'strangely joyless national compulsion'. Sexual behaviour and exper-ience became 'dehumanized'. Sex died a 'slow withering death', giving rise, increasingly, and with greater and less satisfying intensity, to sexual fantasy. And second, it led to the same joyless, dehumanised search for sexual gratification among *men*. Anything even approximating to *personal love* was debased into straightforward appetite – which was no respecter of persons. Indeed, it led to 'sexual disillusionment' among American men, and even to a disillusionment with, and a hostility towards, women. Within marriage and outside it, satisfactory sexual relationships became more rare. 'Women,' wrote one press correspondent, 'are on their way out.' The rich promise of the feminine mystique had given way to an impoverished void, and within this combination of factors, the much-vaunted situation of the housewife had become an empty cul-de-sac, a vacuous dead-end, a trap, a positive danger.

> It is urgent to understand how the very condition of being a housewife can create a sense of emptiness, non-existence, nothingness, in women ... I am convinced there is something about the housewife state itself that is dangerous.

What, then, was the way out?

Betty Friedan's diagnosis was very straightforward. Women needed *more* than domesticity. Like men, they were individual persons, with natures, dimensions, talents, capabilities, which – besides their life within the family – could only find fulfilment in personally chosen work and in activities in shared responsible citizenship within the wider community of which they were members. The over-glamorisation of the role of the wife and mother in domesticity should be shed. The 'veil of over-glorification imposed by the feminine mystique should be brushed aside' to make way for a more matter-of-fact realism. A 'drastic re-shaping of the cultural image of feminity' was needed. Much housework was routine, monotonous, and (in itself) unrewarding. Women had grown beyond the confines of such a limited and limiting domestic role. They needed, in addition, wider self-actualising activities: to become 'fully grown'. They needed to find their own identity, their own direction of creativity, in self-chosen work: 'in large creative purposes', in 'responsible work in society', and for this Betty Friedan outlined her 'New Life Plan for Women'.

This focused crucially upon education and the continuity of it throughout life for as long, and in such ways, as women desired. This, too, had not to be just 'education for family life', but education to the extent that each woman and her talents and interests desired, and to fit women (like men) to become 'complete, and fully part of the world'. For women, as well as men, 'education is and must be the matrix of evolution.' This would have to be coupled with the effective realisation of the demands for occupational and professional and income-earning possibilities, nursery provisions, maternity leaves, and all those other adjustments in social provisions which were necessary for the securing of women's rights. But the most important emphasis – from the point of view of our own essential concern – is to see that nothing in this entire analysis, diagnosis, and proposed plan for liberation and fulfilment *was at all critical of marriage and the family*. On the contrary, it aimed at the removal from them of misleading and fallacious images, at their improved health and quality, and at a more satisfactory integration of women's personal life, domestic life, and wider life in chosen activities in society.

Women must be educated to a new integration of roles. The more they are encouraged to make that new life plan – integrating a serious, lifelong commitment to society with marriage and motherhood – the less conflicts and unnecessary frustrations they will feel as wives and mothers, and the less their daughters will make mistaken choices for lack of a full image of woman's identity.

A woman had to live, co-operate and compete in society 'not as a woman, but as a human being'. Only when their life plans were geared to their real (and real range) of abilities, would they not have 'to sacrifice the right to honourable competition and contribution, any more than they will have to sacrifice marriage and motherhood.' Who knows, she then concludes:

what women can be when they are finally free to become themselves? Who knows what women's intelligence will contribute when it can be nourished without denying love? Who knows of the possibilities of love when men and women share not only children, home and garden, not only the fulfilment of their biological roles, but the responsibilities and passions of the work that creates the human future? It has barely begun, the search of women for themselves. But the time is at hand when the voices of the feminine mystique can no longer drown out the inner voice that is driving women on to become complete.

There was, then – and very clearly and decidedly – no criticism whatever of marriage and the family in Betty Friedan's first formulation of the nature and objectives of the 'second phase' of Feminism. Her concern was only to insist that women needed more than this, and that the very qualities of marriage and the family themselves (and the improvement of them) depended upon a recognition of this.

If any reinforcement was required to justify this judgement of her position (which some might think surprising, perhaps even too extreme) her own second book – *The Second Stage* – provided it. Taking shape during the late 1970s, published in 1981, available in paperback form in Britain in 1983, this, again, was rooted in widespread feelings she detected among American women. But these, now, were feelings of disillusionment, even of bitterness, over what had happened within the ranks, pronouncements, and activities of feminism itself following the impact of *The Feminine Mystique*. The 'second phase' of Feminism marked by that book, and what had taken place since, proved to have been only a 'first stage' in the newly awakened Women's Movement. A 'second stage' of reconsideration and reformulation was now called for. And in this new statement, Betty Friedan found herself having to argue – in a way which she felt might well offend some of her more extreme 'sisters' – that much of her first analysis and many of her proposals had been grossly misunderstood, and that the activities and claims of many supporters of 'Women's Liberation' since that time had been not only too extreme but also even false, misplaced, and misguided. They had, indeed, done great harm and been a great disservice to the position and future of women as she had portrayed them. The women who had seemed to 'have gained so much', now seemed 'to have lost a great deal as well'. In particular, she was at great pains to make it absolutely clear that she had *never* at all been anti-marriage, anti-family, anti-man; that she had *never* thought that women's fulfilment lay in the rejection of marriage and family life, or in the imitation of men by entering the same world of competition in the struggle for security, the fight for promotion, for salary increases, power, success. Men too had frustrations to endure, had restrictions and indignities forced upon them which stood in their way, too, of discovering their personal identity and finding fulfilment in self-chosen activities. Women, she felt, were 'falling into the trap men were trying to get out of,' and she voiced new qualms.

She was forthright in dissociating herself from the more fanatical extremists who had gathered to march under her banner. She found distasteful the new 'female machismo' among some women and their groups. The modern image of the feminist, she complained, with its accompaniment of 'bra-burning' and 'sexual politics' had become:

> that of a career 'super-woman' hellbent on beating men at
> their own game, or of a young 'Ms Libber' agitating against

marriage, motherhood, the family, sexual intimacy with men, and any or all of the traits with which women in the past pleased or attracted men.

But it was just this 'reaction against the family' which, she said, had *distorted* the first stage of the movement. This, she said, 'was not what we meant at all'. Her rejection of these extreme positions was very forceful indeed, denouncing all those who regarded 'man as the *enemy*' – the women's writers who portrayed 'man', for example, as 'oppressor' (Millett), the 'natural predator' (Brownmiller), as being driven by 'metaphysical cannibalism' (Atkinson), and who spoke of the child they had helped to conceive (the foetus) as a 'parasite' or 'uninvited guest' (Shulamith Firestone). It had, in fact, been the male leaders of the radical student movement, she pointed out, who had been 'more blatantly chauvinist pigs than their conservative fathers', and she derided the use of 'all that sophisticated Marxist jargon to make a new revolutionary case for destruction of "the patriarchal nuclear family" and the "tyranny" of sexual biology as the source of all oppression.' Her own statement of feminism, she said, had 'never meant destruction of the family, repudiation of marriage and motherhood (or implacable sexual war against men)'. She attacked the fantasies of SCUM manifestos (Society for Cutting Up Men!) which claimed that 'women would never be free unless the family was abolished and women foreswore motherhood and sexual intercourse with men', and she attacked, too, the way in which journalists and publishers were hungry for the most extreme and extravagant books. The answer for women, she said, lay not in denying marriage and the family but in recognising 'that equality makes it possible, and necessary, for *new* kinds of family ... to recognise, strengthen, or create *new* family forms that can sustain us *now* – and that will change, as our needs change, over time.' And she was not alone in having these feelings; not alone in hating the stridency and intolerance of those who had come to struggle for power among feminists. One woman, herself a former radical feminist, said:

> I came into the women's movement because I wasn't treated right by men in the radical movement, but I was treated in much the same way by the honchos in the women's movement. I've had enough of being told the right way to live as a feminist.

Others, besides herself, were sickened at the sight of some leaders in the Women's Movement 'spending as much energy fighting each other and jockeying for money and power to shore up their own

organizational machines as they were on ERA* and abortion ...'
'You can't count on any woman,' said one ex-president of the
National Organisation for Women (NOW), 'once she gets some
power, not to sell other women out.' Power, it seems, was as ugly and
distasteful – and as corrupting – among women as it was among men;
its evils knew no sexual boundaries. She pointed, too, to the growing
problems, to the disquiet and even agonising experiences of women
as, in fact, they gained what they wanted, and became successful in
securing their new roles. Once in senior positions 'in the Boardroom'
– they found themselves just as lonely and discontented there. 'Is this
what I really wanted?' Coming to middle age, restless in the
continued pursuit of their careers, but not, as yet, having fulfilled
their desire to have children, they were devastated to realise that
now, perhaps, it was too late. They found it impossible – satisfactorily – to manage both a career and a home. With their new-
found freedom and autonomy, too, they seemed to be becoming
victims of the addictions, diseases, and social maladjustments –
alcoholism, drug-addiction, stress-diseases, crime, suicide – hitherto
chiefly found among men; and as though to illustrate and prove the
unavoidable degrees of stress involved in striving for actual equality
with men, Betty Friedan reported, in a telling section, the training of
women and men soldiers at West Point – revealing, as it did, and
despite all the efforts to achieve sheer equality in the conditions,
requirements, and speed of training, many differences between
women and men which could neither be gainsaid nor eliminated.

Repudiating these extremes and excesses, Betty Friedan went to
great lengths, too, to make it clear how much she and her colleagues,
in working hard for the causes of 'the first stage', had been loyally
supported and helped by their husbands and families, from the
secure basis of their homes. The 'founding mothers' of NOW, she
pointed out, 'averaged more than two children apiece.' And quite
apart from the Women's Movement proper, they and their husbands
had mutually helped and supported each other in getting their
university degrees, sharing the leadership (for example) of Continuing Education Programmes and other activities to which they were
devoted.

Muriel Fox, high-powered public relations executive, brought
her two children along to NOW's founding conference in
Washington in 1966, and her surgeon husband put them to

*Equal Rights Amendment

bed in the hotel while she stayed up all night getting out our first press release.

She recorded the joint efforts of herself and her own husband in the support of the Women's Movement whilst, with their equally supportive children, being involved in all the continuing 'stuff of family life ... We took all that for granted' – and re-affirming her own conviction that woman's nature was, in fact, deeply rooted in motherhood, the family and all its bonds of companionship and affection; that these dimensions of experience were essential to womanhood. Indeed (shades of Laing, Cooper and Esterson!), she had dedicated *The Feminine Mystique* to her own family: 'To Carl Friedan and to our children – Daniel, Jonathan, and Emily': hardly the gesture of one opposed to the family! In rejecting extreme and uncaring demands for abortion, she reasserted her position, too, that she was *for* life, not *for* abortion – only for the *right* to abortion. But in all this she was careful to insist that her call for a *Second Stage* was decidedly *not* a negative reaction to feminism; decidedly *not* a going back to Ibsen's *Doll's House*.* It was a necessary reconsideration for a sounder move forward. It was necessary to reconsider the new problems, the new positions, which had emerged to move forward to new alternatives. But in this *Second Stage*, she argued, the focus, strangely enough, had actually to be on the family. 'The Family', she forthrightly declared, 'is the New Feminist Frontier.' We need not go into further detail here. For our purposes it is enough simply to note her plain emphasis: which required a sharing, between men and women, of love and work; a restructuring of home and work.

In the second stage, when women and men share the work of their *days*, on the job and at home, with new equality and autonomy, authentic feelings, on the part of both women and men, will replace the role-playing and the tortuous stifling masks imposed by that excessive dependence, need for dominance, and the resulting hostilities in the family. There will be less alienation, less sexual obsession-revulsion, a diminishing reservoir of frustrated life energies to be exploited by either capitalist, corporate, or communist bureaucrats, for their own profit or power, or to be channelled into sadistic pornographic fantasy or actual violence.

... And this new *human* liberation will enable us ... to

*But: see another interpretation of Ibsen in *The Shaking of the Foundations: Family and Society*, concluding chapter.

erect new kinds of homes for all our dreams, affirm new and old family bonds that can evolve and nourish us through all the changes of our lives, and use the time that is our life to enrich our human possibilities, spelling our own names, at last, as women and men.

This, surely, is perfectly clear.

Betty Friedan, in her articulation of both the first and the second stages of the post-war Women's Liberation Movement, made no destructive criticisms of marriage and the family at all. On the contrary, what she wanted was an improvement and enrichment of them in the light of the promise contained in the full recognition of the new status and rights of women as members of society equal with men.

Criticisms of some aspects of her work could, of course, be made. For example, some of the alternative arrangements she proposes for families living in modern urban conditions – new community-type 'co-operatives'; new 'collectives' in which families would share and manage common facilities, etc. – are, at the very least, questionable, as is the connected idea (put forward by some) that to provide separate domestic equipment and facilities in private households is somehow a 'duplication' and so a 'waste' of resources. But it is not to our purpose to consider such criticisms in detail. One or two points, however, do deserve brief final mention as we shall have to consider them again later.

First – a highly intelligent woman, educated to high standards – Betty Friedan makes much of education in her plan for women, and of the provision, indeed, of continuing higher education. It is in no sense an argument against this to suggest two points for possible consideration in this connection. (1) It is at least possible that her diagnosis of 'American women' may not, in fact, be true of all (or even the majority) of women, but only true, more strictly, of these American women who themselves possess such abilities and who may therefore, in their confinement to domestic life, be suffering the same kinds of frustration. The diagnosis, though true for some women, may be far from true for all. (2) In the same way, it is also at least possible that there are many women (perhaps a majority?) for whom education to the level and extent that Betty Friedan proposes, and even the wider and more active participation in the affairs of citizenship that she advocates, may be beyond their powers and outside the realm of their inclinations. Like many men, they may not find their satisfactions in either. Many women may therefore have been very much affected by the strident and fashionable demands for women's rights, women's autonomy, sexual independence and readiness to seek divorce – without properly understanding their situation (perhaps even their own nature?), and without possessing the necessary resources to deal with any disruption brought about in their family lives. They may not be capable of either education or work on a higher level. They may not have the ability or opportunity to achieve financial security alone. They may not be capable of dealing satisfactorily with the new-found freedom they face. Their new position – though liberated – may therefore be one of irremediable disaster, of final tragedy. The gist of this point is simply the possibility that high-powered reformers may wreak havoc among those with a more limited level of understanding and ability who are, nonetheless, a prey to the loudly voiced 'progressive' campaigns and the fashionable attitudes. They may spread attitudes which are simply ill-informed and 'half baked', resulting in misery, and especially for countless children who, as a result, have themselves to grow to adulthood within a kaleidoscope of domestic anarchy with no secure basis whatever for their own self-identity and self-fulfilment. As I write, for example (1986), it is reported that there are 10 million households in the USA headed by 'lone women'. 35 per cent of these live 'in poverty'. And of all the women 'on the Welfare Rolls', 80 per cent are divorced mothers with children. (Only 18 per cent are unmarried single mothers and teenagers.) Can a focus upon education solve this kind and range of problems?

Second – and quite clearly – Betty Friedan's position stemmed entirely from her appraisal of the conditions and experiences of women *in America*. It was, first and foremost, a cry for and from *America*. Here, I merely note this point, but we shall see later that much of great importance may hang upon it. It may be, for example, that in terms of the experiences, wishes, and adjustments of *British* women during the post-war years, it may well have been – even at the time of its first statement – considerably out of date, and therefore (nonetheless having a widespread impact and influence on attitudes within Britain) have been unnecessarily misleading and harmful. It is commonly assumed that America leads, and the rest of the world follows. But this, too, may be a myth! In this case in particular, America may have been behind the times!

It is most worthwhile, however, to draw attention, finally, to two very definite and positive points on which Betty Friedan insisted in her treatment.

First – sympathising with both men and women in the problems they faced within the all-too-complex conditions of the modern world – she was surely right in emphasising one central fact: that in their personal lives (whether alone or shared with their partners) neither men or women could ever be expected to find fulfilment solely in some contraceptively-safe enjoyment of sexual gratification, in some narrow obsession with 'bed and board' – no matter how luxuriously equipped with gadgetry – or even in some occupational role or career within 'the economic system' or 'the social system'. She surely deserves a serious hearing in suggesting that the entire emphasis on 'sex' and 'sexual politics' has been, in all probability, 'a red herring'. Men and women are beings who – besides working, earning and spending income, and making love (or 'having sex' as the current expression goes) – feel, think, and wonder about the meaning of their very short-lived existence in a world which gives rise to unending perplexities. Deeper life-and-death questions tug persistently at the centre of their natures within the ongoing circumstantial pressures of their lives, and which, no matter how hard their efforts, elude any final understanding. In short – and no matter what implications this might be thought to entail, for none of us can now be sure about this – men and women are 'spiritual beings'. The continual probing into their own nature, with all its doubts, misgivings, uncertainties, calls for profound answers – and, if answers are not forthcoming, at least a serious questioning. Neither sex, nor marriage, nor the family, nor occupation, nor society, nor all of these combined can draw a determinate boundary about man's and woman's nature. No such encompassing territory for 'fulfilment' can be drawn. Much lies beyond all these.

But second: her emphasis throughout is not that women do not need love, companionship, and the satisfaction of fulfilling duties and responsibilities within home and family, in shared adult love and shared parental love and care for children; not that they should not play their own part in establishing, securing, and continuing to uphold all this. She does believe, in fact, that the nature of woman – that womanhood – needs fulfilment in these areas of commitment, conduct, and experience, as, indeed, does the nature of man. Her emphasis is this alone: that each individual woman, as each individual man (in each case – a many-dimensioned person), needs something more. And with this – who could want to quarrel or disagree?

After *The Feminine Mystique*, however, came voices of a more militant kind.

Kate Millett

One of the most noticeable of these – sounding a much louder clarion call from America – was that of Kate Millett, and it was her work, more than that of any other writer, which brought a new focus and formulation to the Women's Movement: that of *Sexual Politics*. Her book of that title (published in America in 1969, in Britain in 1971, and becoming widely available in paperback form in Britain in 1972) enjoyed immediate and widespread publicity.[2] Calling, like Betty Friedan, for the necessity of a 'Second Phase' in the movement for women's liberation; believing, like her, that the first phase of Feminism had tended to peter out with the achievement of 'Votes for Women' – and sharing, therefore, a similar perspective; her formulation was nonetheless much more radical and all-embracing. Yet, in the outcome – apart from her utterance of a resounding war-cry for revolution – it was curiously inconclusive. Indeed, Kate Millett's writing was in many respects a strange mixture. Very radical, her position was nonetheless presented in an apparently well-researched academic manner. Her work was systematically organised. Its detailed bibliographical references covered a wide range of literature. And yet ... in many areas of this it was highly selective and superficial, and, in its survey of literature in particular, focused entirely on what might be called 'the banned books' kind. Indeed, if you had never plunged into the obsessions and obscenities of Lawrence, Miller and Mailer, or the homosexual goings-on of Genet you could now do so. A lavish sample of them was offered here. The pages were stuffed with pornographic quotations: slabs of them. Indeed, Kate Millett's selection of literature invites the immediate criticism that it seems to focus entirely upon the pornographic. The upshot is that though she pores, with much absorption, over lurid passage after lurid passage – meticulously describing lascivious sexual experiences and abnormalities – this never seems to bring us any closer to a consideration of the nature of love between the sexes, or sexual love in marriage; and no one would ever glean from them the idea that this salacious exploration of organs and orgasms (multiple! – to the point of physical exhaustion!) in sexual experience and behaviour had anything remotely to do with offspring, with the conception of children, with parenthood. Motherhood, for example, is scarcely even mentioned in a book of some 380 pages – and then only in sections which either merely note it, or note (in derisory manner) some spurious exaltations of its nature in political policies (e.g. of Nazi Germany and the Soviet Union). Fatherhood does not even enter into the index.

Sexual Politics, indeed, begins and ends with substantial reviews of such modern fiction (dating from the 1920s to the 1960s) – their pages so plentifully supplied with obscene quotations that they provide almost a complete entertainment in pornography itself. At the very outset (on page 1) we are plunged into Henry Miller's enjoyment of Ida (in *Sexus*). When her silk bath-robe falls open (to reveal her silk stockings) burying his head 'in her muff' makes her so lascivious that she begins 'nibbling at his prick', and then, kneeling at his feet, 'gobbling it'. 'Her small juicy cunt fitting him like a glove', he then stands her up, bends her over, and 'lets her have it from the rear' and enjoys biting her all over, leaving 'the mark of his teeth on her beautiful white ass'. A wide readership for the book, one feels, must have been captured at once, and after this promising start – which proves to have been quite moderate and tepid – the pages become more and more lavishly sprinkled with (if you will allow the book's vernacular) ... cocks, balls, and twats, undies, asses and cunt ... opening it up with two fingers, getting a candle right up or shoving up a big long carrot ... all of which is the literary illustration, the evidence adduced, of how men assert their patriarchal power over women, and how women – conned by society's socialization into feminine submissiveness – let them. The closing and more substantial literary section is even more rich in obscenities than the first. But it is between these two exhibitions of modern literature that Kate Millett offered her serious analysis of the nature of sexuality in human society, the war between men and women in the relationship between the two sexes which has come to be written into the very nature of society, a historical account of the partly liberating Women's Movement and the counter-revolution which reacted against this, and a few conclusions – vague and inconclusive though these were – on what was now required if Women's Liberation is to succeed.

What is the distinctive nature of her argument?

The central point – bearing our own purpose in mind – is that this went far beyond any concern with marriage and the family. Kate Millett's concern was no less than to understand and attack the entire structure of power in society; indeed, that hierarchy of power and authority which has come to exist in all historic civilisations; and with sexuality as one of the most important bases of it. Hence her extension of the term 'politics' to embrace sexuality, and her focus, especially, upon 'sexual politics'. The relations between the sexes (like the relations between races, castes, classes, rich and poor) were one form of power – one basic pattern of dominance/submission which ran through all the others; and so deeply had this pattern come to be established that it was now completely taken for granted, unquestioned, as something rooted in the very nature of things: something natural, universal, unalterable. That entire hierarchy of structured power, she claimed, was patriarchy. Patriarchal government was, everywhere, 'the institution whereby that half of the human population which is female is controlled by that half of which is male'. Her concern was therefore to analyse and expose the nature of patriarchy so that it could be changed and destroyed, and for this she believed that the early feminists' emphasis on reform had now to be replaced by one upon revolution. She herself clearly regarded her analysis of patriarchy as the most important section of her book, and her views about marriage and the family were therefore only one part of the much wider range of this argument.

The opening example of Henry Miller's play with Ida in the bathroom led on to an equally lurid (perhaps fetid is the more accurate word) description by Norman Mailer of heterosexual sodomy, and on still further to Jean Genet's treatment of homosexual relationships. They were all introduced as stark illustrations of the intolerable exercise of the 'ascendancy and power' of men over women; and she concluded, with Genet, that:

Sex is deep at the heart of our troubles ... and unless we eliminate the most pernicious of our systems of oppression, unless we go to the very centre of the sexual politic and its sick delirium of power and violence, all our efforts at liberation will only land us again in the same primordial stews.

Radical indeed! But let us now consider – as a contemporary argument – her 'Theory of Sexual Politics', her 'notes towards a theory of Patriarchy', which, she readily concedes (discussing the eight important features of it in just over 30 pages), was just 'a sketch'.

She claims, first of all (1) that the ideology and ideological apparatus of patriarchal societies (polities) is always such as to 'socialise' both sexes into the acceptance of certain desired persuasions about the temperament, role and status which distinguishes them from each other. The supposed differences between the sexes are socially established, and are such as to continue, and further entrench, the power of men. Then follows a discussion of the truth or falsity of the grounds of these supposed differences in seven areas of argument: (2) biological, (3) sociological, (4) those of caste, class, and (in general) social stratification, (5) economic and educa-

tional, (6) those lying in the employment of sheer force, (7) anthropological (inclusive of myth and religion), and finally (8) psychological.
Alas, most of these sections are, indeed, a 'sketch' only, and
questionable on quite fundamental counts.

The biological grounds of the differences between the sexes are
discussed only superficially – with brief references to only one or two
physical features (e.g. the heavier musculature and greater physical
strength of the male) and a few observations on the development of
the foetus, and with only the barest references to the very detailed
modern comparative studies (e.g. of the comparative ethologists). All
too readily it is concluded that 'psychosexual personality is postnatal
and learned' and that the implanted differences are therefore the
result of social circumstances '...male and female are really two
cultures and their life experiences are utterly different – and this is
crucial.' The discussion barely skims the surface of all the available
evidence and arguments. In the 'sociological' section the discussion
of the family chiefly appears. The family, it is claimed, is the 'chief
institution' of patriarchal society, its 'fundamental instrument and
foundation unit'. It is the family which instils values and achieves the
conformity and control of the sexes at a level deeper than that which
could possibly be reached by any other agency of government. Dominated by their husbands, women in patriarchal society have no direct
relationship with society and the state. They are ruled 'through the
family alone'. Clearly, then, Kate Millett regards the family as the
agency for maintaining the traditional pattern of power and control
of the male over the female. Again, however, only the most fleeting
and limited comparative and historical survey of the family in
various human societies is given, and any alleviation of the lot of
women achieved by reform in recent times is emphatically belittled.
Indeed, despite reforms in 'divorce protection, citizenship, and
property'; despite the modification of the power of the male in law;
women still (she claims) possess only 'chattel status' – as borne out in
the continuity of their 'loss of name, their obligation to adopt the
husband's domicile, and the general legal assumption that marriage
involves an exchange of the female's domestic service and (sexual)
consortium in return for financial support.' * Female status described
as being 'caste-like', the family is then portrayed as 'the keystone of
the stratification system ... the social mechanism by which it is main-

*This clearly reflects Kate Millett's conception of the nature of
marriage now, and we shall consider this in detail later (pp. 120–1). See,
too, on 'chattel status', pp. 124–5.

tained', and this is followed by a discussion of past and continui
inequalities of women in property and class relations, in areas or
economic life (employment, earnings, etc.) and in education.

Then there is an itemisation of the kinds of sheer force which has
been employed to keep women in subjection: the various penalties
directed at women's nature as a source of evil, and the many cruelties
and barbarities imposed upon them. This list (limited though it is) –
including Indian suttee 'execution', crippling foot-binding in China,
clitoridectomy, the enslavement of women, their segregation
'behind the veil', involuntary and child marriages – is certainly one
which brings and drives home a sickening realisation (though,
strangely, we shall see that no less a person than Germaine Greer has
come to query the wisdom of denouncing at least some of these
practices). The section on anthropological findings (and on myth and
religion) is also interesting, but is again decidedly slanted.

Evidence is briefly mentioned of the many ways in which women
are separated from men in the life of the simpler societies – sometimes with 'taboos' laid upon them. But these – all put forward
uncritically as the 'politically expedient patriarchal convictions about
women' – are so common throughout the world and so much pre-
date anything we would now call 'the state' that to think of them as
having been deliberately imposed by male power is much too simplistic. Women in pregnancy and childbirth, women immediately after
childbirth, women in menstruation, are almost universally objects of
'taboo', but these things, surely, stem from the very nature of
womanhood. Society did not and does not create the facts themselves. The 'taboos' are connected with the feelings within certain
kinds of contact of the 'unclean' nature, the polluting qualities of
menstrual blood, etc., and the mysteries of their relation to fertility
and creation. Crawley's *Mystic Rose* – which Kate Millett mentions
but does not discuss – is full of such examples, indicating the close
relationship, incidentally, between some aspects of sex and religion.
The 'taboos', the 'purifications', the beliefs and rituals, are rooted in
the perception of the facts. They cannot be held to have been
invented by men to bring about the subordination of women, or be
rationally construed as meriting this, as Kate Millett supposes. Similarly, the extension of this supposed 'misogyny' of primitive peoples
into myth and religion is highly questionable. Certainly, much that
claims the evil nature and inferiority of women leading to the justifi-
cation of their subjection is to be found in the religious doctrines and
practices of developed societies, but Kate Millett's account of these,
too, is far too simplistic. Her interpretation of 'the tale of Adam and

Eve' in the Jewish (and Christian) Bible is a good example. This, she claims, is a 'narrative of how humanity invented sexual intercourse'. All its themes 'revolve around sex'. *Eating* the forbidden fruit was not only directly sexual. Even the Hebrew verb for 'eat' (we are told) can also mean 'coitus'! So ... it is sex, sex, sex all the way through. Even the serpent is an 'objectified phallus'. But it is poor Eve who, 'seduced by a phallic snake', *tempted* Adam, and so ... 'was convicted for Adam's participation in sex.' In a patriarchal society, Adam, being a man, could not be held to be blameworthy for such a low misdemeanour. Now anyone who has read Genesis must know that this is a travesty – and it is particularly questionable upon linguistic grounds. The tree from which Adam and Eve were forbidden to eat was that of 'the knowledge of good and evil', and why this was so, since God had created them in his own image, is a little hard to understand. But ... in general, it is a pity that people either do not read or do not understand the actual myths about which they write and question a little more critically the fantasy-interpretations the linguists and psychologists let loose among them.

The crux of the entire argument, however, is that the object of Kate Millett's attack is patriarchy, and the sexual pattern of dominance/submission (between male and female) which is at the root of all this – on which it rests. The family (and marriage) is seen and criticised purely within this over-all context.

She then offers her historical account of the efforts to change this situation – an account which falls into two parts. The 'first phase' was 'the sexual revolution' which took place between 1830 and 1930 (very similar to Betty Friedan's 'first phase') and ended with the 'Votes for Women' of the Feminist Movement before the Second World War. This, she agrees, was a many-dimensioned and worthy movement of reform. In her account she describes the early Feminist Movement itself, the controversies and debates which arose among eminent men – between Ruskin and John Stuart Mill, for example (and no one in this entire story could be better advanced as an advocate for the recognition of the rights of women than John Stuart Mill), and the revolutionary writings of Engels. All this is unexceptionable, but is also strangely vitriolic in some respects and misleading in others. She is very lukewarm, for example, about the feminists themselves. Realising why the franchise was thought to be 'of central significance', she nonetheless describes it as 'the red herring of the revolution – a wasteful drain on the energy of seventy years ... When the ballot was won, the feminist movement collapsed in what can only be described as exhaustion.' Feminism had 'failed to challenge Patriarchy at a level sufficiently deep and radical to break the conditioning processes of status, temperament, and role.' Marriage, the home, were left intact, and though women had been given new freedoms, patriarchy, though reformed, was: 'patriarchy still: its worst abuses purged or foresworn, it might be actually more stable and secure than before.' Later, we shall question the entire slant and emphasis of this account, but, even at first sight, it can be seen that it is hardly a fair account of those many women who – once the vote had been achieved – continued to work hard in education, government, the professions, fields of employment, etc., to glean the promises and pursue the aims for which political citizenship had been (they fully realised) the first and necessary step.

Engels, too, is misrepresented by selective quotations. Thus, on the basis of his statement that 'the monogamous family will cease to be the economic (or industrial) unit of society ... the care and education of children becoming a public matter', Kate Millett goes on to make the larger claim that '... the radical outcome of Engels' analysis is that the family, as that term is presently understood, must go ...' claiming further, too, that whilst ever a woman continues to be 'the sole or primary caretaker of childhood she is prevented from being a free human being' – as though the liberty of women required the abnegation of motherhood. But, as we have seen, Engels did not say or mean any such thing. He did not predict or advocate the end of the monogamous family. Careful not to prophesy what free and equal men and women would choose, his own judgment (for which he clearly stated his own grounds) was that a newly reformed and enlightened form of marriage and the family would be monogamous. It is crucially important, too, to notice Kate Millett's qualifying clause: '... the family, *as that term is presently understood*, must go.' Precisely! But what Marx and Engels meant was that those forms of the ancient family, and even the 'bourgeois' family, which embodied the institutionalised subjection of women, concubinage, etc., should go. They did not say that monogamy in marriage, or that the family as such, should go. And elsewhere in her book, Kate Millett herself (complaining about the insufficiency of the reforming emphasis of the first phase) seems to expect only alterations in marriage and the family, not their abolition.

The first phase ended in reform rather than revolution. For a sexual revolution to proceed further it would have required a truly radical social transformation – the alteration of marriage

113

and the family as they had been known throughout history. Without such radical change it remained impossible to eradicate those evils attendant upon these institutions which reformers found most offensive: the economic disabilities of women, the double standard, prostitution, venereal disease, coercive marital unions, and involuntary parenthood. A completed sexual revolution would have entailed, even necessitated, the end of the patriarchal order through the abolition of its ideology as it functions through a differential socialization of the sexes in the areas of status, temperament, and role.

Alteration – not abolition! And in her paragraph, the areas in which she believes necessary alterations should be made are stated quite clearly (though it is rather a garbled list to link only with the nature of marriage and the family).

However, as this quotation plainly indicates, Kate Millett believed that the Women's Movement, at the end of the first phase, had faltered and failed long before its radical objectives had been achieved, and she then offers an account of 'The Counter-Revolution' which (she believed) followed – between 1930 and 1960. This (she claimed) had at least three powerful components. The first was political: the policies and succession of events in Nazi Germany and the Soviet Union. The other two lay in the realm of influential ideas: first, those of Freud and some of his followers; the other that of fashionable 'functionalism' in sociology, and, indeed, in the very nature of sociology itself.

The political stories are well known, though even here Kate Millett's interpretation of them is slanted and questionable. In the case of Nazi Germany, the renewed enforcement of patriarchal authority was necessary to secure and uphold totalitarian power and control. The rigid distinction between men and women was therefore re-asserted. 'Sacred Motherhood' confined a woman to 'her husband, her family, her children, and her home'. This was her whole world. Here her whole duty lay. 'The German girl is a State subject and only becomes a State citizen when she marries.' The public world of work – of economic, political, and military affairs – was entirely, and without question, a man's world. Severe campaigns were mounted against all kinds of sexual 'licence' (homosexuality, making available the knowledge and wherewithal to practice contraception, etc.) and all such licence was blamed either on Communism or the Jews. In the Soviet Union the story was very different. There, the initial efforts to eliminate the family had been very extreme – as we have seen (p. 80). Marriage, easily and freely entered into, was just as easily and freely terminated; abortion and contraception could be had on demand; women were to be freed from economic dependence on their husbands, having an equal right to education and employment; nurseries, crèches, maternity leave, were provided, and there were many collective provisions for housekeeping. But ... the experiment 'failed and was abandoned'. Kate Millett's interpretation of this was that the Patriarchal Family was seen to be necessary, after all, to preserve the patriarchal authority of society. 'You cannot "abolish" the family,' said Trotsky. 'You have to replace it.' So ... Marxism was stood on its head.

> The State cannot exist without the family ... There are people who dare to assert that the Revolution destroys the family; this is entirely wrong; the family is an especially important phase of social relations in the socialist society ... One of the basic rules of Communist morals is that of strengthening the family.

Twenty-seven years after the revolution, she says, 'the sexual revolution was over, the counter-revolution triumphant.'

Politics aside, however, she then laid emphasis upon two areas of thought which, in her view, led to a re-assertion of conservative feeling and thinking; a movement back to old-style patriarchy (and its ideology) and the old-style domestication of women. One was the influential teaching of Freud about the nature of women. The other was a wide acceptance of 'functionalism' in sociology, and, indeed, what she took to be the nature of sociology itself. In both areas her analysis was superficial, and in one area quite simplistic and false.

Freud, she claimed, saw the nature of women only in relation to her own perception of the nature of man, and her reaction to this. Predominantly (within the context of patriarchy), this was rooted in 'penis-envy', and the most distinguishing traits of female personality were thought to be: 'passivity, masochism, and narcissism'. Women were 'expected to be passive, to suffer, to be sexual objects' and were 'socialized into such roles'. But psycho-analysis was harmful in one other, perhaps more basic, way. With its emphasis on basic biology, physiology, and the psychological elements of experience and behaviour stemming from these, it was held that woman's nature – just as man's nature – was decidedly not something socially engendered, something having its origin in social conditioning, but something naturally given, essential, universal. No changes in society could or would alter this basic nature. All societies in any place or time would have to take it into account. In a 'matriarchal' or a 'communal' society (just as much as in a patriarchal society) this basic nature would remain the same. Kate Millett rejected this emphasis, and what was later made of it among some of the 'Post-Freudians'.

Her treatment of 'Functionalism' and sociology was just plainly misinformed; so much so, and in so many ways, that it is difficult (in brief) to set out and document all the fallacies it contains and which stem from it. She claimed, for example, that from 1930 onwards the social sciences 'turned away from historical considerations to focus attention upon social structures', providing careful descriptions of how theoretical models operated, the leading school calling itself 'Functionalism'. On discovering that something 'functioned' within society as a whole, functionalists, she says, then became prescriptive. Far from being value-free, sociologists were conservative. Now all this is quite plainly and simply wrong! Sociology had been producing descriptions, analyses, and classifications of the elements of social structure and their interrelated functioning in different types of society from at least the 1830s onwards. From the earlier Kant-Hume juncture, and particularly from Comte onwards, the literature of sociology was full of it. And this – far from being anti-historical – actually formed the basis for its wide comparative and historical studies, indeed for its many theories of social change and evolution (of which Marx's theory was one). Also, far from being ethically prescriptive in its own pursuit of knowledge – let alone being necessarily conservative – it was part of the insistence of sociology as a science that, alone, it could not prescribe; that additional ethical and political considerations had also to enter into any such judgments. All that sociology could do was to provide testable knowledge on the basis of which (hopefully) policies having moral and political aims could be more reliably based. Certainly sociological theorists have been troubled in their awareness of the vast changes brought about by the development and spread of industrial capitalism over the past 200 years, and have wanted to contribute to the amelioration of its attendant inhumanities, but their own central concern has been that of establishing reliable knowledge, so that enlightened change could then take place and be achieved. When Kate Millett claims, then, that:

> sociology examines the status quo, calls it phenomena, and
> pretends to take no stand on it, thereby avoiding the
> necessity to comment on the invidious character of the

relationship between the sex groups it studies. Yet by slow
degrees ... converting statistic to fact, function to
prescription, (possessing) bias to biology ... it comes to ratify
and rationalise what has been socially enjoined or imposed
into what is and ought to be. And through its pose of
objectivity, it gains a special efficacy in reinforcing
stereotypes. Seeing that failure to conform leads to 'problems'
and 'conflicts' ... it counsels a continuous and vigilant
surveillance of conditioning that it may proceed on lines of
greater proficiency and perfection ...

She is simply wrong, as she is when she claims, again simplistically:
'Functionalists, like other reactionaries, are out to save the family.'
Such seriously false misrepresentations are, alas, the misleading
kinds of caricatures which arise from tendentious political reasoning,
rooted in what seems to be superficiality and ignorance. Sociology
may well have much to say about the importance and preservation of
the family in society, but this rests on something far wider and
sounder than the simple-minded slipping from fact to value which
Kate Millett castigates. In her work (as, as we have seen, in that of
Robin Blackburn and others of the New Left) sociology is always
made the whipping-boy of reaction. But suggestions of this kind do
nothing more than reveal the abysmally ill-informed positions of
such authors and the extremely limited and false nature of their per-
spectives. Unfortunately, as Betty Friedan complained, these are the
glib, assertive, sensationalist formulations which appeal to editors,
publishers, and booksellers. They sell books!

Kate Millett's entire analysis, however, had one clear outcome:
which was to decry the sufficiency of earlier achievements and to
insist that revolution, not reform, was now required.

There is no way out of such a dilemma but to rebel and be
broken, stigmatized, and cured. Until the radical spirit revives
to free us, we remain imprisoned in the vast gray stockades
of the sexual reaction.

Where to go was not clear. What constructively to do was not
clear. One thing only was clear: patriarchy had to be destroyed. To
this one end revolutionary thought and activity had to be directed.

The concluding section on literature (similar to the opening
section) returned to the same opening theme – to show that literature
from the 1930s onwards had been such as to reflect and reinforce this
counter-revolution. D. H. Lawrence, Henry Miller, Norman Mailer

were again invoked to illustrate this return to male domination, and
... we are back to pages of pornography. Mr Mellors, Lawrence's
gamekeeper talks to his own prick in the third person, 'coyly
addressing it in dialect', asking it whether it wants 'my lady Jane's
cunt', and crying: 'Lift up your heads ... that the king of glory may
come in.' Despite the saliva dribbling from the corner of one's
mouth, one is jolted into sudden laughter. It is surely comical. 'Who
is the king of glory?' – one might sing in rapture with Handel. The
answer is: D. H. Lawrence's fictional prick. The quotations from
Miller and Mailer are more obscene, Lawrence is mild and all too
much of a sober-sides by contrast, and one can only conclude that in
her selection of these three novelists (see pp. 122–4), Kate Millett
shows some very odd grounds of judgment and principles of selection.
Lawrence, for example, she regards as 'an admirably astute
politician' – despite his frequently dictatorial tone, dripping with
arrogance and conceit – as for example when he addresses himself to
Dr Freud. Yet, at last, she condemns the extremities in the
'Lawrentian sexual religion' – of 'coitus as killing' – and judges his
later writing as having a 'monstrous, even demented air'. Similarly,
she considers Miller as a 'compendium of American sexual neuroses'.
Why, then, exhibit his dehumanised orgies of 'fucking' (altogether
lacking reciprocal consideration between persons, and purely –
indeed obsessively – preoccupied with the organs and orgasms of sex
themselves) as being at all representative of sexual experience and
sexual relationships in America (or other societies) at large? Her final
judgment, again, is: '... to confuse this neurotic hostility, this frank
abuse, with sanity is pitiable. To confuse it with freedom were
vicious, were it not so very sad.' Why, then, select just this work? The
same could be asked about the selection of, and selections from,
Norman Mailer. All this, she finally admits: 'will hardly solve the
dilemma of our sexual politics.' Genet's homosexual analysis of
sexual politics is used rather differently, but ... the upshot is that –
having seen certain signs of hope in 'the spontaneous mass-move-
ments emerging all over the world' for the liberation of races, youth,
and the poor, as well as women, she feels that human understanding
has become ripe for a change, and the call for revolution will sound
in ready, welcoming ears.

> It may be that a second wave of the sexual revolution might
> at last accomplish its aim of freeing half the race from its
> immemorial subordination – and in the process bring us all a
> great deal closer to humanity. It may be that we shall even

be able to retire sex from the harsh realities of politics, but not until we have created a world we can bear out of the desert we inhabit.

But what – coming back to our central concern – are we to glean from this large-scale attack on patriarchy, illustrated by literary examples of depravity, about Kate Millett's criticisms of marriage and the family? And what, in particular, does she advocate? It is to her credit that she does at least try to set out quite specifically the essential elements which she would like 'another upsurge of the revolutionary spirit' to achieve. Summarising, but using as closely as possible her own words, her aims are these:

(1) Crucially: the eradication of sexual oppression.

(2) The end of patriarchy, the abolition of male supremacy, and the traditional socialisation by which it maintains the sexual distinctions of temperament, role, and status.

(3) The end of traditional sexual inhibitions and taboos, particularly those that most threaten patriarchal monogamous marriage: homosexuality, 'illegitimacy', and adolescent, pre-marital and extra-marital sexuality.

(4) The elimination of the negative aura surrounding sexual activity – together with the 'double standard' and prostitution.

(5) The achievement of a permissive single standard of sexual freedom – one uncorrupted by the crass and exploitative bases of traditional sexual alliances.

(6) The re-examination and integration of the sexual 'sub-cultures' at present distinguished. The nature of the 'masculine' and 'feminine' would be radically re-considered. Some features of both – e.g. the violence of male virility and the excessive 'passivity' of the feminine – would be rejected as being useless to either sex. But some – e.g. the efficiency and intellectuality of the 'masculine' and the tenderness and consideration of the 'feminine' – would be *integrated* as being useful and relevant to the character of both sexes.

The achievement of these general objectives, she believes, would have necessary implications for marriage and the family, and her chief points, here, are these:

(1) The authority and financial structure of the family ('the patriarchal proprietary family') would be undermined by the abolition of the sex role and the economic independence of women.

(2) The 'chattel status' of women would end (as, she adds, would any denial of the rights of minors).

(3) The 'collective professionalization' of the care of children would also free women and undermine the family (and she believes, without question, that this would be an improvement).

(4) Marriage might, if this was desired, be replaced by 'voluntary association'.

And she adds the further point, as a benefit which would follow:

(5) The problem of over-population in the world might, as an outcome, be more nearly solved. (The assumption here being clearly that the emancipation of women, as here envisaged, would mean the birth of fewer children.)

Kate Millett's criticisms of marriage and the family were, then, an *attack* upon them as part and parcel of her much more radical attack on the patriarchal structure of power in society and the dominance/submission pattern of power between the sexes which had become entrenched in this. One's acceptance or rejection (or part-acceptance or part-rejection) of her criticisms depends entirely, therefore, on whether one accepts the truth and validity of this wider argument, and of all the elements in it. Here, I do no more than raise a number of questions to which we shall have to return.

(1) Her attack, in her stated aims, is directed at the 'crass and exploitative' nature of 'patriarchal, proprietary' marriage. Would the elimination of all the sexual taboos she mentions apply to, or stand in the way of, a marriage of improved quality between equals? She says that marriage *might* be replaced by 'voluntary association' if so desired. But (a) is marriage itself, as it now exists, not a 'voluntary association'? And (b) besides marriage as it is, and the 'voluntary association' she has in mind, what other alternative could there be? And, whatever the alterations decided upon, on what basis would the rights of the members of the domestic establishment, and the claims and counter-claims they could make upon each other, rest, be upheld, and regulated? (2) In all her points there is no discussion whatever of parenthood – excepting the suggestion that the care of children and 'the young' should pass from mothers to the public and 'collective professionalization' of experts. What, then, would the nature and experience of 'motherhood' be? What would be the rights and duties of the mother of a child? And is it proved reliably that the transfer of the care of children to 'professionals' would be an improvement? – particularly for the children? What, too, in all this, is the place of *'fatherhood'*? Is it not at least possible that a father might

love his children? – and that, having been in part responsible for bringing them into the world, may wish to provide for them as best he can, and devote himself to their welfare and providing a satisfactory basis for their own chosen future? Is it not possible, too, that he and his wife may wish to do this jointly, in affectionate partnership? (3) Is it possible to believe that all the customarily assumed differences of temperament, role, and status between the sexes have their origin in, and are perpetuated by, *social* influences? – and that there are no more basic biological and psychological grounds of the differences between the nature of male and female at all? Can we agree with this? (4) The assumption underlying all these points is that present-day marriage – even after the equal citizenship achieved by the feminists, and all the subsequent movements towards equality in the proceedings of divorce, in education, employment, etc. – is still a 'crass and exploitative' institution imposed by 'patriarchal power', and that women still only possess 'chattel status'. Is this assumption sensible, accurate, reliable, and can we agree with it? (5) No alternative basis whatever is proposed for 'domestic groups' – however these might be envisaged. The picture Kate Millett presents, as far as it is possible to be clear about it, is one of completely free sexual liaisons – among minors as well as among adults – with no regulated basis of domesticity; the care of any children who might be the outcome of the 'voluntary associations' being undertaken publicly and collectively by 'professionals', so that women, like men, can remain individually free. Is this a picture which is at all credible? Is it one which comes anywhere near a complete provision for meeting the realities and responsibilities of the sexual bonds and problems of men and women, and the bonds and problems arising among mothers, fathers and their children?

For the moment, I simply leave these as questions. They are only a few of a number of quite basic questions which can be put, and I shall attempt a considered answer to them later. There are, however, a few general concluding points I cannot resist making before leaving Kate Millett's work. All are related to our own task of moving towards a satisfactory final judgment.

Concluding questions

LITERARY CRITICISM?

We cannot go too far into the field of modern literature as such, but is it not the case that Kate Millett's selectivity must be considered open to serious criticism here? Is it not strange that she should concentrate entirely and exclusively on those three novelists – Lawrence, Miller, Mailer* – whose work is most preoccupied with that kind of detailed exploration of sexual experience which widespread common judgment would hold to be obscene? Even her treatment of the slightly earlier literature shows curious gaps of perspective. Some women writers, for example, were active and influential in the very growth of the social sciences during the nineteenth century. Harriet Martineau, besides writing much in her own right, actually translated and abridged (with his approval) the first large work of Auguste Comte, being largely instrumental, therefore, in introducing both him and his sociology to an English audience, and Comte's work had much to say (though not of a kind of which Kate Millett would approve) about the relations between men and women in a more humane society. George Eliot, too, was much influenced by the 'positivism' and 'humanism' of Comte, some of her poetry being written directly under this influence.** Lesser women novelists, too, like Matilda Betham-Edwards, were roaming alone around London and Europe – hearing Karl Marx and John Stuart Mill lecture in rooms in Red Lion Square, meeting Liszt and visiting the Goethe household abroad, and her *Reminiscences* contain telling accounts of the relationships between men and women in social life and literature then. Women and men were jointly active, in a lively way, in literature, social thought, social science, and social reform. Kate Millett makes no mention, either, of George Gissing, who – late in the nineteenth century and at the turn of the century – was having much to say about the relations between men and women, and marriage, and being very critical of orthodoxy. But ... consider also those novelists who were (at least to a considerable extent) contemporaries of the early and the mature Lawrence, who were writing well into the period between 1930 and 1960, and certainly remained very influential then: Galsworthy, Somerset Maugham (surely, in this, a much underrated writer?), Aldous Huxley, E. M.

---

*I leave Genet aside here not because he is greatly different (in this respect) but because he is used rather differently.
**I cannot help thinking that Kate Millett did not index her own book. In one place, mention of 'Eliot's fear of life' is attributed to George Eliot (p. 155), but there is surely no way in which George Eliot and her work could be so characterised. The reference must really be (coming, in the text, after a consideration of the work of Oscar Wilde) to T. S. Eliot.

Forster, Ernest Hemingway ... and this is by no means a complete list. Did these writers have nothing to say about (or anything which reflected) the relationship between the sexes? Did their books contain no comment on the movement towards the emancipation of women and the social effects of this? Clearly, they did – and much could be said in detail about the work of each. The same could be said of some women writers, too. The difference was, however, that they were still writing about men and women in society, not dwelling on 'pricks' and 'cunts'. They were writing about relationships between individuals in the clutches of social situations and circumstances, not about the minutiae of sexual appetite as such and the exciting sensations of putting sexual organs (and other parts of the body) together and achieving the bliss of one, or two, or three ... or even multiple orgasms – before exhaustion set in! I believe, in short, that Kate Millett's entire argument is open to serious literary criticism proper, but I raise this criticism here to suggest two points for consideration.

First, this very narrow selection, quite apart from seeming unduly biased in itself (so obsessed with eroticism as to be, itself, strangely captive to it), is exactly such as to bear out what Betty Friedan had called the 'dehumanization' of sexuality and the spread of a 'mounting sex hunger' and of women 'reduced to sex-creatures ... sex seekers'. People and their relationships disappeared in a plethora of over-heated pornography; persons were drowned and destroyed in a kind of broth of orgasms; the deadly sin of sensuality had swallowed them whole ... all in the quest for liberation. And it is very strange, too, that Kate Millett scarcely ever refers to Betty Friedan (mentioning her work only briefly in two footnotes). But my second point, I think, may be of much greater general importance, though it is connected. It is this:

Might it not be of considerable significance that, in the main, the literature of Lawrence (certainly the later Lawrence), Miller, Mailer and Genet, is a literature which has sprung out of *a world massively and increasingly at war*? It is true that some of Lawrence's work preceded the first World War, but much of it came after, and Lawrence himself was deeply conscious of it, and deeply conscious, too, of its having been imposed upon the masses of Europe's population without real personal meaning for them. In itself, this new mass-nature of warfare actually *was*, and was *seen*, as being, a massive and appalling kind of depersonalisation. Norman Mailer is perhaps the best (and most direct) example here. *The Naked and the Dead* (the beginning of his literary career) itself began as a vivid, dynamic, explosive exposure of the devastations of modern war, and

Mailer has been exploring the many-sided depredation and destruction of the individual person by the processes of modern mass-society ever since – of the vulnerable woman lifted to stardom to be exploited and destroyed by it, just as of any corpse lying like a piece of abandoned litter on the dried mud of a far-eastern battle-field, burned by a flame-thrower into an anonymous heap of charred bones and rags. Indeed, *The Naked and the Dead* might well be a title – Dostoevsky-like in its vast human significance – fitting and spanning not only the whole of his own work, but also all the monstrous destructivity of our own depraved time: over all the battlefields, the empty lifeless atom-bomb devastations, the barbed wire enclosures and heaped bodies of the concentration camps, the countless scenes of clandestine political corruption – from the manipulations of presidential and ministerial power to the discovered mass-graves of military massacres. It is a title whose dreadful significance fits the entire character of our twentieth century – savaged by mass brutalities. Might it not be that it is within this mounting global context of war that our significance as individual persons, and of the qualities of our relationships with each other, has been largely and dreadfully destroyed? Might it not be that it is in relation to this – the spiritual vacuum of our time – that the literature of dehumanised sexual appetite has come to have its significance? I make the point and ask the question here because it seems one important dimension of what I want to emphasise later: the deeply destructive influence upon our lives and relationships of *the long tentacles of war* during the greater part of our century. It is war, perhaps, and all its many profound connotations, which has destroyed any sense of spiritual significance in us at its roots – in each of our own localities, disrupting all with which we had become familiar, and in societies throughout the world. When people have lost everything of spiritual significance, everything sustaining the meaningful nature and dignity of the individual self, perhaps indiscriminate appetite is all that remains. Perhaps it becomes just one organically rooted drug, one addiction requiring greater and greater but always self-destroying reinforcement, among others.

'MARRIAGE' AND THE 'CHATTEL STATUS' OF WOMEN

I commented, in passing, on Kate Millett's conception of the nature of marriage as it now exists; the insufficiency of her all-too brief reference to its possible replacement by 'voluntary associations'; and those grounds on which she claimed that (despite reforms) woman still enjoyed only 'chattel status': a woman's loss of name on marriage, the obligation to adopt her husband's domicile, the exchange of her domestic service and sexual consortium for financial support, etc. At this point, I want only to say that – however we think initially about these points, whether we think them worthwhile or wrong-headed – we should take note of them as serious points, and be ready to consider them seriously. Later, I want to argue that the spread of 'half-baked' conceptions of marriage and of attitudes towards it stemming from these assertions has been misguided and caused great harm. But, more particularly, there is little doubt that the detailed consideration of such issues as the 'naming' of spouses and children, the choice of domicile, and the detailed drawing up of contracts of 'cohabitation', are very serious matters for some women in the pursuit of real equality, and have given rise to very real complexities and problems in the law. These specific complaints and claims cannot be regarded superficially; they have very far-reaching implications and consequences which must be taken seriously into account.

AN ALTERNATIVE STORY

Earlier, too, I said that Kate Millett's negatively toned story of nineteenth-century reforms and the achievements of the early feminists was decidedly slanted, and that an altogether different interpretation was possible. Here, it is necessary to note the nature of her emphasis in just a little more detail (to see more clearly the full character of it) and then to indicate the alternative I have in mind.

Though conceding that there had been 'some real sympathy for the sufferings of women in industry' and that some improvements in the lot of women had been made, Kate Millett argues, nonetheless, that reforms were chiefly made for the wrong reasons, and were still part and parcel of male domination. Essentially disregarding women's 'human rights as workers', reform 'put its emphasis either on the indecorum of their shocking and disorganised lives, or on the subversive effects their working conditions must have on their breeding ability, their service to infants, their "morals" or "virtue"'.

a great deal of the motivation behind reform was little more than protection of patriarchal culture and institutions: family structure was becoming disrupted (including the authority of the father as provider and head of household); women in industry had access to sexual freedom; they were worked too hard in one circumstance (the factory) to serve properly in another (the home). The prevailing male attitude ... seemed to find the perfect remedy in getting women out of the factory altogether and back into the safety of the 'home'.

Might this, however, be the story of events and motives seen only through 'anti-male' eyes? – through the eyes of 'female chauvinism'? And might there not be at least one other version? – which would go, very simply, like this:

Our knowledge suggests that even before the onset of industrialisation, the lot of men, women, and children among the labouring classes was one of abject poverty. With the development and spread of industrialisation (though some improvement in the material standard of living was achieved) harsh conditions of life continued, and were made even more wretched in the new conditions of work – in mines and factories – and among the massed populations in the unregulated conditions of the new towns. These inhumanities attendant upon the industrial revolution took place and worsened in pre-Victorian times, under the unseeing and uncaring eyes of a remote aristocracy continuing to enjoy their own wealth and culture in their own way. At the turn of the century and during the early nineteenth century – among the churches, among some parliamentarians and government officials, among some eminent individuals, and among some writers and poets – the public conscience was aroused. Governments undertook investigations, established commissions to look into the facts of the matter: into the actual conditions of work-places and towns, housing and sanitation, health, welfare, etc. Karl Marx was among those who saluted and valued their efforts. Reforms were then instituted. Some results (among many others) were that women were removed from the burdens, indecencies, indignities, and sheer cruelties of the heavier labours in which they had been involved. Children, too, were removed from the worst kinds of exploitation (whether in domestic or larger-scale industry). For the first time, certain conditions and expectations of domestic and family life were established and secured (if not, initially, to very high standards). The home as we know it, was created in British society. Motherhood was protected. Fatherhood literally did entail the husbanding of his wife, children, and the wherewithal for the maintenance of his home and family. He was the responsible provider. Childhood, too, was created. A period of protected care and dependence was established, untroubled by economic exploitation (whether by parents or employers), and was shortly to be improved and extended with the provisions of public education. Throughout the rest of the century and into our own, eminent men and women alike took part in the work of furthering this reform and building upon these achievements. The lot of men, women, and children alike has been gradually improved from that time to this. More has been required and provided by state legislation. More has been required of both husbands and wives in the responsibilities of parenthood. The qualities of the home, and of family life within the neighbourhood, have been improved as the general level of wealth in society, and the changed distribution of this wealth, has improved. All this was a long, slow, laborious process, through hard-fought governmental and extra-governmental areas of activity, and many improvements have been achieved only in our own century in reforms following both world wars (both of which have made very clear the importance of the contribution of women). New in some respects, these reforms were, nonetheless, a bringing to completion of those originally set afoot in the early Victorian period. They have all been efforts to gain the promise, whilst eliminating the inhumanities, of industrial capitalism. Given these hard-won achievements, might it not be that to go back on the home so created; to go back on the quality of the life of womanhood so protected; to go back on the committed partnership of husband and wife in their shared work of home-making and their shared duties of parenthood so required would be actually reactionary? – not revolutionary but reactionary? Far from being 'progressive', might it not be in danger of destroying something which has been a long time in the making, which has taken much time and effort to create, and which was only made possible on the new wealth-creating basis of industrial capitalism – since changed by reform? Might it not be that we should, perhaps, be counting our blessings and improving upon them still further, rather than misconceiving them, undermining them, and destroying the possibility of their continued survival for our own children?

At this point, I want to do no more than suggest this as an alternative interpretation of (or account of) the same sequence of facts. Later, we can consider and judge it more fully.

MEN – AND THEIR CONDITIONS

A final consideration stems from the fact that Kate Millett's attack on the patriarchal family within the larger structure of patriarchal authority, is entirely 'anti-man'. There is nothing of the kind of sympathy for the lot of men (as well as that of women) shown by Betty Friedan; no consideration of the possibility that – whatever the historical causes of the present-day structure of society – present-day generations of men are no more to be blamed for them than present-day generations of women, and that men, too, just as much as women, may be victims of them. The thought never arises that for men, too, the collective conditions of the modern world may be oppressive, over-bearing, grinding, destructive of all sense of personal significance; that the conditions of the life, work, marriage, and family responsibility of men may be far from appearing like a bed of roses; and that for men, too, in these conditions, marriage – its duties and its burdens – may have the appearance of 'a trap', even of a 'comfortable concentration camp'? That marriage should be regarded as the giving of a 'hostage to fortune' was written a long time before industrialisation, and by a man to men.

> He that hath wife and children [wrote Francis Bacon] hath given hostages to fortune; for they are impediments to great enterprises, either of virtue or mischief.

May it not be, too, that this hostility towards men has rendered Kate Millett herself too uncritically a victim of stereotypes and caricatures? Are all men virile, violent, domineering, intellectual, efficient ... 'masculine'? Are all women passive, masochistic, narcissistic ... 'feminine'? Are we all really so deluded as to accept such stereotypes without question? – and the assertion that society (in its 'socialization') imposes them? If it tries, one can only conclude that it is remarkably unsuccessful! May it not be, in short, that far too stark a contrast between 'Male' and 'Female' has been drawn, and that the improvement of the quality of relationships between men and women has been harmfully posed wholly in terms of a sex-war which rages between them, and the victory of women in this war? Might it not be (as Betty Friedan really maintains) that the collective conditions of our complex industrial society and the modern world are dehumanising, imprisoning, and limiting for *both* sexes, and that the qualities of sexual, married, and family life may be better improved by considering the nature, problems and experiences of both sexes together? by being approached by both men and women in mutual understanding and partnership?

These, at any rate, are points which seem to deserve a good deal more consideration.

There remains a final comment. Like R. D. Laing and Betty

Friedan – Kate Millett, too, prefaces her book with a personal dedication. She dedicates *Sexual Politics* – her attack on patriarchy, the
patriarchal proprietary family, and monogamous marriage – to ...
her *husband*: Fumio Yoshimura.

Germaine Greer

One other voice, however, was sounding its revolutionary call to
women at the same time: a voice just as militant in tone, just as radical in its message, basing itself on just such an intellectually searching
survey of the facts it thought relevant – and yet moving into the
battle-field of ideas along a different approach-route, and being quite
distinctive. It was the voice of Germaine Greer. *The Female Eunuch*
appeared in paperback in 1971[3] (initially published in 1970),
immediately went into reprints, and from that time onwards
Germaine Greer's has been perhaps the most prominent voice of all
in the Women's Movement – beginning (this time) in Britain, but
becoming rapidly influential in America, and, by now, being well-
known throughout the world. Forthright though her initial attack
was, deliberately bold and outspoken though she has always been,
her position is by no means either clear or easy to assess. Highly
intelligent, intellectually and academically able though she
unquestionably is – in the wide range of well-documented material
she draws upon and draws together; the organisation, critical
appraisal, and clear presentation of it – she is decidedly *not*
dispassionate or disinterested. She is at war. Her declared intention is
to provoke. Women's weapons, she says, are traditionally their
tongues! – and she certainly makes full use of her own. The simplest
way for women to expose the situation in which they find themselves
is:

> to outrage the pundits and the experts by sheer impudence of
> speech and gesture ... to expose masculine pomposity,
> absurdity and injustice ...
> Hopefully, this book is subversive. Hopefully, it will draw
> fire from all the articulate sections of the community ... If it
> is not ridiculed or reviled, it will have failed of its intention.

Her beginning is a declaration of war. She aggressively seeks confrontation.

She is sufficiently intelligent, too, to move quickly, superficially,
unobtrusively, over sections of fact and argument which are

questionable when it suits her purpose to do so – in order to seem to have established her points. In short, she is so knowledgeable a demagogue, so intelligent a combatant, that one has always to suspect, and scrupulously criticise, her every *appearance* of academic soundness. Frequently, this is *not* sound at all, though it is easy to see why it *seems* so to those of her less well-informed readers who are actively wanting to believe what she says. Though, too, there is much about her that makes her a likable antagonist (the antagonism bristles out of *her*!) and much about her argument that is true and worthwhile, her ever-present desire to *shock* leads her to use language, and to launch personal attacks, in ways which are often distasteful. We are very frequently back with the language of Miller, Mailer, and company; back in the business, so to speak, of 'pricks and cunts'. 'We are conceived,' she says, to give just one or two examples:

> somewhere between pissing and shitting, and as long as these excretory functions are regarded as intrinsically disgusting, the other one, ejaculation, will also be so regarded. The involuntary emission of semen during sleep is called a nocturnal *pollution*: the substance itself is viscous and stringy, whitish and acrid, like a more disgusting form of snot, if you regard snot as disgusting.

A man whose sexual gratification is really masturbatory, when making use of intercourse with a woman:

> ... regards her as a receptacle into which he has emptied his sperm, a kind of human spittoon, and turns from her in disgust.

Discussing Anne Koedt's emphasis on clitoral (as against the 'myth' of vaginal) orgasm, she tells us:

> At all events a clitoral orgasm with a full cunt is nicer than a clitoral orgasm with an empty one, as far as I can tell at least. Besides, a man is more than a dildo.

This is her kind of language. Much of it one can accept as part of her deliberately outrageous stance, but much seems unwarranted, and – the worst thing – spoils both her and her points. It is sometimes hard – irritated in the thick of her rhetoric, rendered impatient with it – to assess the truth or value of the point she is making. It is easy to lose or dismiss some dimensions of thoughtfulness and judiciousness in her discussion because of the spate of provocative language which is derisively spat out, and, sometimes, the gratuitously cruel personal abuse which attends them. Sometimes, the points and judgments are *not* extreme or exaggerated, but appear so. Like Kate Millett too (though going beyond any concentration on literature alone) her aim is the very radical one of undertaking a fundamental critique of the long-assumed differences between the nature of the sexes, to question and reject many of the supposed grounds of these, and then to mount a militant argument for the liberation of women on the basis of her conclusions. Criticisms of marriage and the family are couched within this much wider argument, and here again, radical though these are made to appear, it is not at all easy to be clear about them. In some parts of her first book they seem violent and extreme indeed – in other parts not at all so extreme. And all this is made the more difficult by the fact that her position and arguments have changed in various ways. *Sex and Destiny*, her second large book on the subject, presents a decidedly different outlook from that of *The Female Eunuch* – in the range of the subject-matter dealt with, the nature and direction of her arguments, and her specific judgments and conclusions: all of which are surprising, to say the very least. The general responses to these changes, both academic and journalistic, have been to the effect that 'Germaine Greer has mellowed.' That may or may not be. To my mind there is not much sign of it. What is certain is that her stance, concerns, and directions of discussion have changed, and – to focus on our own interest – to be clear about what all this implies for her views on marriage and the family is what concerns us. It is possible to ignore or be relatively brief about some matters because, though her voice is always quite distinctive, many of the points she makes have already been covered in our discussion of Betty Friedan and Kate Millett; but our analysis must be thorough, nonetheless, because Germaine Greer has become, and seems to remain, the most widely publicised and influential voice of all within the whole movement for Women's Liberation. Like Betty Friedan, too, she has presented us with two books with a span of more than a decade between them, so that it is necessary to comment on each.

What is the substance of her argument? And what – particularly on the matter of marriage and the family – is her message to women?

The Female Eunuch could not be a more direct title. The book is, in fact, about the *castration* of women, and this (as with Kate Millett) is seen within the context of tyrannical patriarchy.

> The castration of women has been carried out in terms of a masculine-feminine polarity, in which men have commandeered all the energy and streamlined it into an

aggressive conquistadorial power, reducing all heterosexual contact to a sado-masochistic pattern.

Germaine Greer (like Betty Friedan) saw her book as part of the 'second phase of Feminism', but, though agreeing about the need for a second phase in which 'genteel middle class ladies clamouring for *reform*' should be replaced by young 'ungenteel middle class women calling for *revolution*', she nonetheless displayed at once her more acid nature in being much more disparaging about the early feminist achievements.

> Marriage, the family, private property and the state were threatened by their actions, but they were anxious to allay the fears of conservatives, and in doing so the suffragettes betrayed their own cause and prepared the way for the failure of emancipation ... emancipation had failed.

The time had come for revolution. Even this, however, could not realistically hope to change the world at once. It could not even say, with any precision, what a new world would look like. But women could make a radical beginning by reassessing their own nature. They should embark on a revolutionary journey, and, in advocating this, in both the opening and closing pages of her book, Germaine Greer certainly did have radical things to say about marriage, the family, and related sexual behaviour. She rather sneers at the orthodoxies to which she is opposed. Those upholding conventional morality, she says:

> will find much that is reprehensible in the denial of the Holy Family, in the denigration of sacred motherhood,* and the inference that women are not by nature monogamous ...

– and she identifies, very readily and clearly, the revolutionary woman's enemies. They are: '... the doctors, psychiatrists, health visitors, priests, marriage counsellors, policemen, magistrates and genteel reformers, all the authoritarians and dogmatists who flock about her with warnings and advice.' It is a forbidding list! And, by contrast, the only *friends* of the revolutionary woman she names are ... '*her sisters*'. The revolution is going to be a one-sided struggle! The odds are clearly stacked against it. But though revolution cannot see far, or completely, it provides, at least, some indications. It:

---

*See p. 147 onwards for her own more recent views about motherhood.

hints that women ought not to enter into socially sanctioned relationships, like marriage, and that once unhappily in they ought not to scruple to run away. It might even be thought to suggest that women should be deliberately promiscuous ... Much of what it points to is sheer irresponsibility, but when the stake is life and freedom, and the necessary condition is the recovery of a will to live, irresponsibility might be thought a small risk.

The revolutionary journey is, indeed, one of high idealism. Not easy or pleasant, but it will at least be 'more interesting, nobler even'. And actual revolution, certainly, is what it will ultimately accomplish.

The opponents of female suffrage lamented that woman's emancipation would mean the end of marriage, morality and the state; their extremism was more clear-sighted than the woolly benevolence of liberals and humanists, who thought that giving women a measure of freedom would not upset anything. When we reap the harvest which the unwitting suffragettes sowed we shall see that the anti-feminists were right after all.

This is absolutely clear. Germaine Greer's position advocated 'the end of marriage, morality and the state', and at the end of her books, her conclusion remained just as emphatic:

Man made one grave mistake: in answer to vaguely reformist and humanitarian agitation he admitted women to politics and the professions. The conservatives who saw this as the undermining of our civilization and the end of the state and marriage were right after all; it is time for the demolition to begin.

Again: plain enough! And I leave readers to consider the sound-ness of an argument which can seriously envisage *the end of morality*. But what, then, was the over-all argument with which Germaine Greer attempted the reassessment of woman's nature, and on which she rested her call for a revolution in human relationships? It fell into two chief sections. The first - on 'The Body' and 'The Soul' - questioned the assumptions about the supposed differences between the nature of woman and man. The second - on 'Love' and 'Hate' - considered the distortions to which these mistaken assumptions had given rise, and went on to offer a critical appraisal of the relations between the sexes (including those of marriage and the family). There were, in fact, many virtues in Germaine Greer's treatment; it included many likeable and enjoyable features of both substance and style; and I will come back to touch upon these. First, however, what is to be said by way of criticism?

The entire emphasis throughout the discussion of 'Body and Soul' was the same as that of Kate Millett: namely that the supposed differences between the sexes do not rest on any biologically given nature of 'male and female', but are the outcome of social conditioning.

The 'normal' sex roles that we learn to play from our infancy are no more natural than the antics of a transvestite. In order to approximate those shapes and attitudes which are considered normal and desirable, both sexes deform themselves, justifying the process by referring to the primary, genetic differences between the sexes.

A great deal was said about chromosomes, hormones, orgasms (clitoral or vaginal), the recognition of the sexuality of women, the 'sexual sell' which purveyed a false image of this, etc., much of which has already been touched on, but the chief criticism of this entire section must be that – though it appears to be a detailed, systematic survey – it is, in fact, not so! It is, on the contrary, superficial, and, by way of illustration, just a few examples may be noted.

A section on 'Hair', for example, discussed the length of hair on men's and women's heads; the distribution of hair about the body – pubic hair, arm-pits, chest, etc.; but failed altogether to mention the one feature which most certainly distinguishes the two sexes: *facial* hair. What about beards and moustaches? Are these the outcome of long-established social customs and conditioning? Or have bearded ladies in fairground booths not been freaks after all? A section on the 'gender' of children, too, dwelt on the fact that 'of 48 chromosomes only 1 is different' and '... on this difference we have a complete separation of male and female, pretending as it were that all 48 were different ...' This followed the plain statement that the sex of a child is established at conception – that it is the special chromosome which causes the primary difference – but went on to make much of similarities in the earlier processes of foetal development, only – relatively late – leading to clearly distinguishable 'male' and 'female' individuals. One can agree with Germaine Greer about the variations in the 'male-female' mixture of sexual features in some individuals, but the argument that no fundamental difference of gender is established in chromosomal terms simply does not hold water. An even clearer slant of argument, however, is evident in the consideration of differences in 'mental capacity'. Within the general discussion, mention was made of some brain differences: for example – 'the relative lightness of the female brain ...' (though being 'heavier than that of men relative to total body weight'). Since, however, '... the brain is so imperfectly understood that we simply do not know enough about its physiology and function to deduce facts about performance ...' differences in behaviour patterns were thought to be better established by observations of behaviour. But then ... all that followed was a review of various tests to see whether they did or did not reveal 'the intellectual inferiority of women'. The statements made were about differences in the brain of male and female, and it was acknowledged that these differences were there. Men and women were not the same. But these differences – factual only – might well have implications quite other than differences in 'intellectual' or 'mental' capacity. The different features of a woman's brain might well be related to a different orientation of her entire anatomical structure and over-all physiological functioning – to the periodicity of ovulation and menstruation, reproduction, gestation, lactation, etc. – and (the crucial thing) are simply differences. They may have nothing to do with inferiority or superiority at all – whether in 'mental capacity' or anything else. My point here is that a consideration of differences of facts characterising the two sexes is switched to a consideration of intellectual inferiority or superiority between them. But why? Only because Germaine Greer is herself slanted in that direction of argument.

The section on 'Love' and 'Hate' covered ground already well-trodden by Betty Friedan and Kate Millett. The falsities in the 'romanticisation' of love furthered by magazines, advertisers, and romantic novelists; the simplistic portrayal of the 'Middle Class Myth of Love and Marriage' ('the marrying-and-living-happily-ever-after myth') and the exaggerated adulation of its customary and ritual elements, of 'its chief ceremony ... the *Wedding*',* for example, were all well-criticised, if not lampooned. Attention was drawn, too, to the other side of the coin of these falsenesses: the hate and resentment that can attend the dehumanising actuality of seeking,

---

*It is possible to argue that, despite the still widespread popularity of the *wedding*, it is not so much *marriage* that many modern young people have rejected as the *wedding* – and the two, obviously, are by no means the same.

imposing, or suffering, unfulfilled sexual appetite under the false romantic veil, and being forced to become resigned to a captivity within an unsatisfactory marriage mistakenly based upon it. For both men and women 'sex is their undoing.' The only criticism here, too, is that all this is over-done, sometimes destructively so, painting a completely unrelieved black-and-white picture.

'Altruism' within the family, for example, was dismissed cynically and entirely as being 'chimeric', when, surely, it is by no means entirely so.

> ...We, the children who were on the receiving end, knew that
> our mothers' self-sacrifice existed mostly in their minds ...
> We could see that our mothers blackmailed us with self-
> sacrifice ... that they must have had motives of their own for
> what they did with and to us. The notion of our parents'
> self-sacrifice filled us not with gratitude, but with confusion
> and guilt.

But is that the whole of the story? Is there never other-regarding devotion and self-sacrifice – indeed, sheer love – between parents and children? – or between children and parents? And is it true that 'in sexual relationships, this confusion of altruism with love *perverts the majority*'? This is surely an over-statement, as are similarly extreme statements that much reciprocal love in marriage has really only 'taken the socially sanctioned form of egotism', or that the staple plot of women's magazine stories ('falling in love, the kiss, the declaration, and the imminent wedding') means that 'sexual religion is the opiate of the supermenial'. Germaine Greer's detailed treatment of such points does have much substance and truth – but a continual flow of acid runs along the edge of her blade of criticism which bites into and destroys some truths which are telling (possessing genuine insight), and some half-truths which are, nonetheless, full truths for many. The criticisms often seem too high-and-mighty for many whose lives have to be lived on a much lower plane. Like Betty Friedan, it sometimes seems true that Germaine Greer is the too-unreflective (too-un-self-critical) educated woman speaking to, and for, the educated woman; and that she neither understands nor sympathises with many who are not, and cannot be, of the same level.

The same charge of exaggeration can be levelled at the generalisations about *hate* between the sexes. 'Women have very little idea of how much men hate them.' Is this true? And how confidently Germaine Greer seems able to speak about the sexuality of both men and women. She writes without any apparent doubt in her mind about the thinking and experiences of boys hanging about dance halls who felt as the sexual urge arose in them like 'scoring a chick'; for whom a 'walk to the bus-stop was usually good for a wank', or who, 'getting a fuck standing up against a wall or on a leather coat thrown on the ground in the Woolworth's bike sheds', were still unsatisfied. 'A wank was as good as a fuck in those days.' But – however reliable her sources of information – does she seriously believe that the generality of boys and men feel and behave in this way? One can accept all her anger, disgust, distaste, at the abuse of women in rape, but does she seriously think this is the common experience of men? – that rape is evidence of a general attitude of hatred and violence towards women on the part of men? Consider, for example, the illustration of 'cunt-hatred' she quotes from *Last Exit to Brooklyn*.

more came 40 maybe 50 and they screwed her and went back on the line and had a beer and yelled and laughed and someone yelled that the car stunk of cunt so Tralala and the seat were taken out of the car and laid in the lot and she lay there naked on the seat and their shadows hid her pimples and scabs and she drank flipping her tits with the other hand and somebody shoved the beer can against her mouth and they all laughed and Tralala cursed and spit out a piece of tooth and someone shoved it in again ... and the next one mounted her and her lips were split this time and the blood trickled to her chin and someone mopped her brow with a beersoaked handkerchief and another can of beer was handed to her and she drank and yelled about her tits and another tooth was chipped and the split in her lips was widened and everyone laughed and she laughed and she drank more and more and soon she passed out and they slapped her a few times and she mumbled and turned her head but they couldn't revive her so they continued to fuck her as she lay unconscious on the seat in the lot and soon they tired of the dead piece and the daisychain broke up and they went back to Willie the Greeks and the base and the kids who were watching and waiting to take a turn took out their disappointment on Tralala and tore her clothes to small scraps put out a few cigarettes on her nipples pissed on her jerked off on her jammed a broomstick up her snatch then bored they left her lying among the broken bottles, rusty cans and rubble of the lot and Jack and Fred and Ruthy and Annie stumbled into a cab still laughing and they leaned toward the window as they passed the lot and got a good look at Tralala lying naked covered with blood urine and semen and a small blot forming on the seat between her legs as blood seeped from her crotch ...'

It is true that, every day, the news brings us stories of kinds of sexual abuse and violence which simply take the breath away, which seem incomprehensible and incredible, but this, surely is at the very lowest level of brutality. Everything Germaine Greer has to say by way of exposing, protesting against, attacking the abuse of women and the sheer depravity of ungoverned sexuality removed from a relationship between persons and brought down to the level of sexual appetite alone, and, indeed, the misery of any marriage which finds itself captive to such a level, can be accepted and welcomed. In all this, she totally succeeds in shocking and sickening. But ... is this degree of depravity really representative of what has generally taken place in society? – between men and women? Is it even generally indicative of what lies under the surface of conventional behaviour? Or does it not protest too much? Sometimes, the feeling becomes overwhelming that, throughout, Germaine Greer is too *tough; so* much concerned to maintain a high level of provocation as to over-state the degree of applicability of her points. But ... it is difficult to know whether, or how far, one might be out of touch here. Is she, perhaps, right?

My own judgment, however, cannot help but be that she is not; that, even when she is making sound and important points, she is led by her aggressive rhetoric into over-statement and superficiality, and because of this her first book fails to carry conviction. Indeed, it could be gravely misleading to some women who, under the pressures of fashion, and wanting to find supporting arguments for their demands, accept its survey of both facts and values as being 'the truth'. It is only fair, however, to say quite clearly that many aspects of Germaine Greer's treatment are an improvement on Kate Millett, and worthwhile and likable in both substance and style.

In her entire analysis, for example (though *sometimes* accepting that men are the *enemies*), she does not only sympathise with women or condemn men. Like Betty Friedan, she thinks that *men*, too, in seeking to understand and come to terms satisfactorily (and truly) with their sexuality, may have had their nature falsely assessed, their experience distorted, and been brought into a condition of clandestinity and misery within the clutches of social expectations and demands. Men, too:

> are really frightened of being desired simply as a sexual object. The man who is expected to have a rigid penis at all times is not any freer then the women whose vagina is supposed to explode with the first thrust of such a penis. Men are as brainwashed as women into supposing that their sexual organs are capable of anatomical impossibilities ...
> Men are tired of having all the responsibility for sex, it is time they were relieved of it ... the emphasis should be taken off male genitality and replaced upon human sexuality.

What she attacks is the dehumanisation of sexuality – believing that this applies to both sexes, and that her radical reassessment may (hopefully) lead to an improvement for both. Discussing 'having sex' to experience orgasms (and all that this entails), she writes:

> If women are to avoid this last reduction of their humanity, they must hold out not just for orgasm but for ecstasy ...
> Sex for many has become a sorry business, a mechanical release involving neither discovery nor triumph, stressing human isolation more dishearteningly than ever before ... Jackie Collins and the sex-books show that we still make love to organs and not people ... and those who understand their sexual experiences in this way are irretrievably lost to themselves and their lovers.

Similarly, and again like Betty Friedan, she dislikes feminine 'machismo', and thinks it a total mistake to interpret the aim of 'Women's Liberation' as being that of adopting, imitating, competing for, or striving towards, the 'role of men'.

> We must fight against the tendency to form a feminist elite, or a masculine-type hierarchy of authority in our own political structures ... If women understand by emancipation the adoption of the masculine role then we are lost indeed.
> Women who adopt the attitudes of war in their search for liberation condemn themselves to acting out the last perversion of dehumanised manhood, which has only one foreseeable outcome, the specifically masculine end of suicide.

In all this, too (and despite her extreme language), Germaine Greer has enjoyable touches of humour. 'One wonders,' she writes – when considering Anne Koedt's 'grim satisfaction at ousting the penis' – 'just whom Miss Koedt has gone to bed with.' Attacking Jackie Collins's description of what she, Germaine Greer, calls 'the perfect fuck' (which includes a description of how, under the caressing touch of the man's hands, the woman's breasts 'swelled – becoming even larger and firmer'), she pours her scorn on the heroine '... despite her miraculous expanding tits'. And, quoting one of Barbara Cartland's descriptions of 'romantic love' – when the feeling of her lover kissing the palms of her hands with reverence made the woman 'thrill until her whole body trembled with a sudden ecstasy ...' she comments: 'when hand-kissing results in orgasm it is possible that an actual kiss might bring on epilepsy.' Her spiky humour makes reading Germain Greer an enjoyment.

It is to be noted, too, that though she does not (like Kate Millett) concentrate wholly on literature as her sole range of illustration and evidence, she *does*, in fact, discuss the presentation of sex and love in literature – not only in such modern examples as Jackie Collins and Barbara Cartland, but also in a much fuller discussion of writers from Dante and Shakespeare up to the eighteenth-century novelists such as Richardson – and, brief though this is, it is infinitely better in its breadth, variety and detail than Kate Millett, making much (which is good to see) of Shakespeare. There are curious gaps in this section, however. The essays of Addison and Steele, for example (especially those of Richard Steele), are not at all mentioned. But *The Spectator* must have been widely read during the eighteenth century – and it was full of sensible, down-to-earth comments on the nature of sex, love, and marriage, often ridiculing the 'romantic novel' of the time. The 'middle class myth of love and marriage' was not without its witty, caustic, good-humoured, and above all realistic critics who tried to replace it with something sounder.

It is also important to note that, throughout this treatment, there is no discussion of what I have called (p. 125) the 'alternative story' of the reforms of the nineteenth century: the securing of protected motherhood and childhood, the making of the home supported by the services of society. This, I suppose, came chiefly with the Victorian novelists – but much that is worthwhile could be said about this, and it is strange that Germaine Greer ignores it. In the back of my mind, too, hangs the feeling that much could be said about Jane Austen, who – of all novelists without exception – was morally impeccable in these matters of personal love, marriage, and, indeed, human relationships generally. However, in the ways mentioned above, Germaine Greer has much to be said for her, and in a full appraisal of her work negative criticisms would have to be tempered with such elements of appreciation. But our own criticism has to be deliberately circumscribed.

It was within the context of this entire argument that Germaine Greer had something quite direct to say about 'the family'. 'The real theatre of the sex war, despite the atrocities committed in social situations, is the domestic hearth; there it is conducted unremittingly.' She devoted a separate chapter to the family, and in it she committed all the usual errors. She began in a silly manner: 'Mother duck, Father duck, and all the little baby ducks ...' She committed the error of Leach's 'Reith Sentence' (though without reference to Leach) about the intense and destructive privacy of the family: '... The isolation which makes the red-brick-villa household so neurotic ... the intense introverted anguish of the single eye-to-eye confrontation of the isolated spouses.' She made the usual mistake of believing that 'the nuclear family' (see pp. 19–26) was something altogether new; contrasting it with an earlier state of affairs which was more satisfactory. Only recently, she claimed, has the nuclear family 'dwindled to the stump of community living that it now is.'

> When the largest proportion of the working community was in service in large households, when spinsters and unmarried sons lived in the household, when sons and daughters were most often sent away to work in other households, the family remained organic and open to external influences. Husbands and wives could not indulge in excessive introversion about their relationship which was buttressed firmly by the laws against divorce, public opinion, and the uncontrolled size of families. Ageing parents were kept and cared for in the household.

She wrote in the same mistaken way (in this much too rapid and simplistic speeding through the details of social history) about the transfer of 'functions' from the household to the state: 'more and more of the functions of the large household devolved upon the state: the care of the old, the sick, of the mentally infirm and backward,' and in all this she set out the most simplistic caricatures of the modern family, revealing, too, a curiously low opinion of womenfolk in general. The modern family, she said:

> is small, self-contained, self-centred and short-lived. The young man moves away from his parents as soon as he can, following opportunities for training and employment. Children live their lives most fully at school, fathers at work ... [And

141

within this context] Mother is the dead heart of the family, spending father's earnings on consumer goods to enhance the environment in which he eats, sleeps and watches television ... Her horizon shrinks to the house, the shopping centre and the telly.

And ... much more of the same! Sex becomes either miserably clandestine or a pointless lechery, an attempt – requiring a perpetual increase in intensity – to fill a vacuum. Criticising such practices (for example) as wife-swapping, she wrote:

In such a transaction sex is the sufferer: passion becomes a lechery. Ringing the changes on modes of *getting pleasure* disguises boredom, but it does not restore life. Sex in such circumstances is less and less a form of communication and more and more a diversion ... The overfed, undersexed white mouse is allowed a brief spell in another's cage to perk him up ... Universal domesticity buries all. And, with contraception and family limitation: 'the sterilised parent is the ultimate domestic animal.'

The *conventional order* of society, the surface of orthodox behaviour, is only an appearance. Below it seethes a morass of dehumanised and ungratified lust, and the truth is that the family has, in fact, gone.

The status quo is chaos masquerading as order ... The family is already broken down; technology has outstripped conservatism. The only way the state-father can deal with its uncontrollable children is to bash and shoot them in the streets or send them to a war, the ultimate chaos.

In all this, too, whilst making one other point, Germaine Greer gave a sign of what, in other woman writers, has been a much more deeply felt and more evident source of grievance – powerfully motivating much of their criticism (see the comments of Erin Pizzey, pp. 187–8). 'Our society,' she wrote:

has created the myth of the *broken home* which is the source of so many ills, and yet the *unbroken* home which *ought to have broken* is an even greater source of tension as I can attest from bitter experience.

It is this – the experience of the embittered woman – that deserves note, and to which we will come back later.

Now all this, so far, is a damning tirade against the family, no consideration whatever being given to 'the alternative story' about the making of the home and a new decency of domestic relationships out of the inhuman wreckage of the early industrial revolution, and some of her comments, without any doubt whatever, denounce and reject marriage and the family outright. So that this present judgment, and then our later judgment, can be seen to be correct, it is necessary in more detail to see just how radical these are. What, precisely – in this first book – did she advocate? I summarise – for the purposes of clarity.

Women, she claimed:

(1) Should refuse to marry.

> If women are to effect a significant amelioration in their condition it seems obvious that they must refuse to marry ... It is absurd that people should pledge themselves for life when divorce is always possible ... No worker can be required to sign on for life....

(2) should undermine the guarantee to their menfolk of paternity by ceasing to guarantee fidelity, and be ready to practice promiscuity.

> we might as well withdraw the guarantees (of paternity and fidelity) and make the patriarchal family an impossibility ... The withdrawal of the guarantee of paternity does not necessarily involve 'promiscuity', although in its initial stages it might appear to ...' [and] ... the unwillingness of women to commit themselves with pledges of utter monogamy and doglike devotion might have to be buttressed by actual 'promiscuity' to begin with.

(3) should reject the things associated with the marriage role, such as having:

> to take her husband's name, have her tax declared on his return, live in a house owned by him, and go about in public as his companion wearing his ring on her finger at all times ...*

*These items must be noted as (in agreement with Kate Millett and others) they enter quite specifically in the demands for 'contracts of cohabitation' in place of 'marriage'. See pp. 179–86.

(4) should regard marriage entered into as a means of avoiding inconveniences (e.g. of working to support oneself, of having illegitimate children, of managing a single-parent household) as an *evasion*. However, women who *do* marry or who *have* married must not be abandoned as a 'lost cause'. Married women *without* children:

> can still retain a degree of bargaining power ... Many men are almost as afraid of abandonment, of failing as husbands as their wives are, and a woman who is not terrified of managing on her own can manipulate this situation. It is largely a question of nerve.

Married women with children (mothers) are in a more desperate plight, but:

> women *with* children do break free, with or without their offspring ... [and though most mothers (because of their social conditioning)] would shrink at the notion of leaving husband and children ... this is precisely the case in which brutally clear thinking must be undertaken ... the children are not *hers*, they are not her property ... [and] a wife who knows that if she leaves her husband she can only bring up her children in pauperdom must make a sensible decision, and reject out of hand the deep prejudice against the runaway wife ... A woman who leaves her husband and children could offer them alimony, if society would grant her the means.

(5) should 'reject their role as principal consumers in the capitalist state.'
(6) should use their tongues (as Germaine Greer shows them how) 'to expose the situation'.
(7) should work towards the situation which Marx envisaged. If Women's Liberation:

> abolishes the patriarchal family, it will abolish a necessary structure of the authoritarian state, and once that withers away Marx will have come true willy-nilly, so let's get on with it.

These items set out much of the programme of action for the revolutionary woman, and, for Germaine Greer, there were signs that it was on its way.

Nurses are misbehaving, the teachers are on strike, skirts are all imaginable levels, bras are not being bought, abortions are being demanded ... rebellion is gathering steam and may yet become revolution.

Now all this surely adds up, even more clearly than my earlier quotations, to a very clear and definite call for the abolition of the family and marriage, for the revolutionary transformation of society. And yet, even in this first book, in the thick of this entire spate of argument, strangely, *this was not so*! At one point, Germaine Greer put the question quite directly: 'if a woman is to have children, if humanity is to survive, what alternative can there be?' And her answer was equally clear. It was: *the institution of self-regulating organic families.*

> ... The alternative is not the institutionalisation of parental functions in some bureaucratic form, nothing so cold and haphazard as a baby farm, but an organic family where the child society can merge with an adult society in conditions of love and personal interest. The family understood not as a necessary condition of existence in a system but as a chosen way of life can become a goal, an achievement of a creative kind ...
> [If women, in this kind of family, regarded] ... childbearing not as a duty or an inescapable destiny but as a privilege to be worked for, the way a man might work for the right to have a family, children might grow up without the burden of gratitude for the gift of life which they never asked for ...
> [The point of such an organic family] ... is to release children from the disadvantages of being the extensions of their parents so that they can belong primarily to themselves ... accept the services that adults perform for them naturally without establishing dependencies ... [have] scope to initiate their own activities and define the mode and extent of their own learning ...
> ... Parents have no option but to enjoy their children if they want to avoid the cycle of exploitation and recrimination. If they want to enjoy them they must construct a situation in which such enjoyment is possible.

Such an 'institution of self-regulating organic families' may seem, she thought, like a return to chaos, but 'genuine chaos is more fruitful than the chaos of conflicting systems which are mutually destructive.' A question which one might raise immediately is: if men and women can be expected to move towards changed attitudes like these, why can they not exercise these feelings of love, understanding, and other-regarding interest *now*, as partners and parents, within families as they now exist, seeking at the same time to improve the community conditions of them, and so prevent chaos altogether? But Germaine Greer is adamant: 'it is absurd that the family should persist in the pattern of patriliny.'

What is perfectly plain, however, is that Germaine Greer does not, after all, advocate the abolition of the family. She proposes, instead, an *alternative form*: the 'self-regulating organic family', and I leave readers to consider how credible an alternative this is.* Meanwhile, it can be seen that her position is really very much like that of Juliet Mitchell whose work, in fact, she quotes with approval. What both advocate is a *'diversification* of socially acknowledged relationships' which would mean:

> a plural range of institutions ... Couples living together or not living together, long-term unions with children, single parents bringing up children, children socialised by conventional rather than biological parents, extended kin-groups, etc. – all these could be encompassed in a range of institutions which matched the free invention and variety of men and women.**

Juliet Mitchell, again, deliberately did not try to specify the nature of these alternative institutions. Like Engels, she thought that men and women enjoying equality would themselves decide their own desired form (or forms) of marriage and the family. But Germaine Greer's 'self-regulating organic family' is clearly one idea within this kind of plurality.

But there is one other point we need to emphasise before leaving *The Female Eunuch*. In thinking about this alternative to marriage, Germaine Greer believed that the liberation of women she envisaged would entail a reduction in births. This, however, did not distress

---

*Bearing in mind that nothing is thought through – in terms of the claims and counter-claims which could be made on each other by the members of such families, the ownership and responsibility for property, the question of inheritance ... in short, of all the inescapable elements of morality and the law.

**Juliet Mitchell. 'Women – The Longest Revolution', *New Left Review*, November-December 1966, pp. 36–7.

her, and her position here deserves very careful note in view of her own later pronouncements. In *this* place, at any rate, she was in no doubt.

the problem of the survival of humanity is not a matter of ensuring the birth of future generations but of *limiting* it. The immediate danger of humanity is that of total annihilation within a generation or two, *not the failure of mankind to breed*. A woman seeking alternative modes of life is no longer morally bound to pay her debt to nature ... – to consider herself 'bound to breed'.

Fertility was subordinate to freedom! The *limitation* of the world's population, at humanity's present juncture and for its immediately foreseeable future, was what mattered, not its unbounded and unregulated increase.

We come now to the question: what changes of attitude, conviction, and pronouncements about the nature and behaviour of women are to be found in Germaine Greer's second book?

Leaving aside the suggestion that in writing this book, some twelve years after the first, Germaine Greer had 'mellowed', our judgment, on at least a number of counts, can be more precise than this, and, for clarity's sake, the points deserve listing. In her later argument, it can be said that she has (1) become much more aware of the social and cultural conditions of many societies in the world other than those in 'the West', (2) come to believe that the writers, governments, and countries of 'the West' are guilty of unjustifiable arrogance in classifying societies elsewhere in the world as 'undeveloped, developing, and developed' – and of a hasty and thoughtless destructiveness in imposing their policies in parts of the world that they do not understand, (3) become deeply aware of the universal importance to womanhood (and manhood) of *'fertility'*, (4) discovered the many important dimensions of *'motherhood'* – including the world-wide sharing of women, in their own immediate communities, in its many joys, labours, pains, responsibilities, pleasures, (5) come to be persuaded of the harmfulness and dangers of our methods of artificial contraception as against more natural methods, and, as part of this persuasion, of the value of *'chastity'*, (6) become persuaded of the worthwhileness of those cultures which still retain an institutionalised segregation of women (even when this involves, in many respects, a subjected status), (7) come to believe in the worthwhileness of the *extended* family as against the *nuclear* family, (8) come to be persuaded of both the arrogance and the dangers of programmes of population control (the policies of governments and family-planners), and (9) has discovered that, after all, the notion of the imminent danger of the rapid over-population of the world is a '*myth*'!

In short, she has become by no means more 'mellow' – only *reactionary*. *This* lady decidedly *is* for turning! She has made a U-turn with a vengeance, and is now misleading women in almost exactly the opposite direction to that in which she was misleading them before. A second strong feeling arises in one's mind: Germaine Greer is not only almost always *too tough*; she also *shoots her mouth off too much*. She is a strange blend of a music hall artiste, a platform orator, and a preacher – indeed, a hot gospeller. The jacket blurb of her new book (quoting a review) is not far wrong in describing it as 'a stern lesson from the podium'. She is too readily attracted to the adopting of flamboyant public stances before having considered her grounds and thought through her points with sufficient care. Her argument, in short, and particularly for women less informed than herself, is likely to be dangerous.

This second book,[4] like the first, is written with the grandiloquence of emotionally driven rhetoric. An emotional outpouring of half-digested views resting on a survey of a mass of facts only half thought through, it was written out of compulsion – because (she tells us) she had to. It is a 'plea for a new intellectual order' – no less! – and, still not knowing the answers to the questions it raises, it again seeks to provoke: this time 'to gore the reader slightly with its horns'. It is a breast-beating book, born, chiefly, of wider travel and a wider first-hand acquaintance with other cultures, and a deprecation of 'Western civilisation'. Again, though worthy in many respects, its appearance of academic thoroughness and reliability (covering a wide range of material) is an appearance. Like her earlier book, it is scattered with loose, aggressive, careless, unnecessary and sometimes totally unfair judgments: for example, in referring gratuitously to the '*pseudo*-science' which Sir James George Frazer founded (whilst acknowledging Frazer's own wide influence), or completely misrepresenting the emphasis and implications of Sir Cyril Burt's work – claiming that 'we now know that Burt's evidence was faked'; judgments of a kind no well-informed (as against superficially informed) person would make. But the book's argument is clear.

Beginning with the bald statement that modern Western society 'is unique in that it is profoundly hostile to children'; that it has a life-style having an 'anti-child thrust'; and that the management of pregnancies and births is being taken over from mothers by professionals;

she describes the love for children and the relations between adults and children in 'traditional societies' in warm terms.

> The closeness of adults and children in traditional societies is partly a result of the exclusion of women from the public sphere and their generally low levels of literacy, but these disabilities are in part compensated for by the centrality of the household in daily life. There is little in the way of public or commercial amusement; entertainments and celebrations take place in the household and children are included. Men may go to the coffee-house or the *mudhif* for their entertainment but their freedom to do so is not regarded with envy, for women and children are capable of having riotous good fun on their own. Perhaps the most important difference between mothering in traditional societies and mothering in our own is that the traditional mother's role increases in complexity and importance as she grows older. If she is skilful and fortunate enough to keep her sons and her sons' wives as members of her household, she will enjoy their service and companionship as she grows older. She will have time to play with her grandchildren; her flagging pace will match their unsteady steps. As she sinks into feebleness, her sons' wives still assume her responsibilities and care for her until the last.

Children in such societies may be grubby and less well-nourished than Western children, but:

> ... they will not be found screaming for all the goods displayed in the supermarket (and to make them so scream is the point of the display) until their frantic mothers lose control and bash them, and then compound the injury by poking sweets into their mouths.

We of the West 'do not like children' and are in danger of 'crushing all pride and dignity out of child-bearing'. Elsewhere in the world, however, there is a profound conviction of, and feeling for, the desirability and importance of fertility. Discussing 'the curse of sterility', she then places much blame on such matters as the spread of gonorrhoea, acute pelvic inflammatory disease, various kinds of 'insults to the reproductive system' (e.g. an abortion or two, a curettage or two, the insertion, rejection, or removal of an IUD), and therefore on our sexual behaviour.

There can be no doubt that the high frequency of pelvic disease in Western society is related to the degree of sexual activity and the number of partners that most people expect to enjoy, especially in adolescence and early adulthood. To point out that this is so is not the same as to say that increased and freer sexual activity is wrong, but it might suggest that the people who seek to suppress the expression of erotic desire because it conflicts with fertility are not simply irrationally puritanical in that their practice is justified by an actual connection between increased sexual activity and decreased fertility....

Infertility may be said to be a risk that the Western woman agrees to take when she opts for later child-bearing; the factors that erode her fertility are all aspects of her chosen life-style, although she may well object that no one ever spelt out to her with any clarity what their cumulative effect upon her child-bearing potential would eventually be.

These seem very strange pronouncements, coming from one who had recently advocated the desirability of possible, and even actual, promiscuity.

She points, too, to the unprecedented scale of mass-sterilisation:

... now the most popular form of family limitation in the United States. More than 600,000 sterilisations are performed annually....

More than 75,000,000 women have been sterilised, 9,000,000 in the United States. In 1970 only 20% of contracepting women had been sterilised; by 1975 the proportion had risen to 51%.

She also warns of its dangers.

Female sterilization is not a trivial matter. Whether or not a sterilized woman suffers after-effects of the operation depends on what technique was used and how skilfully it was carried out. She runs an elevated risk of ectopic pregnancy with some methods, an elevated risk of abdominal adhesions with others. If blood supply to the ovary is disrupted she may suffer abdominal pain and menstrual irregularities. In rare cases a tube will recanalise and a normal pregnancy may ensue ...

The whole world is involved in an orgy of cutting and burning human reproductive tissue.

All these, she says, are crimes which 'the white Protestant materialist' of the West is willing to countenance to avert 'that theoretical catastrophe – the death of the world through over-population.' In the face of this, chastity is then upheld as a form of birth-control, and in this she at once throws massive doubt on the ideas of free love (even in self-regulated organic families) advocated in *The Female Eunuch*.

The most straightforward and unambiguous way of keeping population in balance with resources is the denial of reproductive opportunity by the imposition of restrictions upon sexual activity. No human society exists in which human beings may copulate at will; no human community has ever been organised around the principal of free love, or could be, as long as reproduction and sexual activity were inextricably connected. Marriage is a licence to reproduce. Even in societies where sexual experimentation among young people is encouraged, illegitimate birth is rare and regarded as disgraceful. . . .

In the West, we might have come to doubt the sufficiency of such apparently simple methods of constraint, but:

Casual devaluation and contempt for cultural patterns of chastity and self-discipline are not only arrogant, they actually discredit our activities in the eyes of people who are supposed to be impressed by them . . .

It is fatally easy for Western folk, who have discarded chastity as a value for themselves, to suppose that it can have no value for anyone else.

Our assumptions about the superiority of our own methods of birth-control are to be deplored, and the validity of those of other societies have been too readily derided. Indeed, the positive functions and value of chastity have been unrealised:

abstinence has a two-fold function; not only does it keep the birthrate lower than it might otherwise be, it actually protects fertility by placing a high value on the activity which must be foregone . . .

Chastity may be seen, then, to have two contrasting functions. On the one hand, it endows sexual activity with added importance by limiting its enjoyment to special persons and special times. This may be no more than husbanding of the limited resources of human sexual energy by institutionalising the period of detumescence, which amounts to no more than natural chastity as defined by A. E. Crawley. This kind of chastity may actually serve to stabilise marriage unions by maintaining a constant level of sexual interest in a wife who is often unattainable ... natural chastity ... may be said to maintain optimum fertility by spacing sexual activity and sustaining sexual interest over a long period rather than allowing it to burn out in a shorter period of unbridled indulgence ...

If self-control is to be practised with dedication and seriousness, it follows that it must be shown to have a positive function, and there are millions of people in the world who are convinced that it has. In order to challenge this belief, its opponents need better evidence then they have so far been able to marshall.

The thoughtless imposition of our own methods has meant that the opportunity to sustain and spread more natural and safer methods has been missed.

Instead of teaching reverence for the body we chose to teach callousness; instead of exploiting concern for children and the passionate desire for them to survive, we assumed that too many were surviving already. The chance to develop the human propensity for sexual restraint in the interests of the congested world has been missed.

In all this, too, examples are quoted (e.g. from Crawley's *The Mystic Rose*) of the segregation (and distancing) of females from males in the simpler and traditional societies, but it is interesting to note that she does not emphasise, here, that such societies segregate women because of the setting of taboos on certain aspects of woman's nature: the forbidding of certain kinds of contact (e.g. in eating and sleeping together); and, indeed, that they are the kinds of society in which women are subservient to men. Describing abstinence among the Yoruba, for example, and the fact that the great majority of wives do not miss intercourse at all during periods of abstinence brought about by such segregation, she goes on to comment:

The degree of deprivation felt does not seem surprisingly low when we learn that Yoruba women rarely eat with their husbands and forty-eight per cent *never* do, and only 30 per cent join their husbands at festivals and parties. Hardly any husbands and wives sleep in the same bed, and only 27 per cent in the same room. Obviously, the women's principal emotional satisfaction does not come from their relationship with their husbands, and may very well have more to do with their relationships with their children. Yoruba grandmothers, for example, take a very active part in the rearing of their grandchildren. Moreover, the actual physical pleasure that women experience in sexual intercourse, apart from the receiving of attention and affection and the reassurance of attractiveness, can be severely curtailed by quite trivial factors. The Yoruba do practise clitoridectomy upon young women – in a fairly off-hand way. Accidents and diseases of the puerperium are also likely to interfere with their capacity to enjoy intromission, as do a multitude of other infections both trivial and serious.

Similarly, she denigrates the assumptions and practices of Western society and upholds those of other cultures and religious which, strangely enough, are the very societies in which women are held in subjection. In *The Female Eunuch*, for example, Germaine Greer starkly criticised the separation of women among Moslems (among others) because of 'atavistic fears' about menstruation (i.e. the persistence of 'taboo' in this connection.) 'Women who adhere to the Moslem, Hindu or Mosaic faiths must regard themselves as unclean in their time of menstruation and seclude themselves for a period.' But now, she actually extols Islam in its insistence on veiling its women because this actually shows a sensitive concern for their nature and status.

One of the reasons for the success of Islam as a proselytising religion is that it treated the lowest and least prestigious groups as deserving of the same respect as the highest; it covered their nakedness and veiled their women, conferring upon them a new kind of value and hence, self-respect. When the Shah of Persia outlawed the veil in 1937, he did not so much liberate his people as announce their dependency upon the West.*

The chance for realising the true worth of chastity has been missed,

---

*Strangely, however, as we have seen, the attempts of the nineteenth-century reformers in Britain to *protect* women – treating them with a new respect, conferring upon them a new kind of value – was regarded as a condescension on the part of men.

she claims, but then, even so, she goes on to criticise artificial methods of birth-control in no uncertain terms, advocating, instead *coitus interruptus* and the practices in other traditional societies which extend their enjoyment of sexual pleasures beyond that of actual intercourse. Her conclusion is:

> Our culture obliges us to abandon all attempts to control our own fertility by using our polymorphous potential for pleasure, and to give that control up to external agencies on the grounds that they are both more efficient and less harmful. The harmfulness of traditional methods of stereotyped intercourse has often been asserted but never shown. The efficacy of traditional methods has never been studied because they were invariably assumed not to exist.
>
> Our preference for mechanical and pharmacological agents of birth control is irrational. Our position with regard to the function of sex is absurdly confused. The other systems which have occasionally been referred to so far have had a certain internal consistency, outlandish though some of them have seemed. There is no logic in a conceptual system which holds that orgasm is always and everywhere good for you, that vaginal orgasm is impossible, that no moral opprobrium attaches to expenditure of semen wherever it occurs, that considerable opprobrium attaches to the bearing of unwanted children, *and* at the same time insists that 'normal' heterosexual intercourse should always culminate in ejaculation within the vagina. These are the suppositions which underlie our eagerness to extend the use of modern contraceptives into every society on earth, regardless of its own set of cultural and moral priorities. As the basic premises of the position are incoherent, the position itself is absurd.

This is very severe. And, for one who wants to see 'an end to morality', she shows, strangely, no reluctance in condemning these Western attitudes in no uncertain manner: 'Another name for this kind of mental chaos is *evil*.'

There are times, when reading Germaine Greer's latest book, that one has a vision of her moving in stately manner through the grand doors of St Peter's into that solemn interior: received, welcomed, folded at last into the bosom of the Roman Catholic Church. A kind of crypto-Catholicism seems to creep into her pages. 'His Holiness', one feels, is not far off.

There follow short treatments of (i) the history of contraception – in which she deprecates many artificial methods; pointing to the possible (and unknown) dangers of 'the pill', (ii) abortion and infanticide – in which, claiming that abortion is an extension of contraception, she concludes that 'contraception is too often abortion in disguise', and (iii) changing concepts of sexuality – in which she claims that 'the popular religion of sexuality' has centred too much upon 'genital activity', so that if this (and the achievement of orgasm) fails, than marriages are thought to be dead and have to be prodded back into life. This leads her to be scathingly critical even of adultery – as one kind of 'sex-aid' among others.

The seeker after corporeal blessedness should not be deterred by any considerations of taste, emotional consequences, the family or the law. Those marriages deemed 'dead' because they are not dignified by frequent and superlative orgasms must be either rejuvenated with the help of sex-aids, sex therapists, marital guidance and stimulants of various kinds, or abandoned, for to be inorgastic is to be as if in the state of sin, muddied, defective and defiled....

Adultery, if carried out as hygienically as marital sex itself is perfectly acceptable, but adultery with a partner who is difficult of access, in circumstances of guilt and secrecy, will not accomplish the desired purgation ... Because orgasm is everybody's right and bounden duty, progressive couples commend each other to adultery and freely discuss whether or not these adulteries restore them to blessedness, each acting as the other's lay therapist. This is called 'being up front' and usually acts to the disadvantage of the unwitting third parties, who have no notion that their most private behaviours are being anatomised by the cannabilistic couple, who need the input in much the same way as a painted warrior needs to eat the heart or liver of his opponent.

She believes, too, that women are becoming 'masculinised' in their sexuality. We are back to the fateful clitoris! 'Whether women like it or not, current sexual mores are conditioning them to become clitorally centred: their sexuality is being conditioned into the likeness and counterpart of masculine response.' And she then moves on to the statement of her new persuasion that motherhood, with its many dimensions of body-eroticism, is far superior to all this. She refers to the ecstasy of Diana Rigg – 'who was completely intoxicated by her daughter and rhapsodised about how she simply had to bite her bottom from time to time', and of Viva – 'who found it impossible to wean her little girl and kept on giving her the breast for years after everyone around them thought the child had been weaned, mother and child resorting to each other by stealth, like guilty lovers.'

Parenthood, especially motherhood, for Germaine Greer, had come back into its own.

Later sections discuss eugenics and the population policies of governments, but we can now come to the crucial question: what, given all this, is Germaine Greer's judgment about 'The Fate of the Family'? In her answer to this, she is simply astonishing!

The simple truth of the matter is that whilst, in *The Female Eunuch*, she vacillated between advocating the outright abolition of the family or its replacement by the 'self-regulating organic type', in *Sex and Destiny* she quite forthrightly defends, upholds, and – indeed – extols the family. So clear and decided is this that we must note it very particularly – in all its detail and with all its aspects. Her own full statement follows, and I have divided it into shorter paragraphs and italicised certain phrases to bring out the several points in all their significance. Even at the outset, however, we can note (a) that she completely accepts the fact that a husband, a wife, and their children constitute the basic familial unit of society, (b) that she sees this unit existing within a wider context of kinship relationships, and (c) that the qualifications she makes to arrive at her own definition of '*the nuclear family*' are such that this kind of family could never possibly exist – except, perhaps, as a very rare aberration. The truth is that she fully accepts the existence of the nuclear family unit within its wider structure of kinship – which is all that anyone has ever accepted, or ever wanted to accept.

> Almost all discussions of the family founder because of the difficulty in deciding what the family is, as distinct from what it was or will be, because families are always building up and breaking down, acquiring new members by marriage and procreation and losing them by estrangement and death.
>
> Obviously, a man and a woman must get together for a child to be conceived, and we might concede *without too much irritability* that such a link constitutes *the basic unit* in *a system of links we may call the family*. We might indeed, as we are describing something like the dynamic associations which make up living bodies call the procreating couple the *nucleus of the cell in the family structure*.
>
> I will only describe a family as nuclear when the relationship takes precedence over all others, and involves more time and more attention than are given to any blood

relationship; for the purposes of my discussion I will not exclude even the relationship with *the children of the nuclear unit, who are given less time in the nuclear family than the spouses give to each other* and are compensated in other ways. The children of the nuclear family become infrequent visitors to their parents' household, and the least courteous and communicative visitors at that, as soon as they feel that they are grown-up. *Where adult children willingly seek their parents' company the family, according to this definition, is not nuclear.*

It must not be thought however that because the nuclear family gives more energy and attention to the relationship between spouses, it gives more time to conjugal interaction than anything else. *The relationship with the employer takes precedence over all in terms of time, energy, concentration and loyalty.* This clearly cannot be the case for an unemployed partner, but even for the increasingly rare stay-at-home *housewife, the relationship with the children is secondary to her relationship with her husband (and with her husband's employer).*

The woman in a nuclear family who puts her children before her husband is 'asking for trouble': all the advice systems that have been set up to keep her on the right track will warn her that she is heading for disaster. The majority of women in the world do put children before husband, and are encouraged by their own families and their husbands' families to do so, and *the majority of women in the world do not live in nuclear families by my definition.*

Thus, while it may be true that *the copulating couple is the nucleus of the family* and families may be composed of cells all produced around some such nucleus it is absurd to maintain that everyone lives in a nuclear family. *The family becomes nuclear when it is stripped down to this function, all other relations of blood and affinity having atrophied and fallen away* (my italics).

Consider, now, some of the strange wording in this passage, which indicates clearly that it is rhetorical manipulation which is at work, not reason. Conceding, for example, that a man and woman must 'get together' to conceive children, and that this link constitutes 'the basic unit' in familial relationships – is the 'nucleus of the cell in the family structure' – she says, nonetheless, that she does so: 'without too much irritability'. But why does irritability enter at all into the matter? Might it be only because she is having to abandon her earlier arguments? – that she is having to admit the actual and necessary existence of the primary family group? But consider, further, the many qualifications used, despite her 'concession', in her continued attempt to decry this 'nuclear family', to strip it of all dimensions and significance. The children of the nuclear unit, she says, 'are given less time than the spouses give to each other, and are compensated in other ways'. But on what grounds does she assert this? And is it not patently untrue? How, if it is true, have we come to be called a 'child-centred' society, with 'child-centred' families? If children, we are told, visit their parents only infrequently when they have become adult, the family is nuclear. If they *do* willingly visit them, it is *not*. But what sort of definition is this? And are all family communications by letter, telephone, occasional holiday times when holiday breaks permit it, sharing regular festivities (at Christmas, etc.), ruled out?* And (leaving aside the strangely introduced emphasis upon the employer ... on the basis of a different interpretation, *work* could be looked upon as the necessary basis for each family's independence and well-being) the family is said to be nuclear only: 'when all other relations of blood and affinity have atrophied and fallen away'. But on this count *no family is ever, or has ever been, or can ever possibly be, nuclear*! It is of the very nature of the case – and a very elementary point – that since husbands and wives have to be drawn from different families, each of which has its own different network of kindred, the existence of 'nuclear families' necessarily entails, as a matter of sheer fact, the existence of a defined network of kinship. One cannot possibly exist without the other. It is among the most common-place facts within sociological analysis, and this is where the great confusion over the distinction between 'the family and kinship system' on the one hand, and 'the nuclear family and the extended family' on the other, closely reveals its dangers and falsities. In Britain, 'the nuclear family' within its context of 'wider kinship relationships' is what has always existed. The 'extended family', the 'extended household', about which anthropologists and historians of other civilisations speak, is something quite different, and we shall come back to this. The confusion must be clarified – and then abandoned!

---

*Indeed, some writers claim that families are now *more* in communication with each other than they frequently were in times past – aided by the new technologies of communication; remaining in touch with each other, indeed, over greater distances. See *The Shaking of the Foundations: Family and Society*, Part 1.

Germaine Greer's objective, however, is particularly to extol the enriching and supportive qualities of the network of kindred which surrounds nuclear families, and she distinguishes this by calling it the *Family* – with a capital *F*. But despite all her qualifications, what she means by this, quite simply and in her own words, is: 'a working network of kin' which is also of a 'multi-generation nature' – an organic structure of reciprocal relationships which, she says, 'can be shown in law, in genetic examination, in patterns of land ownership and parish records, but *has its realm principally in hearts and minds*'. It can properly and truly be described, she claims, in terms of 'mentalité'. It is a reality of feeling, thinking, motivation, confiding and confident familiarity, in the experience of those who *are* so related; a reciprocal set of relationships which can be confidently taken for granted and relied upon. It is the intimately experienced context of close *community*, even though it exacts its price in terms of the limits and constraints – its own inner regulations – required of its members.

The Family remains the poor man's last resort: it will give him power and authority when no one else will. It will extend to him the palm of success, when no sign of even basic respect is forthcoming from any other quarter. Only the Family can make sense of growing old: only the Family can give shape and coherence to all the phases of human life. For these services the Family exacts a price, a price which some pay gladly and others begrudge every hour of every day. At some stages in the career of any individual the pressure seems unbearable, relentless or vicious. The Family has its casualties, the stranger brides immolated at their cooking stoves, the runaways, the prostitutes, the unpaid labourers for tyrannical kinsmen, the runts, the ill-matched, the childless. Everybody who has ever lived under the yoke of Family has at some time longed to escape from it: the most passionate hatreds have been hatched within it as well as the most enduring love. But Family is a slow-growing thing, its roots sunk in a time beyond the individual's remembrance.

But this description is nothing more than that of the family within its kinship system. It contains nothing new whatever. It is what all of us have been talking about all the time. All Germaine Greer is saying (though with misleading rhetoric and falsely placed exaggeration) is that the collective conditions of modern industrial society have become such as to be disruptive of the stability and continuity of kinship within which families used to be bound in the past, in their own familiar localities, and which continue to exist in some societies today. And this, too, has been said times out of number. The even stranger thing is that she actually *warns* against the misplaced attacks upon family and kinship solidarity which have arisen within 'the consumer society'.

If the Family pits itself against the power of the preachers of instant gratification, it presents itself as a stumbling-block to the establishment of the consumer society, which has resources which can sweep the whole tenacious structure into the void. Among those resources are intelligentsia of every shade of red, pink and blue, who have mounted attacks on the Family from every side.

Yet, surely, she herself (in *The Female Eunuch*) was just such a member of the intelligentsia – indeed, one of the most militant critics – in her case with a decided shade of red!

She then indulges in a critique of some critics of the family – including, believe it or not, Frederic Engels and Jesus. This time, poor Engels is actually *berated* for being a critic of the family, and for getting things all wrong, having focused his attack too much on 'marriage and the sexual relationship of the spouses, and not the family at all'. 'The great apostle of the brotherhood of man,' she says derisively, 'is not at all interested in brotherhood itself, let alone sisterhood or maternity.' Poor Engels! – he was, after all, only supporting the liberation of women. Germaine Greer really must pass on to her sisters (Friedan, Mitchell, Millett, etc.) the fact that the testimony of Engels is so unreliable ... because they so frequently make the mistake of quoting him with warm approval.

Even Jesus (as well as Christianity) was anti-*F*amily (please note the capital *F*): being the champion only of 'the *nuclear* family'; and some remarkable things are revealed about him. Jesus, says Germaine Greer (following an author by the name of Mr Mount), 'had no brothers or sisters'. Furthermore, 'his mother had no brothers or sisters'. Now I lay no claim to biblical expertise, but must suppose that when Jesus was told by one of his disciples (Matthew 12) that 'his mother and brethren stood without, desiring to speak with him', these individuals were, in fact, his brothers. If not literally brothers they must have been kinsmen, and, in either case, Jesus must have lived within a context of *F*amily, despite his own rather cosmopolitan point of view as to who really constituted his relatives. And, indeed, a little later (Matthew 13), we find that when men were bewildered about the authority and wisdom of Christ, since he came from such humble origins, they said:

> Is not this the carpenter's son? Is not his mother called
> Mary? And his brethren, James and Joseph, and Simon and
> Judas? And his *sisters*, are they not all with us?

But there is more. If it does not sound too frivolous, Jesus also had
an Auntie Mary. We are told (John 19) that among the women
present at the crucifixion:

> there stood by the cross of Jesus his mother, and his mother's
> sister, Mary the wife of Cleophas, and Mary Magdalene.

Besides the long line of David on Joseph's side, Jesus was clearly
related to the members of a kinship network on the side of his
mother – and who knows how many people were related to Uncle
Cleophas? It is a decided possibility that Jesus had cousins. The
upshot of all this is that if she does decide to enter the Roman Catholic Church, Germaine Greer would be well advised to spend a little
more time in reading the Bible – and not, in so evidently slavish a
manner, following Mr Mount.

After this, we are treated, yet again, to an account of the taking
over of the functions of the *F*amily by institutions, any resistance the
*F*amily might have had to this having been undermined by the law.
The care for health, including that for childbirth, economic and
educational functions, the holding of property, etc ... all are taken
over by the state, and the modern nuclear family, all that remains, is
stripped of them. It is the old, old story.

We than have again (again – believe it or not) the recourse, as
though a mention of additional evidence and supporting argument,
to the usual sources. Leach's 'Reith Sentence' – the very sentence
itself – is (slightly incorrectly) quoted yet again: that 'Far from being
the basis of the good society, the family, with its narrow privacy and
tawdry secrets is the source of all (our) discontents.' Here, too, are
Laing and Cooper: 'convinced that the authoritarian family has
dominated the formation of personality to such an extent that the
sexual and spiritual independence of the individual has been
destroyed.' All this is introduced as evidence, all to support the deni-
gration of the nuclear family – as Germaine Greer had defined it –
and then, by contrast, she points to the great advantage of retaining
the individual family's place within its wider context of kindred (the
family's place within *F*amily). Children, she says: 'need to grow up in
larger more relaxed groups centred on the community ...'; it is 'a
better environment for children'; and in it women 'are not at the

mercy of their husbands'. A woman there 'is not an object but an agent'.

So ... in this, her latter-day pronouncement, Germaine Greer recognises and wishes to preserve the supporting nexus of kinship relationships within which a man, his wife, and their children form the basic unit. Hardly a cry for revolution! One wonders what all the aggressive argument has been about, and, indeed, Germaine Greer herself feels apologetic about it.

It may seem strange for a twentieth-century feminist to be among the few champions of the Family as a larger organisation than the suburban dyad, for most Families are headed by men and men play the decisive roles in them, or at any rate usually appear to, but there are reasons for such a paradoxical attitude. For one thing, if the family is to be a female sphere, then it is better for women's sanity and tranquillity that they not be isolated in it, as they are in the nuclear family. The Family offers the paradigm for the female collectivity; it shows us women co-operating to dignify their lives, to lighten each other's labour, and growing in real love and sisterhood, a word we use constantly without any idea of what it is.

She clearly favours wider family networks, headed by men who play the decisive roles in them, within which women – protected and supported in their motherhood – are able to lead and enjoy their own shared style of life. I cannot help thinking that there are many feminists who will believe this new position to be misguided and reactionary. But, in addition, there is another major turn-about in Germaine Greer's position which needs the most decided emphasis.

In *The Female Eunuch* she quite specifically brushed aside the probability that the rejection of marriage and the family, and the liberation of women from them, would result in a reduction in the number of births. This, she thought, could only help to solve the problem of the world's over-population. The limitation of births was a good thing. Now, in *Sex and Destiny*, having discovered the import- ance of fertility and the joys and sensuous delights of motherhood, she has also discovered that the very idea of a rapid over-population of the world is a *myth*! And who are we, she asks – out of the context of the depravity of the West – to impose this myth upon the rest of the world? It is here that I think it fair to give the example I promised earlier of Germaine Greer's tendency to launch distasteful, and even gratuitously cruel attacks on individuals with whose views she disagrees. For her, now, strongly defending her U-turn, people who are troubled by the 'problem of over-population' are culture-bound, culture-blind fools: for example, Dr Paul Ehrlich. Ehrlich was once going home to his hotel in India (Delhi) in a taxi which was forced to crawl through the crowded streets. He was moved to the depths by what he saw.

I have understood the population problem intellectually for a long time. I came to understand it emotionally one stinking hot night in Delhi a few years ago. My wife and daughter and I were returning to our hotel in an ancient taxi. The seats were hopping with fleas. The only functional gear was third. As we crawled through the city, we entered a crowded slum area. The temperature was well over 100°F; the air was a haze of dust and smoke. The streets seemed alive with people. People eating, people washing, people sleeping. People visiting, arguing and screaming. People thrusting their hands through the taxi windows begging. People defecating and urinating. People clinging to buses. People herding animals. People, people, people, people. As we moved slowly through the mob, hand horn squawking, the dust, noise, heat and cooking fires gave the scene a hellish aspect. Would we ever get to our hotel? All three of us were, frankly, frightened. It seemed that anything could happen – but, of course, nothing did. Old India hands will laugh at our reaction. We were just some over-privileged tourists, unaccustomed to the sights and sounds of India. Perhaps, but since that night I've known the feel of over-population.*

---

*One is reminded of T. S. Eliot's echo of Dante's Inferno (though he was writing of the crowds on London Bridge): '... I had not known that death had undone so many.' But even Dr Ehrlich's description does not go far enough. I remember a widely experienced foreign correspondent of the *Daily Telegraph* – Llewellyn Chanter – talking to me about his recent visit to India to 'cover' some sort of international conference. In addition to Dr Ehrlich's details, he had seen hundreds, if not thousands of starving Indians, lying on the ground outside the Indian stations to die; having nowhere else to live or die. An urbane man, hardened by much reporting, including war-time experience, he told me it was weeks before he could get the depressing weight of the experience out of his mind, and that, in fact, it never left him. Like Ehrlich, he had *felt* the actuality of the world's over-population – and who can deride such an experience?

What is Germaine Greer's response to this quite obviously sincere and deeply felt impression? It is almost as though she regarded it as a sheer insult to the Indian people and Indian civilisation. People, she says, 'like Ehrlich and his paymasters ... who waste emotional energy in resenting other people's weather (dwelling on his reference to the heat) had better stay out of it.' The taxi was probably going slow, in third gear, she tells us, in order to save petrol. And if Dr Ehrlich 'had been less of a ninny' he could have got out of his taxi, talked to people, and come to a better understanding of them, their culture, and their situation. After castigating him still further, she concludes:

> Still, one can sympathise, for the good doctor has had
> himself sterilised after the birth of one daughter; this matter
> has been made public presumably in order to show the utter
> sincerity of his preaching of Zero Population Growth, only to
> have to contemplate the ghastly vision of the world being
> taken over by thin brown people who eat, wash, defecate,
> and cling to buses in defiance of him.

Can this be interpreted as anything other than gratuitous personal nastiness? Meanwhile, her own judgment about 'the problem' is by no means thought out to any conclusion. She does not need a conclusion. In any event, she believes that 'the West' is arrogantly and insensitively imposing its conceptions on other ancient cultures which do not have the same values. 'Over-population,' she states, 'is not our problem to define and solve,' and, in any case, nothing is to be gained by getting worked up about it.

> I don't know how many people the earth can support, and I
> don't believe that anybody else does either; it can certainly
> support more people on a low calory intake than it can on a
> high calory intake, but as the world is not a huge soup-
> kitchen the fact is irrelevant. It is quite probable that the
> world is over-populated and has been so for some time but
> getting into a tizzy about it will not prove helpful. Nothing
> good can come of fear eating the soul. We cannot take right
> decisions if we are in a funk.

One can come to only one conclusion. Germaine Greer has decidedly not 'mellowed'. Far from it. She has merely undergone (one cannot say rationally argued) a complete U-turn. Fourteen years ago, wanting the abolition of the family, she now defends it against all-comers, simply wanting to see it within its supportive context of kinship. Once advocating the liberation of women from the many bonds of age-old traditions, she now tolerates and even advocates some of these kinds of bonds as the most likely basis on which women might be able to experience a satisfying, female, child-bearing, child-sharing style of life. These are the 'extended families', the kinds of *F*amily, she defends. Once concerned about the perils of an over-populated world, she now denounces the 'ninnies' who waste their emotional energy sympathising with the massed-populations of the poor cities in the world, and who continue to promulgate this 'myth' and remain worried about it. Not only does she now advance no coherent and telling criticism whatever about the family – at least as most feminists conceive of it, she has decidedly ceased to be a voice speaking for the liberation of women. Women may be secluded and segregated behind the 'Veil'; they may, within their own cultures, perhaps suffer clitoridectomy, but, nonetheless ... we must properly understand the qualities of the lives they enjoy within their own traditional contexts. And never once does she stop to reconsider a few simple questions.

Why – whenever and wherever women gain equal citizenship with men – do they opt for monogamy? Why is there no example of women choosing anything else? Why is there no instance whatever where this is not true? Why do they not opt for the retention of the closely knit, extended, organic, family-and-kinship networks which they have, for so long, traditionally enjoyed? And why, similarly, whenever and wherever women are able to exercise choice, do they opt for *privacy*? – to have their own homes, to lead a life of independence for their own families, though retaining still such ties of affection and responsibility with wider relatives as they want to preserve?

Germaine Greer's own answer is that when young men and women choose in this way, it is because of their 'acceptance of Western technology', and she hopes that – among the Yoruba, for example – this will not mean the 'experience of the selfishness, instability and impermanence of the nuclear family along with its higher fertility' of the West. Might she not, however, be wrong about this? Might it not be that liberation from the tight bonds of outmoded traditions is what women in these societies want? – and for good reasons?

All this, however, stems from an analysis of her two books alone. In journalistic and television exposés and interviews, her new-found feelings spill over in a more relaxed and conversational manner. In an interview printed in *Woman's Own*, for example, she was presented as being: 'bored by sex; waxes lyrical about the sensuality of motherhood; prefers more old-fashioned societies where men do their thing and women do theirs; and advocates abstinence as a better form of birth control than the Pill.' The report of the interview was of this kind, but included quotations from Germaine Greer herself.

Quite a turnabout, you might think, for the woman who admits to having had several abortions, the woman who used to rejoice in her own promiscuity, and joke that in a lifetime in the cause of sexual liberation she'd never caught VD ... She gets quite sentimental when talking about family life in traditional societies where men are men and women have more fun.

'I've never been against the division of labour – it makes sense for men to do certain jobs and women to do different jobs. Both are doing work that can't be duplicated so there is autonomy and mutual respect ... And the first thing that strikes you in these kinds of societies is that the women actually have great fun together. They don't want the men around because that would spoil it. I've never understood why in our society we expect our husband to be our best friend.'

She moves deftly on to her other favourite subject – motherhood. She has never had a child herself ... but she goes into raptures about the sensuality of sleeping with her god-daughter, Ruby ...

'It's terribly sensual, absorbing, demanding, interesting and exciting and to just gloss over it is to really miss out. Women have more skills for bringing up children than men. And I don't think it's something you can enjoy if you're trying to combine it with a job. I've talked to women who've tried to do both, and they're nearly going crazy.'

But if motherhood is to be properly enjoyed in combination with a job, how is it possible without *partnership*? And what is wrong with the kind of partnership which modern marriage and the family offers? Indeed, what is the alternative? Is there *any* alternative which manages to secure the autonomy, equality, dignity, status of women (indeed, of all individuals) which feminists want whilst providing a secure context for the shared emotional and practical care of children?

To end, once again, with the matter of *dedication*: *Sex and Destiny* is dedicated to 'My god-children – Baal Krishna and Purrushotta'.

For all her fullness of years and supposed 'mellowing' Germaine Greer gives every appearance of being one thing only: thoroughly confused – with from time to time a curiously inexplicable edge of nastiness. One would not want to exercise the same cruelty in judging her as she herself employs in judging others (e.g. Paul Ehrlich). People do, during their lives, change their minds, and what they have done earlier sometimes makes impossible what they might like to do later. But – given the harshness of her own attacks, and since she has called for so many women to listen to her, she must face the same criticism herself. And it does seem true that her discovery of the importance of fertility and motherhood is a discovery *for others* not for herself.

One of the loudest preachers in the Women's Liberation Movement now faces, herself, the most radical questioning. Meanwhile – both within and outside her own writing – the family remains intact.

Miscellaneous

We have now considered fairly thoroughly the positions of three of the most prominent writers in the Women's Liberation Movement – Betty Friedan, Kate Millett, and Germaine Greer. This in itself gives us a clear picture of the wide range of issues raised and judgments made about the family and marriage within the movement. Obviously, however, these writers are not alone. Over the past fifteen years, the literature of 'Women's Lib' has mushroomed enormously – in quantity, and in the number of points of view and special interests represented. Though it is impossible to cover all of these, it is necessary, no matter how briefly, to give at least some indication of the kinds of writing which continue to be influential in the late 1980s. For brevity's sake, the most important strands of argument can be grouped under three heads.

CONTINUING EXTREMES

Two examples will be enough to show that on both broad and narrowly focused fronts, many of the views expressed are still as extreme as the most extreme pronouncements of Kate Millett and Germaine Greer. One – on the broadest front possible – is the report following the United Nations' Decade for Women (1975–85); the other is the very specific matter of family breakdown and the increase in the number of single-parent families.

On the basis of the materials gathered together for the conference to mark the end of the UN Decade for Women, an official *Report on the State of the World's Women, 1985*[5] was produced – the materials themselves stemming from questionnaires filled in by 121 governments. The entire project was, without any doubt, an enormously important and valuable work of research. It demonstrated the still unalleviated conditions of life for women in many parts of the world. It recorded such progress as had been made, and was being made, in improving their status – making plain what still needed to be done. And, in all this, it marked the continuing strength and vigour of the Women's Movement and the importance of its implications for societies throughout the world – still, of course, far from having been fully worked out. It showed, indeed, that in a world thronging with many factors and situations of crisis, the movement towards the equal status of women was, in fact, a *transforming revolution* which was still afoot. But the publication *Women: A World Report* had an additional dimension. Ten women writers were asked to visit particular countries for a month to form their own impressions of the life and problems of women there: women from poor countries visiting rich countries; those from rich countries visiting the poor. These reports were necessarily personal and impressionistic, but added welcome qualitative detail to the formal analysis itself and to the tables of statistics. Unavoidably, too, they were very varied. It is hard to be critical of such a worthwhile publication, but yet it has to be said that the editor's (Debbie Taylor's) opening introduction and analysis is characterised, in many places, by extremist points of view, and marked, strangely enough, by an almost complete lack of reference to *men* and the part they might (and perhaps *do*) play in families.

Throughout the analysis, women are seen as an exploited, unpaid work-force – compulsorily providing sexual as well as other services – in a pattern of life so much dominated by child-rearing and domestic work as to make any autonomy of work, life, and personal identity impossible. The burden of unpaid labour is all the heavier because men (it is said) refuse to do it. The arrangement:

> suits both husbands and governments very well. They have a ready-made class of labourers providing, for nothing other than board and lodging, a whole spectrum of services that would otherwise have to be purchased in the market place.

This unpaid exploitation also includes the unwarranted and

unsatisfactory sexual subjection of women. For married men – sex is satisfying. For married women – not so!

The physical sensations of normal, male-controlled, penetrative sexual intercourse (which give a man the perfect moist sensual environment for his penis, while a woman's clitoris must snatch at what pleasure it can from crude, dry, pelvic bumping and grinding) are a major reason why so many women get so little pleasure from sex ...* When women get so little pleasure from it, sex becomes simply a service which, along with the work involved in childrearing, married women are expected to provide free.

Prostitution and surrogate motherhood commit the offence of being *paid* – and by more than one man.

... prostitution is not, in itself, any more degrading than any other work. Neither is the related occupation of surrogate motherhood. What the prostitute and the surrogate mother have in common – the characteristic that actually defines their shame – is the fact that they are not the sexual property of just one man. They are offering an independent service to any man who wishes to avail himself of it. At the cost of social censure, they receive an income for services that their married sisters are providing free ... A large number of women are prostitutes. But a much larger number continue to provide sexual and domestic services free of charge to their husbands.

Women are forced to 'accept the terms of the marriage contract' by 'sheer social and economic powerlessness' – and therefore seek to limit births. Fifty million abortions a year are mentioned as evidence of this, but, it is objected, many women would, in fact, like *more* children. *Wanted* children are excluded by this sexual-socio-economic domination, and so ... women who *do* want children should be supported – by the *state*.

Governments who are unable or unwilling to provide services, for dependent members of the community – such as children, the disabled, the unemployed, the frail elderly – tend to

*In a light vein, one might reiterate the question Germaine Greer asked about Anne Koedt. 'One wonders just whom Debbie Taylor has gone to bed with.' But, much more seriously, this conception of sex in marriage is a telling indicator of Ms Taylor's notion of what love in a marital relationship is like.

assume that something called 'the family' will step into the breach and scoop them all up into a warm and all-providing embrace. And it is women – albeit within 'the family' – who are expected to provide these services as part of their domestic role. But basing national plans on this assumption is neither realistic nor just.

The necessity for women to work outside the home, together with the rising rates of divorce, separation, migration, and illegitimacy, demonstrate that it is unrealistic. And placing these responsibilities on women's shoulders alone is unjust.

A society that values both the welfare of its children and the autonomy of its women has a responsibility to ensure that women are able to choose the number of children they have and that they have the support they need to provide for and care for those children without prejudicing their desire to fulfil themselves in areas other than child-rearing and domestic work.

One might suppose that it is families themselves (husbands included) who should decide upon, and then support, the number of children they wanted, but Ms Taylor claims that the family has *failed*.

In theory jobs for men and housework for women should sort people neatly into nuclear families. In practice the trend is for men and women to separate, rather than cling to one another cemented together by their complementary roles in the nuclear nest.

The 'nuclear' unit again! – this time a nest! And it is argued that – with the discovery of man's role in procreation – marriage was the way in which, in allying himself with a woman, he gained power over both her and her children, imposing fidelity upon his wife, and confining inheritance to his own offspring.

the laws of marriage and inheritance are usually superimposed on laws allowing women equal access to land and income, tending to pass control of whatever wealth a woman manages to amass into the hands of her husband. He can then use that wealth to purchase the loyalty of his children (his male children in particular), prising them away from their infant closeness to their mother.

The marriage contract secures for a man control of the wealth accrued through the labour of his wife and children and of wealth amassed previously via inheritance ... In both cases it is the children as well as the wife who are bartered and the man who profits most from the exchanges.

That is Ms Taylor's conception of marriage, and she discusses female circumcision (of various kinds) as the way of ensuring virginity and fidelity.

The aim of the operation (and of that part of religious morality that tends to uphold it and other less drastic restrictions of woman's sexual pleasure) is to ensure that sex, for women at least, is linked with procreation, not enjoyment. If women enjoyed sex they might be tempted to have intercourse outside the marriage contract, thereby undermining a husband's control over her children.*

There is much more of the same kind, all of which is held to demonstrate the continued inequality of the sexes: 'The side marked "woman" is weighed down with responsibility, whilst the side

*I do not know what this implies for Kinsey (et al.), Anne Koedt, and the clitoris, but one interesting fact mentioned is that though Kinsey reported that only between 70 and 77 per cent of North American women had ever experienced orgasm at all, 88 per cent of circumcised Sudanese women (who had had the clitoris *removed) had* experienced orgasm. Sadly, Ms Taylor comments, 'the figures for the sexual pleasure of *uncircumcised* women in the rich world may be lower than figures for circumcised women in the Arab world.'

Similarly, the strange point is made that though the compulsory (complete) virginity of the bride was supposedly something insisted on by the *man* and suffered by the woman, the revolution in sexuality and contraception had not improved woman's lot, but liberated *men* rather then women.

Men are free simply to take advantage of the new free sex. But women find that sex is now a service they must provide outside and inside marriage, at the same time as trying to ensure that they do not prejudice their bargaining position in the marriage contract. Men's continuing social, moral and economic power means that the sexual revolution has not necessarily been good for women. They have lost the bargaining currency of virginity, without the compensation of more sexual enjoyment. While there may be a few more orgasms and a bit less shame around, this is often at the cost of women defining their sexual feelings in male terms, in the services of male sexuality.

As one of the women later insisted in another section: 'we have had the sexual revolution – and *lost!*'

marked "man" rides high with power.' It is very decidedly a one-sided treatment, and it would never occur to a reader that *men* (in *partnership* with women, in *families*) contributed anything to the well-being of women and children in an other-regarding way, or that the commitment of marriage, among other things, actually included duties and undertakings on the part of men. It is a pity that in a report of this kind the emphasis stems so much from the extreme feminist wing of the Women's Movement.

We cannot dwell on the other 'impressionistic' chapters – they are so variable – but, sickening though they are in revealing the continuing ill-treatment of women, they also make some disquieting revelations as to the qualities of attitude and character among women which have resulted from their newly acquired freedom. There is the story of a Norwegian wife, who, living in difficult conditions with her husband (a man of 'a weak and gentle nature') and their children, moved to a healthier locality with the help of a social worker, and had the opportunity of resuming her education, becoming known as a brilliant scholar and doing particularly well at mathematics.

This had given her so much confidence that she divorced her husband and moved to a small flat nearby. She was working as a shopgirl by day and studying computer sciences by night. When she was qualified, she was certain she would get a job in a field that seemed to her exciting and promising.

And her husband? Elisabet smiled. He had always enjoyed housework more than she did; now he had given up his job to stay home and look after the children. His colleagues thought him a martyr and the neighbours (particularly the old ladies) thought him a hero and brought him cakes and sympathy. Old women and wives in the neighbourhood abused her as she went by. She smiled again. 'I have a strong will, I can stand it.' The social workers were helping her, and she had one supporter at home. Who?

She burst out laughing. 'My mother-in-law!'

Hardly a responsible attitude to marriage? – or to motherhood? The 'for better' side of the marriage commitment seems to have attracted a less serious consideration than the 'for worse'. The description of teenage girls and liberated women in Australia, too, makes one glad to be living at the antipodes!

– So how is it?
– Oh, it's okay.

- Do you like making love?
- Yeah, it's okay.
- But why do you do it if it isn't great, wonderful, marvellous?
The four of them look at me from behind their cigarette smoke. I must be some kind of exalted 'oldie'.
- Why do you do it?
- I dunno, the tallest one says.
- I dunno, answer the others.
- You don't know?
- Dunno, dunno, dunno, dunno ...
- And what do you do when you go out?
All four giggle in chorus.
- Oh, movies, dances, picnics, parties, discos, tennis (along with cricket, it is the national sport), beaches, surfing. We watch television, drink Coke, or beers for the boys, eat hamburgers and lollies.

And - discussing attitudes to both menstruation and virginity - a mother, asked if her two daughters have started to menstruate, answers:

Oh, sure. I showed the oldest how to put a tampon in by putting one in myself in front of her.
- A tampon? Straight up like that?
- Of course.
- But what if she loses her virginity?
She looks at me with absolute contempt.
- Who cares? I don't give a damn about her virginity.
- And what will happen when a boy - ?
- She interrupts me impatiently; she is, in fact, always impatient, most women are in Australia.
- What about the boy? To hell with the boy. It's his problem. No one gives a damn about a thing like that anymore. On the contrary, the quicker she loses it the better.

There are other tit-bits of information as to what Australian women get up to.

Now a woman falls into a trance because she can insert a speculum into her vagina and observe her organs in a mirror. Exciting, wonderful, overwhelming, exhilarating, enchanting, vaginal lips, mount of venus, clitoris, vulva, everything can be depicted, nothing is missing, genitals stare back.

All one can say is: thank God for 10,000 miles! But things are said, too – for example on sexual behaviour and relationships in Egypt – which put a different complexion on Germaine Greer's description of the dignity of women and their enjoyment of a shared female lifestyle 'behind the Veil' in Muslim countries. Thus, Angela Davis, speaking to Nawal el Saadawi, says quite unequivocally:

> When she lectures in the United States, she invariably feels compelled to criticise Elizabeth Fernea's film *The Veiled Revolution*, which represents the veil as a positive step on the road to liberation. The film argues that Egyptian women made a profound mistake when they took off the veil at the beginning of this century. Now they have embraced authentic Arab culture and are thus capable of moving forward on their own terms, rather than on the terms established by Western capitalism. This (she says) is an erroneous, apologetic position. The veil does not represent the authentic culture of her people – and indeed, in her book *The Hidden Face of Eve*, she offers a historical analysis of the veil as a product of the Judaeo-Christian tradition – but rather is, in its contemporary expression, a direct result of prevailing socio-economic conditions in Egypt. As unemployment began to rise in connection with Sadat's Open Door Policy, so the veil began to be resurrected. One of its essential purposes was to remove women from the job market at a time when domestic production was declining in response to the saturation of the market with imported goods from the capitalist countries. Rather than functioning as a means of resisting the invasion of Western, capitalist values, the veil serves to consolidate and confirm them as it strengthens the sexist social attitudes which facilitate neo-colonial economic fetters in Egypt.

It seems plainly true, too, that the Muslim segregation of girls and women is to their decided disadvantage in education.

> Economic reasons are not the only ones that prevent girls going to schools or continuing their education for as long as boys. Moral reasons can be equally powerful.
> In strictly Muslim countries, for example, where men and women tend to move in completely different worlds, where better-off families keep their wives and daughters secluded or covered in the *chador* whenever they venture out of the

house, and where pre-marital sex is considered an utter outrage for women, many parents keep their daughters away from co-educational schools as soon as puberty approaches, and attendance at secondary schools tends to be very low. In Ethiopia and Morocco, for instance, there are nearly twice as many boys as girls in secondary school, while in the Yemen Arab Republic and Pakistan boys outnumber girls by well over three to one.

In such countries pubescent girls are prevented from associating with boys altogether. In other countries it is the actual consequences of that association that causes girls to leave school. Pregnancy – wanted or unwanted, legitimate or illegitimate – is another major reason why girls are less likely than boys to complete their education. In every country these costs of adolescent sexuality are borne by girls alone.

Germaine Greer's liking for societies still retaining 'extended families' seems a very strange disposition if it is the liberation of women from patriarchal tyranny she has in mind. But the same extremes are to be found in books which focus their attention on much more specific problems.

There are several such books dealing with the 'breaking up' and 'splitting up' of marriages, and, in particular, the growth of single-parent families, and it is enough to consider just one of these: *Splitting Up*,[6] edited by Catherine Itzin. This – sub-titled 'Single Parent Liberation' – would be better titled 'Single Parent Tragedy'. Claiming that, for many, 'the end of marriage is an important period of release and freedom', its descriptions of most marriage break-downs are so harrowing as to suggest that, in almost all cases, the end came about because of disaster. And this kind of book is a good example of that kind of criticism of the family and marriage mentioned earlier arising from the experiences of the 'embittered' or 'injured and aggrieved' wife. Even the editor's own foreword explains that her book stemmed from 'the crisis' of her own marriage breakdown, when she was 'desperate for moral support, practical advice and a new perspective', and when she felt abnormal among 'everyone else' who were 'happily married and securely nuclear nested'. (The nuclear nest again!) In a short preface, too, Paul Lewis (of the National Council for One Parent Families) speaks of '... the cruel practical difficulties which society puts in the way of one-parent families reaching their potential as whole, happy and well-balanced families', which suggests that society is to *blame* for the breakdown of particular marriages, and goes on to point out how disadvantaged such families are.

One-parent families are, on the whole, poor families. Over half of all families at the poverty line are one-parent families and even those lone parents who work earn low pay – most of them are women – and face extortionate costs to have

their under-fives looked after all day or their five to ten-year-olds outside school hours.

Also:

Poverty has its effects on health – lone mothers are more prone to illness and disability; on housing – half of all homeless families are one-parent families; on children's attainment at school; and, if the mother becomes pregnant again, on the health of her new baby.

But if she is the mother in a one-parent family in such poverty *why* does she become pregnant again? Is society to blame for this, too? Society *is* undoubtedly to blame, claims Catherine Itzin. The problems to which she points:

are inherent in the social system itself, in conditioned expectations and in the institution of marriage ... There is still the widely held notion that men who leave their wives and families are monsters: but they are often forced by the system to behave in ways they would not otherwise choose ... *Splitting Up* calls into question just about all accepted values connected with marriage ... and the problems faced by single-parent families ... reveals the shambles of social, psychological and educational conditioning; the sham of society's assumptions about marriage, and the economic and legal sanctions which support the assumptions ... [They] cry out the need for change in attitudes, changes in the law, changes in the welfare system, and ultimately changes in the social system itself.

The *social system* is to blame for one-parent families! *Society* 'does very little to accommodate them'. And Paul Lewis agrees with her.

when all these problems are too much and social work help becomes involved, too often children are taken into care. About half of all the children in care are from one-parent families, their blameless mothers labelled failures. And smug society takes over the parental rights, and pays a foster mother twice or three times as much as was given the real lone mother or father on supplementary benefit to care for their own children.

The mothers are blameless. The fathers are blameless: 'forced by the social system to behave in ways they would not otherwise choose'. Smug society is responsible. But – even more than that – it is, after all, the nature of the normal two-parent family which is to blame, and, again the vision is offered of ... revolution.

Help for one-parent families is seen as under-mining the dominant two-parent family and with it the structure of society. But if the two-parent family is so weak an institution that it has to be bolstered up by a layer of poverty-stricken parents and children, perhaps it is time to re-assess its real strength and importance ... Perhaps this book will help us all to see one-parent families not as a growing problem but as the vanguard of a revolutionary change in the structure of society.

These assertions are so lamentably insufficient in their degree of thoughtfulness and in their one-sidedness as to call for no comment. *Society*, and *the family and marriage* in it, are blamed for the break-down of those marriages and families which *fail!** But the absurdity of the position is made even more clear in the dozen 'case-interviews' which follow. These are prefaced by the astonishing statement:

Both the women and the men came to realise how arbitrary was their decision to marry, how little consideration they gave to it before embarking upon it, how little they understood the effects it would have upon their lives. They came to understand how marriage had trapped them in rigid roles and frustrated their personal expectations. They came to realise how little thought they had given to having children and how monumental the consequences.

But if so little forethought had been given preparatory to entering into marriage and parenthood, this, surely, in itself, was part of the explanation (at least) of the failure of these marriages and the break-

---

*The entire argument is rendered even more strange by Ms Itzin's statement that: 'despite the hardships, these single-parent people are – without exception – happier as single parents than when they were married, even the "happily" married.' But if they have won through to such happiness, why all the protest and the complaints?

down of these families? But no! Catherine Itzin wants to see 'single-parent familyness' given a 'properly serviced status'. Referring to Lee Comer's Marxist analysis* which claims that marriage is part of the economic base of society, she claims that changes in it will necessarily change the structure of society itself, and so (again): 'the radical implications of single-parent familyness within the social structure will force revolutionary changes in society.' The casual, careless attitudes towards marriage and parenthood mentioned in this opening statement are amply borne out in the case-studies which follow.

In one of these – in which Eleanor (19) married Harvey (25) – they not only had had no pre-marital sexual experience, they did not even know that sexual intercourse entered into a marital relationship. Their marriage was not consummated for five years! After that, Eleanor was 'pissed off'.

> This friend of mine who lived just across the road had just recently got married and it was all happening ... wallop, bang every night, you know ... randy scenes, orgies. And she was really ramming it down my throat twice a day, you know, and that wasn't helping ... Mini skirts had just come in and I thought, oh sod it, I'm going to get a bloke ... I was really fed up. I thought, bugger it, I'm going out and have some fun. So I went to this New Year's Party and Harvey stayed at home looking after the kids ... I looked around and I thought, 'I'm going to pick the randiest looking bloke I can find.' And I saw this absolutely crazy looking man sitting in the corner, so I went over and got him. And that was it, the beginning of the end.

A long time afterwards, Harvey found himself a young girl – Carol – but this, said Eleanor:

> really got me down, I couldn't cope with it at all. It was really painful. You see, I could dish it out, but when I was getting it back, that was something quite different. And it really made me miserable and sick ... I'd kick him out as soon as he'd come in and say: 'Go back to her, go on piss off'. In the end, we had a big row and I told him to go. He went, and didn't come back, and that was it.

Wedlocked Women. Juliet Mitchell's Marxist analysis regarded marriage and the family as part of the *ideological super-structure* of society. Lee Comer regards it as part of the *economic base*. So much for Marxism as a 'scientific' study of society.

Later, discovering a diary he had kept, she found that he had referred to her as a 'gut-sucking bitch', and she recalled that she herself had (for example) written things on the mirror like 'FUCK OFF'. 'He saw it when he came in. It was hideous.'

This ... was one family; one broken marriage – with children. Later in the book, the editor comments: 'one wonders if it is the people involved who fail at marriage or whether marriage fails them.' Is there really any room for such wonder? Another person driven into the condition of a single-parent family concluded:

> I have created an alternative family structure because the one that society offers is inadequate. *That is society's fault, not mine.* So I resent the fact that I, or my child, or her mother should suffer unnecessarily for it (my italics).

Society's is the fault!

Another marked feature of these case-studies is the often expressed view (it is hardly a conception) of marriage as 'just a bit of paper'.* 'When we signed *the bit of paper*...' says one man. 'Marriage doesn't come into it really,' says one of the women. 'I think I'd be too scared that *just that piece of paper* can make so much difference.'

These, surely, are just immature, ill-informed, and irresponsible attitudes? I do not want to leave the impression, however, that this book (and those like it) are entirely without value. They make interesting revelations – as, for example, the fact that sometimes *men* are treated unequally and unjustly when compared with women (e.g. on the amount of maintenance for children they are able to claim.) My essential point is only that they are based upon an extreme feminist position on which even the facts they themselves present throw radical doubt. What is certain is that no persuasive criticism of marriage and the family emerges from them; only – instead – a picture of how unbelievably ill-informed many people seem to be about them, and how ill-prepared they are for entering into them.

LEGALISTIC CONSIDERATIONS

We come now to that kind of contribution which I have no more than indicated from time to time before, though at the same time intimating that, despite my limited comments then, it was the one

---

*See again *The Shaking of the Foundations; Family and Society*, Part II, Chapter 4 (iii) on the nature of marriage.

which – among all the contributions to the literature of the Women's Movement – might well prove ('for better, for worse') to be of the greatest and most far-reaching importance.[7]

From time to time, in the thick of all the heated and weighty arguments about sexuality, the sex-war, etc, we have noted that a concern was voiced about certain insignia of inequality. Why, on marriage, should a woman adopt her husband's surname? Why should she, in particular, be given a ring in the ceremony of marriage, and be expected to wear it? Why should she be expected to live in her husband's domicile? Why should her property, her income, be merged or even taxed in conjunction with his? Why should the children of the marriage, too, adopt her husband's surname? – perhaps bringing to an end the continuity of her own family's name? Why should all these things be an assumed and expected part of marriage? Why should the woman, in particular, have to relinquish so much which, so far in her life, has been her own: of her own family background and tradition; of her own nature? On the face of it, these seem the trivia accompanying the union between a man and a woman which they both mutually desire and to which they are deeply committing themselves. But ... are they trivia? Perhaps not. And though it might be said that these things are merely customary – matters of established convention – and that it would be easier and more comfortable if these sanctioned usages continued, it is perfectly reasonable for women who want equality of status with men to question them. It is, therefore, not only the evident inequalities of income or property, of opportunities in education, employment, career, professional advancement, but *all* such signs and corollaries of women's inequalities with men which have come to be put in question, and such questions require answers.

Clearly, this – in itself – is an enormously complicated aspect of Women's Liberation. It is impossible to consider it in anything approaching full detail, and, indeed, in all its specialised areas goes far beyond any one person's competence. But it is so serious and fundamental a matter that something must be said about it, and here I want to comment on only *one* development: the desire on the part of those wanting to clarify and secure the rights of women to draw up a new *Domestic Law* providing for the contractual regulation of private relationships going beyond those in what we might call conventional marriage, and, indeed, their efforts to do so. Whether for good or for ill – and it may well have elements of both – this desire and these efforts have already produced a detailed *Cohabitation Handbook*, and it is a book of great interest. We have seen that – though without attempting to specify detail – Juliet Mitchell and Germaine Greer (perhaps it might be said of Betty Friedan too) have really wanted not so much the outright *abolition* of marriage and the family as a new diversification of forms of cohabiting relationships within which all people might more fully work out and satisfy their own actually existing needs, wishes, and differences. It is this – a new diversity of commitments among members of households, of domestic groups – which this particular direction of effort has endeavoured to formulate, whilst at the same time offering guidance on the law as it now exists and advice to those who wish seriously to consider their new proposals. Clearly, this is a different kind of literature from the rhetorical arguments we have considered so far – of a different temper and requiring a different temper of consideration.

Elsewhere, I shall want to argue (as mentioned earlier) that the general influence of the literature of the Women's Liberation Movement has had the one harmful consequence, at least, of spreading abroad a half-baked conception of marriage (well evidenced in the *Splitting Up* book just considered), and that this has created an unfortunate tangle in both the law and the social services.* Meanwhile, however, people still *want* to live, and *do* live, in *families*: in small domestic groups within their shared homes, or households. The half-baked chaos of marriages and their breakdown is a conspicuous surface appearance which belies the more fundamental underlying fact that people need and desire to live in families, and do, in fact, live as families. For the present, however, I want only to note what is maintained within this 'legalistic' position itself; in particular the general position which underlies all its specific and detailed formulations.

One quite basic fact seems true: the entire approach of the 'Rights for Women' group is *not opposed to the family*. It is centrally opposed to one thing only: *conventional marriage* (and is critical of the *nuclear family* as defined by marriage as it now exists). And it is opposed to this on two chief grounds: first, that it is in this life-long-binding commitment (as it now exists) that women suffer a loss of status – have to submit to inequalities; and second, that it stands *alone* as the *one* regulated way for the founding of families, of domestic units or groups, when, in fact, people wish to live together in many different forms. Whilst single, following divorce, following bereavement (as widow or widower); as lesbian, as male homosexual;

*In *The Shaking of the Foundations*, I have tried to *defend* the correct conception of marriage – which is, contrary to much current thinking, *more* than a contract.

or as groups of like-minded individuals desiring a collective, communal style of life . . . people wish to cohabit without entering into the bond of conventional marriage, which, in any event, is inappropriate in some of these cases. It is one of the plain facts of social life today (say the authors):

> that more adults and children are spending more of their lives
> outside marriage and the traditional family unit. These
> changes raise new issues. Who should support women with
> children if there is no husband to provide for them? What
> rights should fathers have if they are no longer living with
> children, maintaining them or caring for them? These are now
> central problems in law and social policy . . . (but) . . . in
> England no general principle has been formulated. Changes in
> the legal position of cohabitants have been piecemeal and
> erratic.

The attempt is therefore made to set out proposals which might form the basis for a new and comprehensive domestic law, and in this some of the elements clarified are important.

First, it is made quite clear (and which is true) that in English law there is no such thing as 'common law marriage'. There is no such thing as a 'common law *wife*' or a 'common law *husband*'. These terms are simply euphemisms which seem only to be some kind of seeking of respectability. *Why*, indeed, anyone who has deliberately rejected marriage and chosen to live with someone outside the defining bounds of its commitments and regulations should wish to use the words 'wife' and 'husband' at all is a mystery. But again, I shall argue later that this, too, is one of the absurdities of the present-day state of affairs: namely, that people reject marriage, but, when they encounter difficulties in their relationships, want, nonetheless, to lay claim to all those elements of the law pertaining to marriage – claiming the right to the same (and equal) treatment. The 'Rights for Women' group has the merit of plainly pointing out this misconception.

But second, they show equally clearly what a tangle the law has become. In *some* law (e.g. The Housing (Homeless Persons) Act, 1977; The Inheritance Act, 1975; The Domestic Violence Act, 1976) relationships between cohabitants outside marriage have been recognised; and this is even more true – but in a thoroughly confused way – in the social services. The 'Family Income Supplement' regulations read: 'You can claim if you are single, married, or living with someone as if you are husband and wife – it doesn't matter which one of you is working.' The wording in the Supplementary Benefit leaflet says: 'If you are a couple (married or unmarried) either the man or the woman may be able to claim.' For Child Benefit, too: 'If you are unmarried parents of the child and are living together, the mother should make the claim.' You cannot claim 'One Parent Benefit', however, if 'you are living with someone as husband or wife', and the 'Child's Special Allowance' *ends* if 'you live with a man as his wife'. The law, then, is in a state of confusion. Specific regulations are what they are, and the law can rule clearly on them, and yet they all seem to derive from differing (or at least unclear) foundation principles. Some clarification of domestic law certainly does seem to be required.*

A third obvious point – very clear and simple – is that in all cohabiting groups, whatever form they may take and whatever the desires, beliefs and opinions of the parents in them, the rights of children need protection. This leads these reformers to aim at a domestic law which would recognise both a variety of cohabiting forms and the rights of the individual children (as well as those of adults) within them.

> Central to all our proposals for changing the law is the belief that *all* domestic relationships should be treated equally and unconventional relationships should not be ignored.

Against the claim (or perhaps the fear) that any social widening of a 'law of cohabitation' would undermine marriage itself and the stability of families, it is pointed out that 'common law marriage' or 'marriage by habit and repute' has long existed in Scotland and in France (the *'union libre'*), and within which claims and counter-claims between the partners have been recognised in case law. Swedish family law, too, provides for the problems which arise from 'the cohabitation of a man and a woman with family functions' and aims 'not to give a privileged status to one form of cohabitation over others'. In the United States, too, cases of cohabitation are arising (e.g. the Marvin Case) in which the claims of the partners will be considered in the courts, which will 'try to give effect to individual intentions'. None of this would satisfy English law at present, or the English conception of marriage, but it is interesting to know that such legal recognition of a wider law of cohabitation can and does exist.

*The movement towards a fully clarified *Domestic Law* could well parallel the movement (already very clearly in evidence) towards a single *Family Court*.

The final, and extremely important recognition and insistence is that no new form of cohabitation can be, or can be allowed to remain, a purely *private* matter.

> Whatever your personal reasons may be for the way you live, private relationships, especially those between men and women, are a public matter. The law has always been concerned with marriage. People who 'cohabit' do not avoid this public concern.

The casual and irresponsible attitudes towards 'cohabitation' which sometimes seem so widespread, receive no support whatever here. And the new system of domestic law which is set out to protect the equality of women:

> which gives women individual access to waged work and benefits regardless of their domestic circumstances ... Women should not have to look to individual men for their livelihood. The inequities between men and women in society generally cannot be resolved by private redistribution ...

– nonetheless focuses upon '*the household unit and its members*' (whatever form this might take besides that of the orthodox family).

> Our aim has been to define *the key subject for domestic law as the relationship between individuals in a shared home.* In contrast, the cornerstone of family law has until now been the dependence of married women on their husbands. Understanding the position of women within the family is a central task of the women's liberation movement.* By tracing the legal position of cohabitants outside marriage much light can be thrown on marriage itself. In suggesting changes in the legal position of cohabitants we have been concerned not just to give legal status to previously unrecognised relationships, but rather *to try to create a framework in which women and men can achieve free, equal and independent relationships* (my italics).

This, clearly, is an entirely positive and constructive approach. The entire system then outlined is very complicated. Rules are

---

*Strictly speaking, this makes *the family* (rather than *marriage*) the key focus of domestic law – echoing the emphasis of Westermarck. It also reflects the most recent emphasis of Betty Friedan: that '*the family is the new Feminist Frontier*'.

proposed covering, for example: the changing or retention of names, the nature of homes (rented or owned), homelessness, domestic violence, the sharing of living costs, the bringing up of children, death and inheritance, etc ... in particular outlining the possibilities and forms of 'Cohabitation Contracts'. It is impossible to enter into all these details, but only two concluding points need to be made at the moment.

First, it seems clear that it is in *this* way, more perhaps than in any other, that all the many implications (apparently large and apparently small) of the movement towards equality in the status of women may be clearly worked out; and in *this* way that social changes may come to be fully recognised, considered, and evaluated, and the regulatory structure of society be appropriately and effectively transformed. A *transformation*, too, it will most certainly be.*

And second – perhaps the most interesting consideration of all – it *does* seem that a new and entire system of domestic law can at least be envisaged in provisional outline: a kind of Bill of Rights for individuals in familial relationships; a comprehensive framework of recognised forms of cohabitation and the statuses of persons within them. These might, for example, include (i) marriage and the family as it now exists, (ii) marriage of a more limited nature – with more specifically defined commitments, (iii) cohabitation – with specific

---

*It is bound, too, to be a transformation attended by many detailed and perhaps unforeseen difficulties. For example, the very recent decision of the European Court that, in England, women as well as men may not be compelled to retire until the age of 65 has raised curious problems – not the least being that of a new inequality of men! The court's ruling was conceded in the Government's consultative document *Sex Discrimination and Retirement*. But on 5 April 1986, the Equal Opportunities Commission condemned them both as being 'unfair to men'. *The Times* reported:

> The situation arises because the European Court ruling and the Government's document say nothing about pensions ... Nor do they say anything about giving men the option of retiring at 60 instead of 65. ...
> 90% of Britain's company pension schemes work on the basis that women retire and take their pension at 60 and men at 65. If a woman was allowed, under the new law, to carry on working until 65 she could still take her pension at 60 while her male counterparts would still have to wait an extra 5 years for theirs.

The transformation of the law (which both *reflects* and *is* a change in the entire structure of society) is bound to be a long and troubled process.

definitions of the interrelationships and chosen name, (iv) a shared household – with members and names, (v) kinds of 'collectives' or 'communes' – again with specific contractual definitions and obligations, (vi) lesbian or male homosexual relationships – with the commitments and degree of permanency desired. A comprehensive set of categories might be gradually drawn up, with specified kinds of contractual and legally recognised rights and duties, social service entitlements and claims; and perhaps *all* of these (not only conventional marriage) could be declared ('solemnised') before the Public Registrar. Private and public responsibility could therefore be required and insisted upon; personal irresponsibility and a casual arbitrariness among relationships carrying serious consequences could be removed – or at least minimised. Such a possibility is, at least, an interesting consideration, and – bearing in mind, for example, the variety of provisions in Roman Law and those made in the common law of some modern societies – within the bounds of realistic achievement. Indeed, it is difficult to see how the many claims for change of our own age can possibly be met without some such over-all drafting of a new Domestic Law. All the piecemeal developments which are being forced upon the law – in terms of sheer practicability – to deal with the scale and complexity of 'family and matrimonial proceedings', are increasingly moving towards the creation of a single Family Court. Perhaps the time has come, alongside this, to formulate an entire system of Domestic Law on the basis of which this court could adjudicate.

However all this may be, it does seem that it is these legalistic considerations and efforts within the Women's Liberation Movement – though making least noise – which may prove to have the greatest effect and most important long-term consequences. They have, too, the great merit of insisting upon care, thoughtfulness, and the important consideration of making written contractual agreements when entering into relationships which have recognised public implications – so eliminating 'half-baked' notions; and in recognising, too, the importance of primary domestic groups whilst individual rights are being protected.

There is no flamboyant rhetoric, no irresponsibility, here.

RECONSIDERATION AND MODERATION

Finally, we can briefly note, too, some substantial and significant continuity in the more *moderate* positions within the Women's

Liberation Movement as well as in those which are more extreme. Two examples will be enough: that of Erin Pizzey, who has reconsidered her earlier extreme feminist position and changed her mind, and that of Elaine Morgan who stands in a class of her own.

(i) Erin Pizzey

We saw how Germaine Greer had 'suffered a sea-change' ('into something rich and strange!') and had made a U-turn in certain quite basic respects on her earlier position. Erin Pizzey is an example within this same category. Her own stance has never professed the same intellectual thoroughness as Germaine Greer's; her U-turn has been more frank and complete; and she probably represents, more generally, the views of many women who – certainly desiring an improvement in their status – are nonetheless themselves put off by the extremists in the movement. And again, more openly than most, she readily concedes that the earlier protest of many women stemmed, strictly speaking, from the pain and embitterment of their own experience of a failed marriage rather than any well-considered judgment about marriage as such. Erin Pizzey, having herself had a miserable experience in her first marriage was, for a time, a member of a battered wives refuge (in Chiswick) and shared a house with women friends in Bristol. She joined the first feminist march through London, and – almost to her disbelief – found herself appalled at the sheer hatred of men which was then displayed. Soon, too, she found their group invaded by feminist 'organisers' who insisted that they were a 'collective' and that they should call each other 'comrades'.

> 'Women don't need men' was the main underlying message
> behind all the reasonable talk about equality. 'You can have
> it all' was the second message. 'Divest yourself of your
> boring, ordinary husband. Take the house, keep the children
> and as much of his income as you can grasp, and boot the
> bastard out.'

Objecting to this kind of position, she was officially banned from collectives and from the Women's Liberation Movement, but then saw her friends, under this kind of influence, sacrifice their husbands and children for their own freedom – only (literally) to take to the bottle and find themselves alone – and unbearably lonely. Furthermore, the revolution which had taken place from the early 1970s had had the consequence of turning men away from women, and they, she felt, were coping with their new situation more satisfactorily than the wives who had left them. For her, and – in her judgment – for many of her early feminist friends, the revolution had been a misguided tragedy, a mistake. Happily re-married now, she concedes that the whole protest (for many women – though by no means for all) was falsely based. Concerned still about equality of status for women, more nurseries, better contraceptives and choice and control over childbirth, more play groups, etc., she cannot believe that to pursue these ends satisfactorily means the destruction or abandonment of marriage and family life.

> I look at my beautiful daughter who is a single parent, and I, at 46, feel that her generation have been the casualties of an incoherent philosophy that grew out of rage. The concept of equality never seemed to include keeping and improving what was finest in family life – the support system that enabled us as women to achieve our own aims.
> Now ... I see the tide receding. We must ensure that all we have gained, such as the right to choose our own contraception and the right to control what happens to our bodies, must not be swept away with all that has been destructive ...
> The relationships between men and women have to be a compromise. I don't want a feminised man for a husband ... A man who truly loves a woman wants to marry her. Marriage is a compromise between two very disparate human beings ... and now I have what I always believed possible – an equal partnership.

For some feminists, at any rate (as with Betty Friedan), to seek the improved status of women does *not* mean a negative criticism and abandonment of marriage and the family. On the contrary, for them it can only be achieved with the preservation and qualitative improvement of them.

(ii) Elaine Morgan

The last writer we have to consider stands quite alone within the women's movement. Moderate, balanced, judicious, her arguments always deeply considered and intellectually well-founded, but always down-to-earth and rooted in (and tested by) the firm actualities of common experience, she is – compared with all the others – a positive joy to read. It is Elaine Morgan, and the book I have in mind is *The Descent of Woman*.[8] Her position deserves a far fuller critique than space here allows, but, so different is she from other writers, that some of the major points within it will be enough, alone, to indicate her soundness.

Her book differs chiefly from others in that it is not just a rhetorical outpouring of argument about the problems of women (is not narrowly concerned with this alone) but offers, and rests upon, a very profound outline of the nature of evolution (including a specific theory of it) and, in particular, of the evolution of humankind. Indeed, her discussion of evolutionary theory is far more acute and profound than (in her down-to-earth language) it seems, and than orthodox (academic) scholars in biology and ethology will admit. It is, I repeat, a sheer joy. With a humour and style which, on occasion, closely resembles that of both P. G. Wodehouse and Thurber,* she quietly, rather mockingly, but altogether correctly, points out the superficiality and weakness of many of the enormous (and yet unquestioningly accepted) generalisations of orthodox evolutionary theory, and the utter paucity of evidence for them. Scholars themselves will neither make nor concede these kinds of criticism, but she – non-academic as far as the biological and human sciences are concerned – makes them in a delightful non-academic way which is, nonetheless, *true*. She then moves to the theory which she finds most intriguing and satisfactory – that resting on the suggestions of Alistair Hardy – and which she has more fully expounded elsewhere,** but it lies, alas, too far beyond our own purpose to consider this here. It is enough, perhaps, to say that her general conclusions about much that is claimed in the over-all theory of evolution, and, in particular, what has been said on the basis of it (and by Freud and others within psychology) about the nature of 'the female sexual response' can be summed up in two of her sentences.

Most fair-minded readers will agree that the status quo as outlined above could reasonably be described as foggy.*** I can think of only one other subject which in the same period has spawned so many experts all heatedly contradicting one another, and that is economics.

*Those who know Thurber's fables will find the flavour of him in, for example, this kind of description of the sea cow: 'Only instead of staying there for ten million years she stayed forever, and grew soggy and torpid, and lost her legs and most of the features of her face and degenerated into a great fat ugly six-foot blob of glup.'
** *The Aquatic Ape* [9]
***Those who know and love Wodehouse will find his flavour in this.

But on the basis of her own (and Hardy's) version of these matters, she has telling – and again quietly stated and well-founded – things to say about the two sexes and the nature of marriage and the family in human experience.

Without dwelling too much on the validity or otherwise of the rootedness of her points in her general sketch of human evolution, it is possible to itemise some of them which are so firmly grounded as to compel consideration. She believes, for example, that there is a decided *difference* in the sexuality of men and that of women; a difference, too, which marks the human species off from other closely related animals. In particular, as distinct from all other primates, *oestrus* disppeared during the course of evolution and 'never returned to the female of homo sapiens'. The marked periodicity of undiscriminating readiness for presenting and intercourse vanished. In men, however, sexual desire continued as before, resulting in a certain discrepancy or lack of it. Somewhere in the deep layers of the male mind, she suggests:

> is a deeply buried conviction that there is something prissy and phoney about the way women carry on, and that if they weren't so damned hypocritical there should be times for every one of them – say one week in four – when she careered round the streets gaily admitting that she was mad for it, soliciting sex from all comers like a young howler monkey, and pursuing her prey until the sun went down. . . .
> Alas for homo sap., we don't behave like that anymore. We are not the match for him that we were originally designed to be. We chase after him for love, companionship, excitement, curiosity, security, a home and family, prestige, escape, or the joy of being held in his arms. But there still remains a basic imbalance between the urgency of his lust and ours, so that when it comes to the crunch the prostitute is always on a sellers' market.

Along this same line of argument, discussing the contemporary emphasis on sex, orgasms, and the like, she comes to the matter of *love*.

> We have now taken the reckless step of admitting into the discussion what many scientists tend to treat as the ultimate four-letter word. Masters and Johnson are pretty outspoken, but they know where to draw the line, and you don't often catch them bandying terms like that around. There is a

widely held belief that while 'sex' has a nice hard edge to it, 'love' is wishy-washy, and that women tend to talk about love while men tend to talk about sex merely because women are too mealy-mouthed to say what they really mean.

Very few thinkers have seriously explored the hypothesis that perhaps they tend to say love because they tend to *mean* love.

Perhaps, after all, it is *love* which women want? And perhaps men, too? But this then comes to be considered in relation to the family and marriage. Pouring gentle, good-humoured scorn on what she calls the 'Tarzanist-type' theories of 'Man the Hunter', she nonetheless makes some firm points about the origin and development of the human family – one might also say of the 'nuclear family' (i.e. of the kind of family natural to man within the pressing environmental conditions within which he had to struggle for survival) – during the era of 'Man the Hunter': the Pleistocene era. 'True man, homo sapiens proper,' she says, 'is the child of the Pleistocene,' and she believes it probable that the evolution of the human family had 'more to do with economics than with sex'. She points to three chief factors which, together, interestingly enough, point to the *father*, as well as the *mother*, as an *essential* member of the family.

Firstly, pointing to the development of the brain and the size of the skull of the human child, she claims that children had to be born 'at an increasingly "premature" stage*' (or they would never have passed through the pelvic ring at all) and so (the important point) had *a longer period of complete helplessness*. The young male (as well as female) child would spend a long period of infancy and pre-adult life closely dependent upon and associated with his mother and her other offspring. Secondly, in the hunting-gathering economy, when food – when plentiful – had to be securely stored, and when, gradually, tools, implements, and methods for dealing with it (cooking it, sharing it, etc.) were cumulatively developed, came the importance of *the lair*. The intimate 'matrifocal' group – for shelter and security in all respects – would establish a *home*. The relationship between mother and male offspring, even among some apes, lasts eight years or longer. This would most probably be extended between

---

*This bears an interesting relationship to theories of 'neoteny' – something which is probably of crucial significance for an understanding of the nature of man, and of the part played in the evolution of man by *culture*.

human mothers and sons, and so – Elaine Morgan suggests – the *habitual orientation* of a male towards a female-centred kin-group and towards a home would be established; as would be the desire (and continued habit) to continue and re-establish such a group when the mother died, or when adulthood came.* Within this context of attachment and habitual usage, the sense of *property* and *jealousy* could be expected to arise,** and, within the male, the disposition towards both the *protection* of his own and the desire for the *exclusivity of the bond between himself and his own*. As Elaine Morgan puts it in her matter-of-fact way:

'This is *my* woman,' he told himself, '...this is *my* place ... these are *my* children...'. He had horned in good and proper on the matrifocal family group, and was well on his way to becoming Daddy.

But the third fact is very specifically rooted in the environmental conditions (the *collective conditions*, the *life conditions****) of the period, and is very telling indeed. It points to the establishing of the *father* as an *essential component* in the human family. Speaking of the Pleistocene era, Elaine Morgan says:

In those turbulent millennia when the hominid wandered over the face of the earth, when the northern hemisphere pendulumed between ages of ice and ages of greenness, and the southern hemisphere between dusty dearth and torrential rains, then the third factor came into play. *If the nuclear family had not acquired a father by that time it would have been necessary to invent him.* Again and again the human family must have passed through eras of climatic crises when almost every living child had a father whose devotion to the

---

*Again, interesting conjectures arise here about the possible element of 'seeking a mother' in the adult male's sexual desire for a mate and a home, and of the possible element of 'protectiveness towards a son' in the adult female's sexual desire for a husband and father of her own children. Much more could be explored here about these components and dimensions of human 'love'.
**Again, it is interesting to consider the possibility that *jealousy* (often frowned upon) performs, in fact, a positive function.
***I emphasise these terms to indicate their relatedness to the positions of some important sociological theorists – notably Durkheim, who claimed that social institutions originated in 'the collective conditions within which the group as a whole is placed'.

family group was unshakeable – not because there is some reserve of nobility in the human heart which adversity invariably calls forth, but simply because a baby with any other sort of father would have died (my italics).

This, to my mind, is a point of crucial importance. It says that as soon as *homo sapiens* proper emerged in the long evolutionary history of humankind, the nuclear family was *the* distinctive domestic human group (whatever the wider and various networks of kindred which came to be socially and culturally developed). And, to move right back to one of our starting points, it will be seen at once that this view is entirely in keeping with the specific view arrived at after long comparative study by Edward Westermarck – whose claim was:

> it is originally for the benefit of the young that male and female continue to live together. We may therefore say that marriage is rooted in the family rather than the family in marriage.

The conjugal and parental sentiments came to be founded and deeply established within the necessitous bonds of these relationships. Far from being a domestic group brought into being very recently by 'exploitative capitalism', so requiring demolition, there are firm grounds for supposing that the nuclear family – within all the complexities of modern society – might well be that small remaining group which has been the most natural for human beings from their very first emergence as *homo sapiens* onwards. To destroy this group would therefore be to destroy what has been the most basic and abiding context for the making and realisation of human nature from time immemorial – from mankind's very beginning.

So much – and very important it is – for Elaine Morgan's suggestions about the nature of the family group and the emergence of marriage from it. It is equally important to note, however, that she is far from holding the view that 'nature' and even 'human nature' are such as to guarantee the everlasting survival of the family, and she goes on to analyse other psychological dispositions (e.g. of aggression in the nature of the male) which, within the collective conditions of modern society, are dangerously destructive, and could, without successful curbing, become even more so. We come then, however, to Elaine Morgan's observations on the issues of the status of women, and women's liberation, and what – in her view women actually want. In all this, too, she is decidedly on the side of 'the moderates'.

She is decidedly *not* moderate, however, in her appraisal of the extent to which (given the origins of the family and marriage) women have subsequently come to be subjected to the power of men, and it is here that her chosen title – *The Descent of Woman* – becomes significant: having, now, not only evolutionary implications, but implications, too, for the long historical story of decline and social inferiority.

> The phrase 'the descent of woman' had ... acquired a more than genealogical significance ... Woman had descended so far that in many, perhaps most, human communities she was regarded as congenitally inferior – physically, mentally, and morally. Sometimes this conviction went so far that it amounted to what is called 'pseudo-speciation' – she was thought of as not quite part of the human race. Men would debate in sober earnest the question of whether women could be held to have souls.

She believes, however, that most of the past wrongs and sufferings of women are being put right.

> So many lies about the inferiority of women have been exploded that she now sometimes believes that except in strictly physical terms there is, or need be, no difference at all between women and men. She has equality before the law (or very nearly), and she has the vote, and earning power, and education, and the pill.

Why is it, then, that it is particularly in the countries 'in the capitalist world' where the new freedoms have gone furthest, that women are:

> most strident, most discontented, most ready to march about with banners and complain about the dreariness of their lot, and their frustrations, and about being sexual objects, and about their need of liberation...?

At least three things, she believes, have gone wrong: the relations of women (1) with their children, (2) with men, and (3) with other women, and we can note her comments on the first two of these as being (in her view) the most important.

One thing which women actually want, she insists, is their children – and she criticises as an outright mistake and foolishness the rejection of motherhood and all that it offers to the nature of women on the part of many of the 'Women's Libbers'. She is very decided about this. Why, she asks, do liberationists:

> groan and growl when they hear people croon about the joys of motherhood? Has a yuch reaction really crept into this relationship, like the Victorians' yuch about intercourse? Having more or less exploded the myth that some women are frigid to the delights of sex, are we now to discover that some are frigid to the pleasures of maternity? ... There is a vague idea floating around that only dimwits can really enjoy bringing up babies.

– and she proceeds to describe the pleasures of motherhood in a way which – *now!* – would meet with the entire approval of Germaine Greer. But in earlier days, Germaine Greer, Shulamith Firestone, and Kate Millett were very different, and Elaine Morgan shows here impatience with them all. Kate Millett's suggestion of devolving the care of children on to 'trained professionals' receives short shrift.

> does she really believe the average city school, any more than the average conveyor belt, is really staffed by idealistic trained practitioners who have 'chosen it as a vocation'? Most of them become teachers for the same reason that Jane Eyre became a governess, because they have to earn a living, and this seems the least distasteful of the avenues open to them.

And as for Germaine Greer:

> Germaine Greer urges the runaway wife to leave her children behind if necessary because 'he is more likely to be able to pay a housekeeper or a nanny than a woman is'. And when she suggested liberating women by the pleasure principle – 'it is possible to use even cooking, clothes, cosmetics, and housekeeping for *fun*' – it just never came into her mind to include the baby as one of the fun things. The best way to deal with *him*, failing a nanny, is by a communal household, so that women can take turns in 'liberating' one another from him.

As we have seen, however, Germaine Greer has now turned her back on all of this.

The most unfortunate aspect of the relationship between women and men which has gone wrong in both the family and society is, she believes, *economic*. If the domestic work and the care devoted to children was evaluated in monetary terms, it would, she says, 'amount to a whacking great chunk of the gross national income', but she is not extreme even in this.

I do not suggest that the contribution made to society in this way should necessarily by evaluated and paid for. But the fact that the occupation of housewife and mother is *not* economically evaluated – and it is pretty well unique among occupations in this respect – has had far-reaching consequences.

One major result has been the creation of 'a discontented work force', and one further result of this could be 'that you will end up with an inferior product. That's going to be a very bad day for everybody.' If her contribution *was* sufficiently recognised, however, a woman within the family 'might begin to feel that her job was as important as his' (her husband's), and 'might even rediscover that this job is far more rewarding and creative than most'.

It is in her recommendations for the future that Elaine Morgan's moderation becomes particularly clear. Like some others we have mentioned, but more clearly and directly, she points to the dangers for both men and women of a 'sex-obsessed society', and of the position of the more extreme feminists. Strangely, she points out, women are becoming more and more – not less and less – 'sexual objects', and are being increasingly treated as such by the advertisers and the media.* Strangely, too, this, far from making liberated women more attractive to men, is turning men against them – is creating an active distaste and dislike for them. And for *both* sexes, the focus on sexual appetite alone is something which, yielding diminishing returns, needs continual 'super-normal' stimulation which has to feed upon itself in order to be continually effective.

In some of its more extreme aspects the sexual revolution seems to have passed the point of campaigning for the liberation of a natural appetite, and reached the vomitorial stage of trying to reactivate an exhausted one.**

---

*It may be of parallel significance, too, that sexual assault and rape seem to be increasing rather than decreasing – as though the assertion of power in getting sheer sexual gratification is more, rather than less, insistent, and less, rather than more, restrained.
**A reference to the practice of the Romans in keeping alive their appetite for food: the building of vomitoria where they could go and empty their stomachs – and then come back for more!

All, she concludes, are likely to 'end up losers on the deal'.

She also condemns the tendency in Kate Millett and others towards 'feminine macho' within the Women's Movement: 'alleging the whole male sex to be a ferocious leopard and whipping up hatred for it'. As part of this, she also deliberately finds room for those women who actually and positively *like* being housewives.

what on earth is wrong with being house-proud if that's what turns you on? Keeping a house beautiful is no more barren or 'stultifying' a job than a professional gardener's keeping a garden beautiful.

What she *does* call for is a greater *respect* for women *as* women (i.e. the recognition that being a woman carries with it something of which to be proud); an effective economic independence of women so that her agreement to marry (if that is what she chooses) is *not* regarded as a contract for 'a meal-ticket for the rest of my life'; and the *certainty* of having no more children than she wants (including none at all – if that is what she wants). None of this at all stands in the way of the normal (traditional) division-of-labour nuclear family – which she has shown to be so deeply grounded in conditions of the past – and, on the question of marriage, she is eminently sane.

What about marriage? The more way-out liberationists seem to be hell-bent on destroying the institution. I can't quite see why there has to be a 'policy' about this. When we're just getting loose of one lot of people laying down the law that we *must* get married, it's a bit rough to run head on into another lot telling us we mustn't. It is surely, as Oscar Wilde ruled about the tallness of aunts, a matter that a girl may be allowed to decide for herself.

Anyway, marriage is going to be with us for a long time yet ... It can sometimes be tough for two people of opposite sexes trying to live permanently at close quarters without driving each other up the wall. But it can be equally tough trying to do it with someone of the same sex, or with a child, or a parent, or a sibling, or a colleague; or with a succession of different partners; or with a commune (for the rate of failed communes is at least as high as the rate of failed marriages). And it can be toughest of all trying to live in an empty house or apartment quite alone.

And, pointing to the greater maladjustment of single people as against married people (and particularly of single *men*) – in 'indices of unhappiness, severe neurotic tendencies, and anti-social tendencies', her conclusion is:

> Marriage (or something less legalistic but the same in essence) will certainly endure until the people who say it is a miserable institution can come up with a convincing answer to the question, 'Compared to what?' I haven't been convinced by any of the answers yet.

This brief note is far from doing justice to the many qualities of Elaine Morgan's work, but she is undoubtedly one of the best exponents of the more moderate positions within the Women's Liberation Movement, and this without at all minimising the problems which women face or her own desire for a solution to them. In her position, again, the family and marriage remain intact, and we are now in a position to draw together a few conclusions.

Conclusions

It seems sensible and worthwhile to divide these into two groups: first, those which make, perhaps surprisingly, quite positive statements about the family and marriage; second, those which seem to be explanations of the questions arising from these.

Five positive conclusions seem clear beyond all doubt and are very important.

(1) *It is not true that the Women's Liberation Movement rejects marriage and advocates the abolition of the family (even of the 'nuclear' family).*
The widespread notion that this is so turns out to have no foundation; to be a plain mistake. We have seen that even the most extreme 'revolutionary' writers (such as Juliet Mitchell and Germaine Greer) argue only for greater *diversity* in the forms of cohabitation recognised by society and the law, and want, in particular, to see all such nuclear families, domestic groups, or households (whatever their form) living within the wider contexts of their 'extended' kinship relationships or improved and supportive community conditions. Even Germaine Greer (initially with her 'self-regulating organic families' and later with her analysis of the 'nuclear cells' within the entire network of 'familial relationships') agrees quite decidedly in this. When we turn to the more moderate writers, however (including the 'founder' of modern Women's Lib – Betty Friedan – and Elaine Morgan), the truth of our conclusion is over-

whelmingly clear. For them, the family as the primary domestic group within the community, and marriage as the institution by which partners commit themselves to its foundation, continuity and stability (particularly, but by no means only, for the care and well-being of their children), remain of the most fundamental importance and value for both society and individuals. Betty Friedan, indeed, sees the family as 'the new frontier of feminism', and Elaine Morgan can so far see no alternative which satisfies her. Elaine Morgan, too, has provided quite crucial grounds for believing that – despite all the obscuring dust stirred up by recent extremes of argument – the family proves to have been, throughout far and away the greater part of human evolution and history, the most basic and most abiding group in society. Despite the considerations from all points of view – throughout the whole spectrum of opinions from the most extreme to the moderate – the importance of the family and marriage remains fully recognised in the literature of Women's Lib, and this conclusion deserves the firmest emphasis and the widest possible dissemination. There are still many to whom it will come as a surprise; many for whom Women's Lib has been thought to be synonymous with the rejection of the family and marriage. But such an interpretation is quite *false* – and can no longer be held.

(2) *It is not true that the Women's Liberation Movement denigrates the desire for fertility and the nature of motherhood.*
On the contrary, within the continued positive appraisal of the family, there has been, too, an almost universal recognition of the importance to women of fertility and motherhood – and not only with the welfare of children in mind, but also for mothers themselves. Indeed, it has come to emphasise the joys (as well as the pain, problems, and work involved) of motherhood, and the deeply satisfying pleasures to be found by women in sharing the concerns and delights of motherhood. This is so clear as to need no further emphasis, but again it deserves reiteration that even Germaine Greer – so often thought of (from the influence of her earlier writings) as the extreme denouncer of marriage and the family – has come to be fully in agreement with this. The very positive evaluation of fertility and motherhood is now perhaps the most central emphasis in her position.

(3) *It is not true that the Women's Liberation Movement rejects the place and importance of the father in the family.*
This conclusion stems from many sources. One thing widely agreed is that – whatever may be claimed as to the right of people to establish single-parent-families, whatever may be claimed concerning the

rights of the members of such families, and whatever the increase in the number of them – these families generally face grave and perhaps insuperable difficulties. In general, they have to struggle with conditions pressing them towards poverty, and are in many ways disadvantaged. Again, even Germaine Greer believes it impossible to have a child and to care satisfyingly and satisfactorily for it whilst at the same time trying to hold down a job (and, presumably, uninterruptedly pursuing a career). This points, surely, to the sanity of *partnership* between a man and a woman in the family. Elaine Morgan quite definitely and conspicuously (but it is true, too, of Betty Friedan, Erin Pizzey and others) claims that there is no difficulty in sustaining the 'division-of-labour nuclear family' whilst at the same time insisting on the equal status of men and women. The two things are not incompatible; not mutually exclusive. Indeed, she, in particular, has not only demonstrated the firm grounding of the family in the struggle for survival within the earliest environmental conditions of mankind, but also – within this context – the *essential* place and functions of the *father*. Without the father, she claims, neither families nor children could have survived. Part of this same conclusion too – one other source of it – is the recognition of the fact that there are *differences* in the nature of men and women; differences in their *sexuality* too; and that these differences, and their *complementarity*, require recognition and understanding, and in no way prevent the achievement of the equality of status between the sexes. As in other areas of claims and counter-claims (education, etc.) in the many issues surrounding the relationships between the sexes, *equality*, as a principle of social justice, is decidedly *not* an insistence that men and women are, *in fact, the same*. The extreme rejection of men, and of marriage, by a few vocal 'Women's Libbers' is not only ill-considered nonsense, but carries grave dangers in the deliberate advocacy of 'one-parent families': dangers of sacrificing the rights, interests, and happiness of children on the altar of some supposed 'principle' of women's freedom. *Partnership* – with equality of status and equality of consideration and mutual respect – is surely the recommendation which emerges strongly here.

(4) *It is not true that the Women's Liberation Movement focuses upon sexuality alone, or advocates a free indulgence in sexuality alone, without reference to other dimensions of human nature, feeling, and companionship.*

On the contrary, there is a wide agreement among women writers that the obsession with sexual excitation and gratification alone may well have become distorting, increasingly unsatisfying for both women and men, increasingly destructive of their relationships, tending to blind both to other important and deeply felt aspects (perhaps *needs*) of their nature. This conclusion can be mentioned only briefly because it is one of the most profound points of all, and difficult to write about satisfactorily. A book in its own right would be necessary even to approach doing full justice to it. Elaine Morgan touches on it in her suggestion that when women talk about 'love', perhaps they actually *mean* 'love', and that this may entail something more than (for example) 'experiencing multiple orgasms until the limit of physical exhaustion is reached'. The natures of men and women have dimensions going beyond their sexuality (though, no doubt, being intimately related to it), and it is difficult to see how any relationship between a man and woman which fails to see, know, or find close communion in these, can possibly be a full relationship of love. And marriage, properly conceived, requires such a relationship of love. One can do no better, again, than refer to Shakespeare, and, indeed, a brief contrast between what extreme Women's Libbers have to say about 'sex' and what Shakespeare has to say about 'love' will at least serve to indicate the gulf that I have in mind. Compare, for example, Germaine Greer's statement that 'a clitoral orgasm with a full cunt is nicer than a clitoral orgasm with an empty one' and that 'a man is more than a dildo', or Debbie Taylor's – that penetrative sexual intercourse 'gives a man the perfect moist sensual environment for his penis', whilst a woman's clitoris must snatch at what pleasure it can from crude, dry, pelvic bumping and grinding' – with Shakespeare's portrayal of the love between (say) Othello and Desdemona, thrown into disarray and wrecked by the calculated poison of Iago, or of Hamlet's anguish over a nobility of love between his father and mother soiled and brought down by deceit and wantonness, or with his sonnet on 'the marriage of true minds' ... and the gulf between 'sex' and 'love' is very plain. The mystery, indeed, is how anyone could ever have failed to be aware of it. And Shakespeare was quite sure about the ideality of love and the reality of this ideality in love's actuality. He was philosopher enough to see and know clearly the reality of idealities in the actuality of human experience.

> If this be error and upon me proved,
> I never writ, nor no man ever loved.

A comment of A. E. Housman's, reiterated by Philip Larkin, is also relevant here: 'anyone who thinks he has loved more than one person has simply never really loved at all.' Some may not have known love. Some may therefore lack the eye that can see. But this does not mean that love in human experience does not exist, or that – whether within marriage or outside it – all its dimensions can be reduced to, or are to be equated with, 'sex'.

Stated in its simplest terms, this conclusion is – quite starkly – that sex (with all the liberation, stimulation, and heightened excitation of it) is not enough. As in Plato's picture of the human soul, the hydra-headed monster of our appetites and desires – if ungoverned – can usurp, displace and despoil all the elements of spirit and reason in us – leading, through the growing tyranny of its insatiable and all-engulfing hunger, to shapeless and undiscriminating anarchy.

(5) *It is not true that the Women's Liberation Movement (including the Rights for Women group) advocates casual and freely chosen cohabitation which is not responsive to public obligations and responsible to the law.*

On the contrary, the most exacting examination of the detailed legal considerations necessary to ensure the equality of women in relation to all the 'insignia' of their status (their name, domicile, property, income, etc., on marriage or cohabitation) has proved such as to insist upon the greatest degree of care and responsibility in entering into *any* form of cohabitation. It has made it quite clear that no such thing as 'common law marriage' exists in English law, and that such terms as common law 'wife' or 'husband' are mere euphemisms. It has made it clear, too, that private relationships, especially those between men and women, are a public matter, having public consequences and entailing public obligations. Also, and in particular, it has found it necessary to focus its attention upon *the domestic group within the shared household* in order to define and secure the rights of all the individual members of them. Critical of *conventional marriage* (and its implications as it now exists in the law) it has therefore not been destructively opposed to *the family*, but, again, has explored the possible *diversity* of contractual forms of cohabitation believed necessary to give effect to the existing diversity of needs, wishes, and intentions among all the members of society. There is nothing in the specifically *legalistic* literature of the Women's Liberation Movement to advocate or uphold attitudes of irresponsibility towards society and the law. If new forms of cohabitation are to be considered – then they deserve careful definition, serious undertakings and responsible commitments between the individual partners within the law. Nothing of a casual nature receives any support.

Certainly *some* women writers have – in their aggressive, revolutionary rhetoric – adopted exaggerated and extreme positions, but when the whole literature of the movement is taken into account, the five positive conclusions outlined above can be seen to be true. They are also firm and important, giving a picture quite different from that which has come to be thought the aim of Women's Lib: i.e. the *demolition* of marriage and the family. But this conclusion itself gives rise to another question. How – if it is true that these conclusions are validly drawn from the literature – has such widespread misunderstanding come about? The answer leads to a number of quite different but equally telling conclusions.

(1) *Attacks – not criticisms* Firstly, the most conspicuous public outbursts of the extreme Women's Libbers were not considered *criticisms* of the family and marriage so much as *attacks* upon them. Spreading out widely through public opinion from the Women's Lib Movement – like the ripples spreading to all parts of a pond from a stone splashed violently into the centre – the caricature assumption came to be established that the pursuit of equality for women meant the denunciation and derogation of the family and marriage. The same is true of attitudes towards men. Among the extremists, these rested not on any serious appraisal of the place of the father in the family (and an appreciation of his *own* difficulties within the collective conditions of modern society), but were an outright attack on 'Patriarchy', the tyrannical power of men, entailing – among the most extreme writers – a virulent hatred of men and of male sexuality. Attacks – not criticisms – were the rule.

(2) *Sensationalism – the media* The vehicle for the spreading of this assumption was the passion for sensationalism of the middle-men-of-communications who feed on the 'newsworthy problems' of society and flock to 'a good story' like rootless iron filings tugged to the nearest face of the strongest magnet. The publishers, editors, critics, producers, journalists who form the collective filter of 'knowledge' and opinion in our mass society are attracted not primarily to the truth but chiefly to what – in their own particular medium – will *sell*. The most forceful, glib, clever-seeming, up-to-the-minute fashion; the headline-catching phrase or stance or story ... these attract their attention: those things which will advance their own reputation, career, viewing audience, sales. Within this field the women's columnists and editors of women's magazines loom large, though they are by no means alone. It was, therefore, not *all* the literature of *all* the women's writers which was read (by and large it is not *books* which are read), but the most conspicuous ripples passing through the media. Women and girls who would never buy a book could not fail to be aware of these.

(3) *The loudest noises – the most extreme sources*   It was, therefore
– and understandably – the most extreme position within Women's
Lib which spread most widely and rapidly, and, as we have seen, the
Women's Liberation Movement was not lacking in extremists only
too ready to feed and use all the avenues of the media open to them.
The more extreme sources made the loudest noises, and some of
these sources have become clear. One was that of those embittered
wives (and, more rarely, embittered husbands) who attacked
marriage and the family in part because their own marriages had
failed, because their own families had broken down, and they had
been left in traumatic conditions of stress, hardship, and loneliness.
Another was that of lesbians and others who harboured a positive
hatred of men. A third was that of the political ideologues (chiefly
Marxists) who always seize on any strand of social discontent or disorder to further their aim of the revolutionary transformation of
society. The simple truth here is that when a band-wagon is seen to
be moving, all kinds of fellow-travellers eagerly jump on to it to
enjoy their own kind of exhibitionism and to try to move it in the
direction of their own purposes, whatever the purpose of those who
first set it in motion. Again, the truth is hidden, is not so much
noticed as the most simplistic slogans and the loudest cries.

(4) *False perspective*   Given the attacks, the journalistic sensationalism, the extremism from various sources, and the ideological
wrappings – a questionable perspective on the nature and history of
the family and marriage came to be thought established. The 'nuclear
family', in particular, was made to appear something *new* in society,
something of recent growth, a creature of the 'exploitative
capitalism' of the nineteenth century (almost a Victorian creation),
peculiar to the modern industrial world, and the confinement of
women to marriage, home, and the care of children – who were themselves now confined to their homes throughout childhood, was seen
as something imposed on women by the wilful desire and the dominating power of men. The aim of women – in seeking their freedom
and equality – was therefore seen, and advocated, as the *rejection* of
this confining marriage; the *destruction* of this 'nuclear prison'; and
the *liberation* from this exploitative family role of wife and mother.
Any other perspective – for example: that the family had been
founded much earlier in the history of human society; that the
conditions of early industrialisation had been brutalising and oppressive; that women and children had been removed from the hardships
of heavy wage-earning labour and protected from exploitation; and
that an improved basis for home and family life had been created –

which could be, and had been, reformed and improved ... and that, indeed, it was the spread of this throughout the modern world which was perhaps now making possible an improvement in the conditions and status of both children and women ... such an alternative perspective was never considered. It would not call people to the barricades. It would not make such good headlines.

(5) *Half-baked conceptions* With this perspective and these extremes – voiced initially in flamboyant rhetoric, and lacking the detailed consideration of legal implications which came much later – came the spread of a 'half-baked' conception of marriage which has proved ruinous to so many young people: the notion that it was merely 'a piece of paper' of no consequence; that relationships of co-habitation ('just living with somebody') were no more than a matter of casual personal choice – 'of no concern to the public'; that 'private' relationships were of no concern whatever to other people, and had no moral, legal, or public considerations (to think so was to be 'square' and old-fashioned); that being a 'common law wife' or 'common law husband' deserved – and should get – just the same consideration and treatment in the law and social services as those who had entered into the status of marriage. Such notions became, and remain, common-place. I shall come back to the conception of marriage elsewhere*, but it is enough, for the moment, to see that these irresponsible attitudes towards familial relationships reflected only the most extreme positions within Women's Lib, and that the Rights for Women Group itself has now come to remedy this – placing their emphasis very decidedly upon public and legal obligation.

But two other conclusions emerge from our survey of the Women's Liberation literature which might not have been thought of, and which are of considerable interest and importance.

(6) *American* The first is the quite striking fact that modern 'Women's Lib' is predominantly *American*. The earlier, most influential, most misunderstood (e.g. Betty Friedan), and most extreme version of the 'Second Phase' of Feminism originated in *America*. Its roots were in the collective conditions of post-war *American* society, just as the development of its organisation and the publicity which was mounted about it were American in character; indeed, one might say, derived its character from that of the American sex-researchers and from the professional women of the American college campuses. This, in itself, is not to condemn these origins in any wholesale fashion, but only to point to the fact that modern Women's Lib, with

*See *The Shaking of the Foundations*, Part II, Chapter 4.

its much-popularised extremes, came to Britain from America with a character quite different from that of English Feminism.

(7) *Out of date* A final interesting and connected fact is that when it did arrive in Britain – in its origins in the mid-to-late 1960s, and in its developments from the early 1970s – this American emphasis was already *out of date*. Already by the late 1950s – as evidenced in the surveys of Geoffrey Gorer, Mark Abrams, Michael Young and Peter Willmott,* and very decidedly by the 1970s as reported in Gorer's repeated investigation – men and women in Britain had already both wanted and in large part achieved the kind of egalitarian partnership which came increasingly to be called 'the companionate marriage': the kind of marriage which the insistence on women's rights envisaged and desired. It may be this approximation to the new sense of equality and partnership in marriage which had come to exist soon after the Second World War which makes writers like Elaine Morgan so much more moderate than her American counterparts. Because of it, too, perhaps *some* women, particularly the *younger* generations of women in Britain may well have come to be sadly misled by the first wave of American exaggerations and led to ignore, or perhaps not even properly to understand, the strides which had already been taken in post-war British society. It may be that, as we suggested earlier (p. 105), the idea that America leads and the rest of the world follows is another myth in the modern world that needs exploding. In this case, at least, the Americans were behind the times and inflicted their superficial and strident attitudes upon generations in Britain who would have been much better off without them. In such ways, the extremists among the Women's Libbers may well have done (and may still be doing) their sisters a great disservice.

What remains quite certain, however, is that when the whole range of the literature of Women's Liberation is taken into account, no damaging criticisms of marriage and the family emerge from it. No grounds at all are given for the abandonment of marriage or the abolition of the family: perhaps a surprising conclusion, but nonetheless true. Attacks there are in plenty, but, as we have seen – and as was the case with Leach; Laing, Cooper and Esterson; and Marxism and the New Left – these really reflect the *strength* of the family in society – stemming from an *impatience* with it and *rebellion* against it

*In addition to books already mentioned, see: *The Symmetrical Family*, Routledge & Kegan Paul, 1973, Penguin Books, 1975.

simply because it so strongly resists the many problems attending social change and instability, even withstanding the social cataclysms such as war; and because, to such attackers, it seems so firmly founded, so traditionally entrenched, so immovable an obstacle to the achievement of their own aims. The sexual revolution, the extremists hoped, would transform society – and so it may well come to do in many welcome ways. But the family and marriage, though permitting of change and improvement, are *not*, it seems, to be transformed out of existence.

An alternative to the family: The commune

One last source of criticisms of the family remains for our consideration – the 'Commune Movement': the *apparent* rejection of the 'nuclear' family as being too self-contained and intense a group, an emotionally possessive, choking, impoverishing prison, and the advocacy of larger 'communes' – with perhaps freer patterns of sexuality and parenthood – as providing a better alternative for personal health, fulfilment, and happiness. This, however, requires only brief treatment as Elaine Morgan's earlier comment: that 'the rate of failed communes is at least as high as the rate of failed marriages' has already implied a fair and accurate judgment. Indeed, in all probability, the failure rate of communes is much higher. My emphasis on the word apparent, above, is also important, and two clear points can be made.

First, a fundamental mistake and confusion frequently underlies arguments about families and communes. It is often claimed that communes like the Israeli 'kibbutzim' or those of China are *opposed* to the family, setting themselves up as *alternatives* to it. This, quite simply, is false. These communities are *not* alternatives to the family, nor are most of those in other parts of the world – in America, Britain, and the supposedly more extreme countries of Scandinavia. They are, in fact, groups of families living in *new and closer community conditions.* But that does not support arguments for the destruction of the family, but for the remaking of the nature of our communities – to provide a better context for familial and wider social life – and from such experiments there may well be much to learn. It is obviously of the first importance, however, that this underlying confusion should be made quite clear.

We have already seen (pp. 80–2) that the Chinese communes actually take pride in having provided a context of improved conditions for families, for a firmer security and better quality of family life; but this, now, deserves renewed emphasis, especially with some of the views of the Women's Liberation Movement – concerning 'extended' families – fresh in our minds. The truth is (almost exactly in keeping with the writings of Marx and Engels) that it was the ancient, patriarchal, extended family system which the Chinese attacked and eradicated, and the monogamous, conjugal family which they have upheld. Nothing makes this more clear than their Marriage Law.

The new democratic marriage is based on free choice of partners, on equal rights for both sexes, and on protection of the lawful interests of women and children. . . .

Marriage shall be based upon the complete willingness of the two parties. Neither party shall use compulsion and no third party shall be allowed to interfere.

Husband and wife are companions living together and shall enjoy equal status in the home.

Husband and wife are in duty bound to love, respect, assist and look after each other, to live in harmony, to care for the children, and to strive jointly for the welfare of the family.

Both husband and wife shall have the right to free choice of occupation and free participation in work or social activities.

Both husband and wife shall have equal rights in the possession and management of family property.

Both husband and wife shall have the right to inherit each other's property.

Parents have the duty to rear and to educate their children; children have the duty to support and to assist their parents.

Children born out of wedlock shall enjoy the same rights as children born in lawful wedlock. No person shall be allowed to harm or discriminate against children born out of wedlock.

Facing enormous population and transitional (political, economic and social) problems, China practises some family policies (such as a severe restriction on the number of births per family) which must seem to us repressive, but the above outline of their family law is perfectly plain. Clearly, it rests on the same values and principles – ooolcing to occurc the same rights for men, women, and children, and the same attitudes of responsibility towards familial and wider social behaviour – as our own. Following his own detailed studies, an American sociologist came to this conclusion:

> The most controversial of the communist innovations were the *communes* which were established on a large scale between 1958 and 1960. Westerners often interpret the communes as an attempt to destroy the family. In reality the communes were intended as a substitute for the *clan** and the *extended* family, but *not* for the conjugal family upon which the communist government already depends ... With increasing economic and political stability, the conjugal family seems destined to receive more official support.[1]

Clearly, communes were in no sense alternatives to the family here.[2] Indeed, it is important to see (given some of the neo-Marxist arguments we have considered) that it was the extended family the revolution particularly wished to displace, not the conjugal ('nuclear') family, which the communes serve and support, and it is interesting to note that in present-day China there is even an apparent emergence of 'romantic love' as the basis of personal choice in marriage as against the earlier tradition of the arrangement of marriages by elders. Perhaps, after all, it is the conjugal family which is destined to become universal in our era of global social change.

A similar picture emerges from a careful study of the Israeli 'kibbutzim', especially when their growth in size and complexity is taken into account. Initially founded as agricultural 'collectives', the early emphasis was upon the identification of individual members with the community as a whole rather than on a too-narrow preoccupation with (and absorption in) the private world of the family. The entire pattern of work and life was 'collectivised'. Men and women participated equally. 'Marriage' as a formal institution was not emphasised. Children were brought up communally. Even then, however, men and women did form permanent relationships as partners (applying for and being allotted a room of their own), and, as parents, spent time with their own children during certain periods of the day. Indeed, M. E. Spiro – to give one example – claimed that closer parental and familial bonds were established within these closer community conditions; that the attachment of young kibbutz children to their parents was greater than in our own society; and that, providing security and love, parents played a crucial role in the

---

*The '*tsu*': all persons with a common surname who could trace their descent from a common ancestor.

psychological development of their children.* Families undoubtedly remained. But as the kibbutzim grew in size, some becoming urbanised with increasing specialisation, the place of the private family became more marked. Parallel with these developments, there came to be an increasing emphasis on the family group: on formal marriage, the ownership of private belongings, the privacy of family life, the making of each family's particular home; and, of course, as was inevitable, there came to be a continuity of generational ties. Even, then, in this most radical example of the voluntary and deliberate creation of closely knit communes by people who shared deeply held religious beliefs and clear social and political objectives, and who were motivated by great zeal – there was never an abandonment of natural conjugal and parental bonds; and these natural familial relationships gradually, but quite decidedly, re-asserted themselves as the communities developed. A growing clarification of the conjugal form of the family seems to be correlated, almost bound up with, certain developments in society, and we shall have more to say about this. There have, by this time, been many studies of the 'kibbutzim'. Lawrence Fellows, for example, traced their history, noting changes in them as urbanisation and complexity grew, and as early simply formulated ideals had, to some extent, to be modified or abandoned.

The old spirit of the kibbutz movement is fading away in Israel.

The members of these collective settlements have been pulling up their stakes and leaving at a faster rate than new members have been coming in. A few of the settlements have shut down altogether....

To the dismay of the old Zionist pioneers, a growing number of the settlements have found that the happiest solution to their problems was simply to turn away from the concept of a collective, classless society.

Of the 250 kibbutzim in Israel, ninety-eight have turned away to the extent that they have become tiny industrial towns....

It was largely the rebellious women who forced the changes that have already taken hold in the kibbutzim. The mothers are gaining increasing responsibility for the care of their own children. The apartments are being increasingly furnished with

*M. E. Spiro, *Children of the Kibbutz*, Harvard University Press, 1958.

211

radios, paintings, individual wardrobes and electric kettles for brewing tea or coffee at home.*

The home was reasserting itself over the communal living and eating places. The conclusion was plain. As the initial communal spirit of the 1930s and 1940s faded, the kibbutzim came 'to accord a more prominent place to the conjugal family'. As though to reinforce this conclusion, as recently as December 1984 the researches of Dr Uri Leviathan of Haifa University were reported in the English press under the headline: 'MOTHERS' THREAT TO THE KIBBUTZ'.** The socialist structure of the kibbutz, it was said:

> is being endangered by the women, who want their children back home.
> In the kibbutz system, from the moment they are born, children live in communal homes and their parents are allowed to take them home for only two or three hours in the evening. The women have rebelled against this time honoured system which was useful during the period when members lived in primitive huts and were fully dedicated to back-breaking draining of swamps and reclaiming the desert.
> Bourgeois habits have now penetrated the kibbutz where homes are equipped with modern conveniences and families are offered free meals, schooling, and cultural life ...
> Women are the leaders of a strong campaign to remove children from communal homes, a campaign which has become an ideological challenge to kibbutz leadership ideologists ... They wage a war of attrition within the kibbutz first by influencing other women and then by putting pressure until the majority of men fall into line.

It was always a mistake, then, to think of the kibbutzim as being totally opposed to, or alternatives to, the family. They consisted of families living in new, small-scale, close community conditions. But as these community conditions changed, the family came increasingly to the fore, and again it is interesting to see that it was the conjugal ('nuclear') family, within its own home, which was conspicuously wished for and re-established. The evidence for the emerging universality of the conjugal family becomes firmer with every case considered, and there are clearly firm reasons for this.

*L. Fellows, *Spirit of Kibbutz Fading in Israel*, 1961, New York Times.
**Sunday Telegraph*, 23 December 1984, reported by Maier Asher from Jerusalem.

It might be thought that the situation would not be the same in the rather more secular and humanistic developments in the Scandinavian countries; that these societies (not so much fired by zealous political ideologies or religious beliefs) might present a different picture; but, perhaps surprisingly, this is not so. An interesting report of the early 1970s* on the 'collectives' in Denmark showed that here, too, the collectives were by no means *alternatives* to the family. Some were groups of families who had come together to create and share their own small community conditions. Some contained a mixture of married and unmarried couples. And though all were founded on the basis of a deeply felt dissatisfaction with the values and pressures of large-scale modern society, and a rebellious reaction to them:

> Most are content to retain traditional marriage ties (at least for the present), but in a wider setting, where couples live together to stimulate cross-inspiration and also to economise on their household expenses. One washing machine, one television, one dish-washer can be used by several families, and this saving can be put aside for the day when the group can squeeze themselves into a jointly-owned car – giving a higher standard of consumer amenities than the individual couples could normally achieve.
>
> This very logical and inviting prospect is savoured by many collective members as a way of slapping the face of the capitalist system, but it also has its drawbacks. In most, cleaning and other chores are dealt out systematically, but friction can quickly develop over relatively insignificant things ...

And one interesting point here is that one problem was that of the sheer preponderance of community experience over private experience.

> Tension is hard to avoid between members ... jealousies and rivalries can quickly develop if collective living takes too much of the available time, cutting down togetherness in marriage.

Too continual an experience of *community* could clearly become *too much*! There was also a need for *privacy*. And privacy in marriage – 'togetherness in marriage' – was something still desired.

*Danish Journal, 1970, 'Doubling Up Togetherness' by Geoffrey Dodd.

Developments of the 'Commune Movement' in the United States and Britain have been far too varied to allow of brief *and* satisfactory discussion, but a little can be said about each country's experience. It is far too simplistic, first of all, to depict the members of American communes as flocks of long-haired, filthy, drug-taking, guitar-playing, flower-decorated hippies living out their 'dropped-out' lives in the dark and shadowy highways and byways of American society. Beginning in 'The Haight' in San Francisco, the commune movement did soon acquire this disreputable image, and in some cases this was no doubt deserved. But communes differ, and to 'drop out' was by no means necessarily to adopt a negative, spiritless, defeatist point of view. For some, it was their first committed step towards the making of a new world in an age which otherwise offered no hope, in which the mass-societies of the world were already destitute of worthwhile values, and were, within the very near foreseeable future, doomed to the destruction they were bringing upon themselves. To move towards an 'Alternative Society' required the outright rejection of the grossly materialistic values and ways of life of the modern 'consumer' society, of the senselessness of greed, ruthlessly competitive commercialism, and war. It rested on a desire for a simpler life – of personal experience and personal relationships – in which the full nature of the created world could be enjoyed in the living moment. It was a rejection of the whole pretentious perspective – the perspective which was a great and growing burden – of a false history, a false culture, a false civilisation which was culminating not in the high ideals which dripped from the pages of its textbooks but in perpetual conflict, napalm bombing, and the disgust and disgrace of Hiroshima. There was much in the thought and feeling underlying the Commune Movement of Thoreau's statement of personal sanity in 'Walden', and more than an echo in it of Thomas Hardy's cynical but terrible comment.

> 'Peace upon earth!' was said. We sing it,
> And pay a million priests to bring it.
> After two thousand years of mass
> We've got as far as poison gas.

Certainly, throughout America, many of the communes which hoped to establish an alternative society were seriously founded – aiming at a simple life based upon the cultivation of the land, self-sufficiency, and resting on quite specific religious beliefs and values.* And again, far from rejecting the family, many of them sought a kind of community life in the context of which they and their families could experience the richer kind of life they desired and felt was possible. They sought an enrichment of family experience. Quite decidedly, the American commune movement – as a total movement – was *not* opposed to the family as a domestic group, and *The Alternative: Communal Life in North America*** gives a detailed account of the wide range of such communes in America.

In Britain, the situation has been more variable, scrappy, and – overall – short-lived. The rate of breakdown of communes certainly bears out Elaine Morgan's estimation, and is borne out, to some little extent, in my own experience. In the early 1970s – seeking knowledge of the communes in England – I was in correspondence with some officials of 'The Commune Movement' which then published its own journal *Communes*. In (1985/86) I sent letters off again in the hope of learning about their developments over the past ten years, without result. The one man I traced in London by telephone had recently returned from a period of 'squatting' in Norwich (the City Council had just taken over the street of derelict buildings in which he and others had been living) and simply commented that (with one exception) the communes he had known at the time of my earlier enquiries had ceased to exist; that communes usually had only a short life; and, indeed, that – given the pressures of our large-scale society – an 'alternative society' was impossible. In the absence of any overall knowledge, nothing conclusive can be said,*** but, judging entirely from the earlier (1970) journals, it is again quite plain that, in essentials, the commune movement was decidedly not *anti-family*. On the contrary, many of the opinions and wishes expressed came from families who were themselves wishing to escape

*It is sometimes forgotten that the founding of communes has a long history, and that many early communities of this kind rested on a firm Christian basis. In America, during the nineteenth century, the Putney Community of 1846 later became the well-known Oneida Community, and in England, even just before the Second World War, the Cotswold Bruderhof was set up – resting on a much simpler Christian basis, itself stemming from communities of the same kind established elsewhere (in Europe and Paraguay).
**By W. Hedgepeth and D. Stock, Macmillan, New York, 1970.
***Understandably, individual communes – sensitive to publicity and irresponsible invasion – were reluctant to have their addresses given to enquirers, and so any firm and extensive knowledge proved difficult.

the social isolation they were experiencing within the impersonal conditions of post-war affluent society. One quite typical letter (but with changed names of people and places) is:

> We are thinking of setting up a community here, and are on the look-out for a couple of people with perhaps one or two children. 'We' consist of Robert, Angela, Margaret and Pamela – 28, 26, three and eleven months respectively, and 'here' consists of a nine-roomed house in an extremely isolated position in the middle of a windswept boggy moorland in Radnorshire. There is a barn capable of renovation as a workroom/studio and an acre of land, which given the right treatment could be fairly productive.
>
> Robert is at present teaching but wants to have more time to paint, and to make this place more productive and self-sufficient. To me, a commune-type set-up seems to answer many of the problems of the conventional isolated family structure and to be a means of being independent of a society which is heading for collapse.

Here is another.

> Would you wish to live, on a permanent basis, with others who have suffered? have similar difficulties? have great needs? a longing for commitment? Do you badly wish to express your anger? aggression? frustration? tenderness? care? all your feelings?
>
> Would you move to a place and help start a community? where would you like it to be?
>
> If you feel that your heart has been broken all along the line, it could be worth all kinds of risks to get back to your feelings again, now.
>
> PS. Do you know anyone who should be reading this?

Clearly, the desire to set up communes stemmed from certain deeply felt kinds of discontent with society as it now exists, even from sufferings within it, and from a desire to find a basis for life on a more personal and human scale. The experiences, the discontent, the sufferings, and the desires actually emphasised familial values and came, in fact, more often than not, from families and groups of families.

This fundamental confusion aside, however, a second point can be made. The direct evidence which does exist of those communes which *did* reject the conventional family, and *did* try to become an

216

alternative to it, is such, so far, as actually to demonstrate the *weakness of the communes* and the *strength of the family*. The evidence from various countries is very similar, but one example can be given from Denmark. One group of a dozen people of both sexes – the Dyveke Collective in Copenhagen – did (said the 1970 report) take the collective idea further in at least the sexual direction by eliminating the 'ownership' barriers of conventional marriage and living as a group family. After less than a year, this collective 'broke up completely' and the break 'was caused by less mundane things than housekeeping and economy, two standard dangers for collectives'.

> The Dyveke group found that after a half-year of hectic activity repairing their house they had not really changed in themselves. In spite of their original intentions, the tendency towards formation of couples became more and more noticeable.
> The 12-square-yard mattress obtained in an effort to collectivise what are usually considered to be more private activities failed to fulfil its purpose. Pairing became more popular; and when this prickly subject cropped up during a group meeting, the distaff side in particular had the moral courage to reject the attractive theories of the project for a more old-fashioned approach. To be the member of a pair gives security, said one female collectivist who did not wish to be named ...
> The theoretical answer to this quite obviously is group security in the collective, but a male member of the group admitted that the feeling of security had not flourished in step with multiple togetherness or group development. On the contrary, the need for a fixed point of reference in the otherwise very fluid emotional state of a group marriage had become more urgent than ever before.
> The collectivists were unusually and commendably forthright in admitting that their experiment may not have given a patent for all marital ills. 'You need the assurance that ultimately a single one is there always. It's true ...'[3]

All in all, then – given, firstly, the full weight of the first basic confusion, and, secondly, the direct evidence of the weakness of those communes which have departed most from conventional family relationships – it can be seen that there is no telling criticism of marriage and the family here. Indeed, any consideration of the nature and history of 'communes' points to the strength, endurance, and even re-emergence and survival of the conjugal family unit, despite quite deliberate efforts to diminish its influence within wider social relationships, and, sometimes, to do without it.

6

Conclusion

The conclusion reached at the end of this book can be as simply stated as the aim with which it began. It is that all the new criticisms which emerged in the late 1960s and gathered strength throughout the 1970s and into the 1980s can be safely laid to rest with the old. Still exercising some influence, still enjoying, among many, a certain vogue, they have been shown, nonetheless, to be insufficient in many and quite fundamental ways, and do not affect our estimation of the nature and importance of the family and marriage at all.

Some – like those supposedly arising from the commune movement – turn out, on close examination, to rest on a misunderstanding. Properly understood, they are not anti-family at all. The same is true of what its many proponents choose, very variably, to call 'Marxism'. The position of Marx himself, and that of Engels, is decidedly *not* opposed to the family or to marriage, and decidedly does *not* advocate their abolition. Strange though it may well seem to many, Marx, on the contrary, considered the moral relationship existing between man and woman in a society the most significant index of its level of civilisation (and humanity), and Engels believed that *monogamy* was the relationship which men and women, freed from their social and economic inequalities, would most probably choose. Some criticisms supposedly stemming from *one* position – like 'the New Feminism' – turn out, in fact, to be rooted in a number of very variable positions (some moderate, some extreme) containing no overall unity or consistency of judgment, and not being uniformly negative in their appraisal of marriage and the family. Others – like Leach's 'Reith Sentence' – are simply superficial, resting on no sound evidence at all. They are merely assertions. And those of Laing, Cooper and Esterson, though such as to be taken much more seriously (as a new and deeply considered re-orientation in psychiatry, and having much of real interest to say), nonetheless prove unacceptable in the ways we have mentioned, and remain questionable at the very deepest level.

It was possible, in the 1960s, to defend the nature of the British family against the older criticisms (see Note 2, p. 222), and we have now seen that the newer criticisms offer no serious challenge. One thing, however, is plain.

Our reflections on *all* the criticisms – old and new – and the very fact that we have continually to take issue with them, shows, beyond doubt, that they stem from a very deeply rooted sense of apprehensiveness. Profound anxieties from the past (rooted in the old persuasions) have continued even as the new concerns have arisen and the more radical challenges and accusations have been made. For whatever reason, from whatever approach, every consideration of the changing nature of the family and marriage in Britain, of the new collective conditions they face, of their changing relationships with other institutions in the wider social order, seems to be rooted in a sense, which all share, of some profound malaise. Something, somehow, somewhere in our society, it is felt, is seriously wrong. This sense of the gravity of the situation can be pressed even further. There seems to be at least one identifiable source of perplexity at the heart of it: a curiously mixed awareness and evaluation of both *progress* and *crisis*. Many things have undoubtedly been improved. Many worthwhile reforms have been made. Progress in many directions has unquestionably been achieved. Yet ... the range and intricacy of our social problems seem not to diminish but continually to increase. Our sense of crisis grows. Far from solving and eliminating social and personal difficulties, progress – curiously – seems to increase and intensify them: creating new problems, the sources and nature of which we are very far from understanding. Progress, far from eliminating crisis, seems strangely coupled with it. It is almost as though they were two sides of the same coin – apparently separate, apparently different from each other, but, in social actuality, being two intimately related aspects of the same process. What are we to make of this? How are we to understand it?

What is certain is that to discredit the criticisms of the family and marriage in society, as we have done, is far from being enough. To do justice to these questions, to try to understand our predicament as legislation expands in ever more detailed ways and social changes become ever more complicated, something more is required: a careful scrutiny of the facts and a searching enquiry to discover the most satisfactory explanation of them. But this is a kind of study different from the one we have just completed, and one that must be conducted elsewhere.[1]

Notes

Introduction. New and radical criticisms: a strange reversal

1 J. Rumney and J. Maier, W. J. H. Sprott, W. Goodsell, Carle C.
   Zimmerman, and even Bertrand Russell were notable examples, but
   among social theorists the declining importance of the family in
   society was a very common theme.
2 A detailed discussion of these criticisms and a defence of the
   modern family against them is to be found in *The Family and
   Marriage in Britain: A Moral Assessment*, Penguin Books, 1962 and
   subsequent editions. A historical perspective and careful analysis
   of the past century of social changes and reforms was enough to
   show that these judgments and accusations rested upon a
   completely false diagnosis, and that the family had *not* declined,
   was *not* less stable than hitherto, and that the standards of
   parenthood and parental responsibility had *not* deteriorated.
   Neither had the functions of the family been 'stripped away' as the
   State had instituted its many reforms. On the contrary, the family
   was made responsible for more, and more demanding, functions
   with every new piece of legislation. This conclusion was also fully
   in agreement with the *one* public report to which the moralists
   seem to have paid scant attention. In *The Family in Contemporary
   Society*, a committee of the Church of England Moral Welfare
   Council reported their finding that 'the modern family is in some
   ways in a stronger position than it has been at any period in our
   history of which we have knowledge'.
      The Shaking of the Foundations: Family and Society (Routledge,
   1988), gives additional support for these conclusions, examining
   the changes since the Divorce Reform Act, and taking the analysis
   further.

221

Chapter 1 'The source of all our discontents': Edmund Leach

1 'Ourselves and Others', *The Listener*, 30 November 1967, vol. 78, no. 2018, p. 693.
2 'Liberating Acts', G. M. Carstairs, *The Listener*, 21 September 1972, vol. 88, no. 2269, p. 362.
3 CIBA Foundation Symposium, *Comparative Family Patterns*, J. and A. Churchill, 1970, p. 7.
4 Methuen, 1968 edition.
5 Ronald Blythe, *Akenfield, Portrait of an English Village*, Allen Lane, The Penguin Press, 1969.

Chapter 2 The family as destroyer: Laing, Cooper and Esterson

1 For these quotations, see *The Leaves of Spring: Sanity, Madness and the Family*, R.D. Laing and A. Esterson, Penguin Books, 1970.
2 Tavistock, 1971.
3 Tavistock, 1964.
4 A. Esterson, *Schizophrenia, Family and Sacrifice*, Penguin Books, 1972.
5 Allen Lane, The Penguin Press, 1971.
6 Indeed, this gives rise to a much more fundamental criticism which might well strike at the very basic of this research. The complete concentration upon *pathological* individuals and families alone might mean that Laing, Cooper and Esterson have got their causal explanation the wrong way round. If schizophrenia, for example, had a *chemical* cause (as some researchers maintain), it is at least possible that the existence and development of this condition in one individual could cause the related tensions, patterns, and 'knots' within the family – and not the relationships which cause the onset of the 'disease'. This, at any rate, seems an important and quite fundamental criticism to which their analysis is open, and which seems worth pursuing.

Chapter 3 The abolition of the family: Marxism and the New Left

1 *Student Power*, Penguin Books, 1969, pp. 163–213.
2 Penguins Books, 1971.
3 English translation, with a preface written by Engels in 1892, Allen & Unwin, 1950 reprint.
4 William Glaisher, 1918, p. xviii.
5 Ibid., p. 473.
6 Ibid., p. 467.
7 Ibid., p. 505.
8 *Conditions of the Working-Class in England in 1844*, 1892 translation, p. 264.
9 Ibid., p. 129.
10 Ibid., Preface, p. xviii.
11 Foreign Languages Publishing House, Moscow, 1961.
12 Ibid., p. 100.
13 *The Origin of the Family, Private Property, and the State*. Charles H. Kerr, Chicago, 1902 Edition, p. 79.
14 Ibid., p. 81.
15 Ibid., p. 89–91.
16 Ibid., p. 97.
17 Ibid., p. 99.

Chapter 4 The family as prison: the New Feminism

1 *The Feminine Mystique* (USA 1963), Penguin Books, 1965. *The Second Stage* (USA 1981), Abacus, Sphere Books, 1983.
2 Abacus, Sphere Books, 1972.
3 Paladin Books, 1971.
4 *Sex and Destiny, the Politics of Human Fertility*, Picador, Pan Books, 1985.
5 *Women: A World Report*, Methuen, 1985.
6 Virago, 1980.
7 See *The Cohabitation Handbook, a 'Rights of Women' Guide to the Law*, Pluto Handbooks, 2nd Edition, 1984.
8 Souvenir Press, Revised Edition, 1985.
9 Souvenir Press, 1982.

Chapter 5 An alternative to the family: the commune

1   Gerald L. Leslie, *The Family in Social Context*, Oxford University Press, 1967, p. 122.
2   A recent letter from the Chinese Embassy in London (1986) confirmed this:

> As far as I know, the Chinese Government has not drawn up a new code of marriage law since 1980 (though some amendments might have been made to the law.) It is an entire misunderstanding that communes in China set up since 1958 were ever opposed to the family. The People's Commune then served as the lowest government level in rural areas. Its function combined local authority and production. Since 1980, the *responsibility system*, a new productive system, farming on a household basis, has been introduced in the countryside. The 'commune' does not exist in China now.

3   *The Danish Journal*, 1970, p. 19. Again, confirmation that very little has happened in the commune movement since 1970 came from the Royal Danish Embassy in London (June, 1986):

> In fact, nothing much has changed since the 1970s, and the embassy is unaware of any public planning or financing of 'Communes' ... [though] ... on a smaller and more private level many Danes, married couples as well as singles, and people just living together, have formed groups which will take over a large house and share the expenses.

Chapter 6 Conclusion

1   See *The Shaking of the Foundations: Family and Society*, Routledge, 1988.

Suggestions for further reading

This bibliography refers to the specific topics dealt with in this book. A much wider book-list on other aspects of the family and marriage (both historical and contemporary) is to be found in *The Shaking of the Foundations: Family and Society.*

Anderson, M. 'What is New About the Modern Family?' *In the Family*, Occasional Paper 31, Office of Population Census and Surveys, 1983.

Barrett, M., *Women's Oppression Today*, Verso, 1981.

Barrett, H. and McIntosh, M., *The Anti-Social Family*, Verso, 1981.

Central Office of Information, *Women in Britain*, Pamphlet 67, HMSO, 1964.

Cockburn, A. and Blackburn, R., *Student Power*, Penguin Books, 1969.

Cooper, David, *The Death of the Family*, Allen Lane, the Penguin Press, 1971.

Cooper, D. and R. D. Laing, *Reason and Violence*, Tavistock Publications, 1964.

Dicks, H. V., *Marital Tensions*, Routledge & Kegan Paul, 1967.

Elliott, Katherine, *The Family and its Future*, CIBA Foundation Conference, Churchill, 1970.

Engels, F., *The Origin of the Family, Private Property and the State*, Charles H. Kerr, Chicago, 1902.

Esterson, A., *The Leaves of Spring*, Penguin Books, 1972.

Esterson, A. and Laing, R. D., *Sanity, Madness and the Family*, Penguin Books, 1970.

Fletcher, R., 'The Making of the Modern Family', *The Family and its Future*, Churchill, 1970.

Fletcher, R., 'The Marriage of Good Friends', *Marriage Guidance*, 1972.

Fletcher, R., *The Family and Marriage in Britain*, Penguin Books (3rd edn), 1973.

225

Fletcher, R., *The Shaking of the Foundations: Family and Society*, Routledge, 1988.

Greer, Germaine, *The Female Eunuch*, Paladin Books, 1971.

Greer, Germaine, *Sex and Destiny, the Politics of Human Fertility*, Picador, Pan Books, 1985.

Hedgepeth, W., and Stock, D., *The Alternative* (Communal Life in North America), Macmillan, 1970.

Home Office, Working Party, *Marriage Matters*, HMSO, 1979.

Itzin, C., *Splitting Up: Single-Parent Family Liberation*, Virago, 1980.

Jenner, H., *Marriages are made on Earth*, David Charles, 1979. (Interesting insights into the workings of a modern Marriage Bureau.)

Jephcott, P., Seear, N. and Smith, J., *Married Women Working*, Allen & Unwin, 1962.

Kiernan, K. E., 'The Structure of Families Today: Continuity or Change?' *In the Family*, occasional paper 31, Office of Population Censuses and Survey, 1983.

Klein, V., *Working Wives*, Institute of Personnel Management, 1960.

Klein, V., *Employing Married Women* (Occasional Papers No. 17), Institute of Personnel Management, 1961.

Laing, R. D., *The Politics of the Family*, Penguin Books, 1976.

Laing, R. D., *The Divided Self*, Penguin Books, 1965.

Laslett, P., *The World We Have Lost*, Methuen, 1965.

Laslett, P., *Household and Family in Past Time*, Cambridge University Press, 1972.

Mill, J. S., *The Subjection of Women*, 1869.

Millett, Kate, *Sexual Politics*, Abacus, Sphere Books, 1972.

Mitchell, Juliet, *Women's Estate*, Penguin Books, 1971.

Morgan, Elaine, *The Descent of Woman*, Souvenir Press, Revised Edition, 1985.

Morgan, Elaine, *The Aquatic Ape*, Souvenir Press, 1982.

Myrdal, A., *Nation and Family*, Kegan Paul, French & Trubner, 1945.

Myrdal, A. and Kein, V., *Women's Two Roles: Home and Work*, Routledge & Kegan Paul, 1956.

National Marriage Guidance Council, *Relating to Marriage*, 1985.

Paterson, Dorothy, *The Family Woman and the Feminist*, Heinemann, 1945.

Plumb, J. H., *England in the Eighteenth Century* (Part II, Ch. 2, and Part III, Ch. 1), Penguin Books, 1950.

Plumb, J. H., *In the Light of History*, Allen Lane, The Penguin Press, 1972 (especially Part Two, Chs 3, 4 and 5).

Plutarch, *On Love, The Family, and the Good Life*, Selected Essays translated by M. Hades, Mentor Books, 1957.

Prickett, John (ed.), *Marriage and the Family*, Lutterworth Press, 1985. (Standing Conference on Inter-Faith Publication.)

Puxon, Margand, *The Family and the Law*, Penguin Books, 1963.

Rapoport, R. and Rapoport, R., 'Work and Family in Contemporary Society', *American Sociological Review*, vol. 30, 1965, pp. 381–94.

Rapoport, R. and Rapoport, R., *Dual-Career Families*, Penguin Books, 1971.

Registrar General (Review) *Marriages and Divorce Statistics, 1981.* Series FM2 no. 8, HMSO, 1984.

'Rights of Women' guide to the law, *The Cohabitation Handbook*, Pluto Press, 1984 (2nd edn).

Social Trends, All numbers up to No. 17, 1987, HMSO.

Spring Rice, M., *Working Class Wives (Their Health and Condition)*, Penguin Books, 1939.

Stone, Olive, 'The Family and the Law in 1970', in *The Family and its Future*, Churchill, 1970.

Study Commission on the Family, *Families in the Future*, Final Report, 1983.

Swedish Institute, Stockholm, *Sweden Today: The Status of Women in Sweden* (on Family Law, etc.), Report to the United Nations, 1968.

Taylor, Debbie (ed.), *Women: A World Report*, Methuen, 1985.

Westermarck, E., *The History of Human Marriage*, Macmillan, 1921.

Westermarck, E., *The Future of Marriage in Western Civilization*, Macmillan, 1936.

Index

Index

Index

morality, 133, 154
Morgan, Elaine, 186, 188–98, 199, 200, 208, 215
Morgan, Lewis H., 68
motherhood, 107, 114, 120, 132, 141, 147, 155, 199
Mystic Rose, The, 111, 152

Naked and the Dead, The, 123
National Housebuilders' Registration Council, 18
Nazi Germany, 107, 114
neo-Marxists (ism), 9, 53, 210
neoteny, 191
New Feminism, The, 3, 83–207
New Left, The, 48–82, 206
nuclear family, 20–1, 40, 141, 147, 156–7, 161, 170, 181, 192, 210, 212
nuclear war, 4, 43

one-parent families, 88–90, 199
Origin of the Family, The, 68

pathology, 31–4, 38–40
patriarchy (and patriarchal power), 112–21, 131
Pizzey, Erin, 142, 186–8, 200
Plato, 202
Pleistocene era, 192
Politics of Experience, The, 45
Politics of the Family, The, 33
Poor Law, Victorian, 21
population problem, 146–7, 162–4
praxis, 34–8
privacy, 15–9, 27–8, 213
property, 192

Report on the State of the World's Women, 1985, 167
Reason and Violence, 35
Reith Lectures, 10
Rogers, Rev. E., 4
Roman Law, 186; the Romans, 196

Sanity, Madness and the Family, 31, 37, 49
Sartre, J. P., 34, 37, 42, 48, 53
schizophrenia, 28, 32, 38–40; schizophrenogenic mothers and families, 31–4
Second Sex, The, 93
Second Stage, The, 100–4
Second World War, 1, 85, 112, 206
self-regulating organic families, 145–6, 198

Sex and Destiny, 131, 162
Sex and Marriage in England Today, 17
Sexual Politics, 91, 107–29
Shakespeare, 140, 201
Shawcross, Lord, 6
social class (es) 12, 17
Social Science Research Council, 17
sociology (ists), 2, 31, 32, 41, 116–7
Somerset Maugham, W., 122
Soviet Union, 80, 107
Spectator, The, 140
Spencer, Herbert, 75
Splitting Up, 175–9
status of women, 67–76
Steele, Richard, 140
sterilization, 150
straw plait schools (and family conditions), 59

Taylor, Debbie, 168–71, 201
Thoreau, Henry David, 214
Thurber, James, 189
Trevelyan, G. M., 71–5
Trotsky, Leo, 115

unisex, 91–2
United Nations' Decade for Women (1975–85), 167
Urwin, Rev. E. C., 5
Utopianism, 52

venereal disease, 149
Victorian novelists, 122, 140

Walter, Rev. C., 4
war, 123–4
Weatherhead, Rev. Leslie, 4, 6
Weber, Max, 30
welfare state, 5, 6
western civilisation, 148
Westermarck, Edward, 184
westernisation, 153
Wodehouse, P. G., 189
Wolfenden, Sir John, 5
Woman's Estate, 50
Woman's Own, 165
Women: A World Report, 168
Women's Liberation Movement, 9, 18, 83–207
women's sexuality, 86, 97–8, 115–6, 169
Woodford Green, 20
workers (and families), 17, 22–5, 55–64
World We Have Lost, 19–21

Yoruba, 152–3

230